Market forces
China.

D0083409

DATE			

© THE BAKER & TAYLOR CO.

Market Forces in China
Competition and Small Business –
The Wenzhou Debate

edited by
Peter Nolan and Dong Fureng

Zed Books Ltd.
London and New Jersey

*Market Forces in China: Competition and Small Business –
The Wenzhou Debate* was first published by Zed Books Ltd.,
57 Caledonian Road, London N1 9BU, UK and 171 First
Avenue, Atlantic Highlands, New Jersey 07716, USA, in
1990

Typeset by Photosetting and Secretarial Services, Yeovil
Cover designed by Andrew Corbett
Printed in Great Britain by
Billing & Sons Ltd, Worcester

British Library Cataloguing in Publication Data

Market forces in China : competition and
small business : the Wenzhou debate.
1. China. Economic policies
I. Nolan, Peter II. Dong, Fureng
330.951′058

ISBN 0-86232-832-2
ISBN 0-86232-833-0 pbk

Library of Congress Cataloging-in-Publication Data

Market forces in China : competition and small business—the
Wenzhou debate / edited by Peter Nolan and Dong Fureng.
   p.   cm.

ISBN 0-86232-832-2.—ISBN 0-86232-833-0 (pbk.)
1. Wen-chou shih Region (China)—Economic policy.
2. Wen-chou shih Region (China)—Economic conditions.
3. Small business—China—Wen-chou shih Region.
4. Competition—Wen-chou shih Region. 5. Wen-chou shih
Region (China)—Industries. I. Nolan, Peter. II. Tung, Fu-jeng.
HC428.W46M37 1989
338.6′42′0951242—dc20   89-70608 CIP

Contents

Preface   vii
Map   viii

1. **Introduction** *Peter Nolan*   1

2. **Petty Commodity Production in a Socialist Economy:**
   Chinese Rural Development post-Mao *Peter Nolan*   7
   The Reform   8
   Performance of the rural economy post-1978   20
   Problems   28
   Conclusions   34

3. **The Wenzhou 'Miracle': an Assessment** *Chris Bramall*   43
   Introduction   43
   Explaining the 'miracle'   46
   Towards an evaluation   60
   Appendix   74

4. **The Wenzhou Model for Developing the Rural Commodity**
   Economy *Dong Fureng*   77
   The development of a commodity economy is essential to
      socialist modernization in China's rural areas   77
   The Wenzhou model is one alternative in developing a rural
      commodity economy   81
   The Wenzhou model for developing the rural commodity
      economy: some issues requiring research   86

5. **Developing the Commodity Economy in the Rural Areas**
   Zhiang Lin   97
   Main features of Wenzhou's open market network   97
   The benefits from Wenzhou's open market network   102

6. **The Growth of Household Industry in Rural Wenzhou** *Li Shi*   108
   The emergence of a new economic landscape   108
   Qualitative improvement and technological transformation   110

An analysis of causal factors and key elements in the growth
    process   112
The wider impact of household industry   116
Conclusions   123

7. **Income Differentials in the Development of Wenzhou's Rural
    Economy** *Zhao Renwei*   126
    Based on increased output, income has risen and differentials
        have widened   126
    The positive aspect of widening income differentials   129
    The negative aspect of widening income differentials   133
    Certain measures which have already been taken and others
        which could be taken   135

8. **A Preliminary Analysis of the 'Big labour-hiring households'**
    Chen Ruiming   140
    The basic circumstances   140
    The characteristics   141
    The trend of development   146
    The advantages and disadvantages   147

9. **Small Town Construction: an Alternative Path** *Pei Xiaoge*   156
    Longgang's economic and geographical situation   156
    Financing small town construction in Longgang   158
    The lessons from town construction in Longgang for other
        parts of China   160

10. **Privatization, Marketization and Polarization** *Lin Zili*   165
    Concerning socialist scientific knowledge   166
    What is the significance of the present widening of income
        differentials?   168
    'Privatization' or diversification of mocro-economic forms?   170
    The necessity of 'marketization' for the socialist commodity
        economy   174

Glossary   176
Notes on the Contributors   177
Index   178

Tables

2.1   Proportion of China's basic accounting units   8
2.2   Compound annual growth rate of different industrial sectors   17
2.3   Stocks of industrial 'incentive' goods per 100 peasant
      households   17
2.4   Index of gross value of agricultural output   21
2.5   Chinese agricultural output, 1950's–1980's   21
2.6   Changes in supply in farm inputs, 1978–1986   23
2.7   Growth of the rural non-farm economy   24
2.8   Food intake of the Chinese population   25
2.9   Changes in peasant living standards   26
2.10 Share of rural income   31

3.1   The composition of retail sales by sector   44
3.2   The range of incomes in Wenzhou   45
3.3   Comparative growth rates of GVIAO   47
3.4   Trends in peasant incomes   48
3.5   Distributed collective income in Wenzhou relative to other
      provinces   50
3.6   National income per head by *xian*   51
3.7   The share of small business in OECD retail and industrial
      sectors   57
3.8   Population growth by *xian*   63
3.9   Growth of real GVIAO   64
3.10 GNP growth and sources of tax revenue in Japan   69
3.11 Tax revenue in Wenzhou by sector of origin   70
3.12 Pre- and post-tax differentials   72

6.1   Average income earned in each process of plastic bag
      production   114
6.2   Character of main goods in seven larger bases of commodity-
      production   119
6.3   Enterprises by scale in Japan   121

7.1   Distribution of the incomes of trading households   129
7.2   Distribution of incomes (industrial or processing work) 129
7.3   Distribution of people at different income levels   132

In memory of
Wang Lin

Preface

The core of this book consists of six articles written by members of the Economics Research Institute of the Chinese Academy of Social Sciences in Beijing, following a research trip to Wenzhou in 1986. They were published originally in that institute's Economic Research Materials (*Jingji yanjiu ziliao*) vol. 94, 1986, no. 8, and made available publicly (in slightly revised form) in Economics Research Institute of the Chinese Academy of Social Sciences (ed.), *The organisation and development of China's* xiangzhen *enterprises* (*Zhougguo xiangzhen qiye de jingji fazhan yu jingji tizhi*) Beijing, Chinese Economics Publishing House, 1987. Lin Zili's article was published originally in *People's Daily* (*Renmin Ribao*), 21 November 1986. The articles were translated by Chris Bramall, Peter Nolan, Wang Hong, Wang Lin and Zhang Xunhai, and revised by Peter Nolan. Peter Nolan is extremely grateful to Chris Bramall for his assistance in editing the book. The idea of publishing the articles emerged in the winter of 1986–87 when they were discussed in detail by the Cambridge Research Group on the Chinese Economy, and it became clear that they were of considerable value to anyone interested in economic reform in the socialist countries.

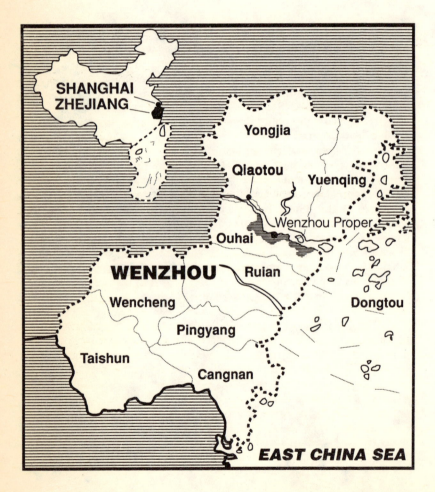

1. Introduction

Peter Nolan

In the 1920s in the USSR there was enormous debate about the appropriate institutional framework for a socialist economy. The Stalinist view was confident of the enormous gains to be won through eliminating markets and competition, and directly administering economic activity rather than leaving decision-making to individual entrepreneurs. In this way, it was thought that not only could capitalist inequality be eliminated but so, too, could its waste, and a sustained high rate of savings, investment and growth could be achieved, without the fluctuations associated with the capitalist economies. The Stalinist view, also, believed that in most economic activities there were benefits associated with large size. 'Economies of scale' were thought to operate in all sectors from steel making to farming. On the other side of the 'Great Debate', the 'Bukharinists' argued powerfully against such a vision. They felt it contained potentialities for concentration of economic power in the hands of a few people. They doubted the wisdom of attempting to eliminate competition from the economy. Competition was likened to a 'magic whip' which spurred entrepreneurs to cut costs of production, improve product quality and introduce new products. Without it, there was a danger of 'parasitic decay' among monopolistic state enterprises. Bukharin and his followers also were deeply uneasy about concentrating resources in large-scale 'gigantic' units of production. This might be appropriate in power supply or steel production, but could be quite inappropriate in large areas of farming, building, light industry and the service sector. Bukharin himself likened his economic model to 'an enormous socio-economic salad', in which there would continue to be a wide variety of institutional forms, pursuing their own economic interests within a much looser form of state planning than was visualized by the Stalinists: 'guidance' as opposed to 'directive' planning. The Bukharinist model probably meant accepting a greater degree of economic inequality than in the Stalinist model, but Bukharin and his supporters considered this an acceptable price to pay if the system was able to generate faster growth of living standards than the alternative: 'What good is equality in poverty?' Bukharin asked.

As is well known, the Stalinist vision of a socialist economy triumphed in the Soviet Union in the late 1920s, and dominated economic policy in that country right through to the mid-1980s. Only under Gorbachev has it been called seriously into question by Soviet leaders. Indeed, Gorbachev harks back explicitly to the Soviet New Economic Policy of the 1920s as a period from which the present-day reformers have much to learn. It is no coincidence that Bukharin's contribution to Soviet history is now being reassessed after decades of official vilification. The Stalinist model of comprehensive administrative planning was, however, dominant not only in the USSR but also in virtually every 'socialist' country. One economy after another took the path of centralized, administrative planning, self-sufficiency based on heavy industry, legal elimination of markets (black markets could not be fully suppressed), large-scale enterprises and agricultural collective farms. Despite some important contrasts, the Maoist path in China was not fundamentally different. For example, even though at certain points much planning was carried out locally (province, *diqu* or *xian*) rather than in Beijing, the relationship between the enterprise and the plan was no different: the enterprise's 'entrepreneurial' decisions were taken by the planners. Only for brief periods did an alternative, 'Bukharinist', view surface in China under Mao: during the early 1950s, at the end of the First Five Year Plan (1953–57) and in the early 1960s.

It has become more and more obvious that the Stalinist model can achieve only limited goals. Its successes have been its ability to sustain a high rate of investment, to achieve quite rapid growth of industrial output, to maintain near full employment, to ensure that incomes are fairly equally distributed and to insulate the economy, to a substantial degree, from world market fluctuations. The economic costs have, however, been considerable. Absence of competition has resulted, as Bukharin anticipated, in a system in which enterprise managers are profligate in the use of resources, so that a large amount of inputs are required to produce a unit of output. It has resulted, too, in a system with an appalling record in relation to technical progress, and with little incentive to improve product quality. Thus, throughout the system, old, heavy, energy-inefficient machines are used which often break down. Apart from the incentive problems stemming from lack of competition, it has proved impossible for planners to obtain either truthful or complete information from subordinate enterprises, and 'approximate' plans, which never truly balance inputs and outputs, create a permanent tendency to hoard resources since no one can rely on supplies arriving on time. This, in turn, exacerbates the situation in a vicious circle of 'shortage', which drives up costs of production (e.g., by lengthening the 'gestation period' for constructing projects and contributing to enterprises operating below full capacity). Large-scale collective farms, too, have their own peculiar problems arising principally from the difficulty of supervising large numbers of workers in farm work (even 'large' farms in the West are, typically, 'large' only in area and capital, but small in terms of numbers of workers, except at harvest time when simple easy-to-supervise operations come into play). Agricultural growth, in consequence, has been achieved only at a cost of massive additions to the rural capital stock, sucking in capital that could have been used elsewhere in the system. There is now a rich literature analysing these (and other) problems in the socialist economies. The result of their micro-economic problems has been that the socialist economies have become locked into a 'heavy industry' development path. The whole economy is profligate in the use of capital goods, and that sector itself is a heavy user of its own products. The result of this vicious circle of heavy industrial production has been a series of economies in which total industrial output value has grown quite fast, but in which the standard of living has grown at an unsatisfactory pace – in terms of the quantity and quality of light industrial products, food supply, housing and a wide variety of services. Far from eliminating waste, these economies have 'wasted' on a grand scale, in the sense, principally, that with a different set of institutions it is likely that the same labour effort could have produced a great deal more in terms of the population's standard of living. There are, however, other types of 'waste' associated with this system, not least that a huge amount of exhaustible resources are required per unit of final production; com-parative data for energy consumption per unit of output in the socialist and Western economies make disturbing reading for believers in administrative planning.

Apart from the early defection of Yugoslavia, no serious attempt to reform the Stalinist economies was made until the tentative experiments which began in the late 1960s in Hungary, and, until the late 1970s, the experiments were confined to that country. The Soviet Union's own 'reforms' in the mid-1960s and late 1970s achieved nothing in terms of the system's fundamental characteristics. The death of Mao Tsetung (Mao Zedong) and arrest of the 'Gang of Four' in 1976 transformed the balance of forces in China's leadership, and opened the way to a fundamental reconsideration of the nature of socialist economic institutions. After the historic Third Plenum of the 11th Central Committee of the Chinese Communist Party in 1978, it became clear that the Chinese leadership intended to move the economy away from the old Stalinist-Maoist system: fundamental 'system reform' was on the agenda. That is not to say that there was a clear blueprint for reform, or agreement about the methods and pace of reform. Indeed, the path of China's reform since then has been characterized as one of moving cautiously from one step to another: 'Feeling for the stones in the water to cross the river' (*mo shi guo he*). There was, however, fairly widespread agreement that there were fundamental problems with the old system.

By 1987/88, massive institutional changes had taken place in agriculture – principally contracting farmland out to individual households – and radical changes to the marketing system. Considerable elements of competition had been introduced into light industry, with, for example, many smaller state enterprises contracted out to groups or individuals, and the price of a large number of products determined by market forces. There were, however, still large areas of industry, especially heavy industry, where the reforms had progressed much less rapidly. For example, it is estimated that by 1987, 56 per cent of non-agricultural consumer goods sold in China's cities had state fixed prices and over 80 per cent of industrial means of production were sold at state fixed prices. Moreover, despite the passage of an Enterprise Bankruptcy Law in 1988, the threat of bankruptcy in practice was very small for state enterprises.

Western, Chinese and Eastern European literature is now replete with analyses of the problems of Stalinist administrative planning. There is, however, only a small amount written about the concrete politico-economic problems of putting into effect fundamental reform of the Stalinist systems. The problem of how to combine the dynamism of market forces with the attainment of socialist goals in relation to the distribution of income, power, wealth and life opportunities, as between classes, strata, regions, sexes and races within a given country is of immense complexity, and cannot be solved by slogans. The series of articles in this book represents one of the first attempts by Chinese authors to look in detail at their reform experience in a particular sector and locality, and to analyse the thorny theoretical and practical problems involved.

The Wenzhou area is in Zhejiang province in southeastern China. It is a largely coastal district, containing approximately six million people (i.e., the size of many developing countries in terms of population) centred around Wenzhou city. In the past few years Wenzhou has gained nationwide fame for its rural reforms. In most parts of China, an important part of the rural reforms begun in the late 1970s had been the lifting of legal restrictions on individual and group non-farm undertakings. The mid-1980s saw a rapid expansion of rural employment in these activities. This was a dramatic change after more than two decades in which rural cadres had condemned such activities as 'capitalist' and attempted to suppress them; capitalism had been likened to a 'dog in the water' which should be 'beaten with a stick'. The collective non-farm sector, however, despite changes in its method of operation, still remained dominant overall, especially in terms of its share of rural non-farm output. What distinguished Wenzhou was that the collective non-farm sector had been weak to begin with, and within a short space of time private non-farm activity eclipsed that in the collective sector. This sector showed immense dynamism, and appeared to be pulling along with it at a rapid pace the whole Wenzhou economy. Prior to the reforms, Wenzhou had been a relatively poor area, but the average income of its residents grew extremely rapidly after the early 1980s. This extraordinary example of a competitive economy based on small-scale private ownership aroused, unsurprisingly, intense national interest, including TV programmes, books and newspaper articles. In 1986–87 the 'Wenzhou model' spread quickly into poor areas where the collective non-farm economy was weak.

In 1986, under the leadership of Dong Fureng, a research group from the Economics Research Institute of the Chinese Academy of Social Sciences in Beijing visited Wenzhou and wrote a series of articles based on their findings. Those six articles form the basis of this book. They constitute a fascinating chronicle of the dynamics of economic reform in a planned economy, rich both in theory and descriptive detail. Dong Fureng's article provides a broad-ranging examination of all the major issues investigated by the research group, chronicling Wenzhou's extraordinary achievements and weighing in the balance the problems to emerge in the wake of the reforms. Zhang Lin analyses the proliferation of market systems and the complex division of labour that has grown up around them. Most striking has been the emergence of a large specialized button market in Wenzhou, probably the largest in Asia. Li Shi provides a detailed analysis of the economics of small-scale household industrial production in Wenzhou. He finds that from an overall, national point of view, many of Wenzhou's small-scale enterprise activities make good economic sense (as is the case with such enterprises in most poor economies) but he also identifies certain activities in which the rapid expansion of small-scale production is more problematic, such as those which have grown mainly by taking advantage of the slow progress of reform in certain sectors of state industry. One of the most striking aspects of the 'Wenzhou model' has been the emergence of privately hired labour, which is, still, an extremely contentious subject in China. Some of this hiring has been on a relatively large scale, and Chen Ruiming's article is based on a detailed analysis of a sample of these households. Prior to 1976, one of the key slogans in China was 'Serve the people', and during the Cultural Revolution China was probably one of the most egalitarian countries in the world in terms of income distribution (as well as in other respects). No slogan marked more dramatically the shift to a new set of policies after 1978, than that of 'Take the lead in getting rich', exactly the slogan used by Bukharin in the Soviet Union in the 1920s, and for which he was vilified by the 'Left'. The removal of restrictions in Wenzhou was, indeed, accompanied by a rapid widening of the range of incomes, as Zhao Renwei's article reveals. Zhao examines, also, the degree to which one might expect the differentials to alter through the operation of market forces and state action respectively. A most important issue in China is the compatibility of the 'competitive small entrepreneur' model with what might loosely be termed 'municipal socialism'. Pei Xiaoge's article focuses on the degree to which it has been possible to pool capital (either voluntarily or through local taxation) generated by Wenzhou's economic dynamism, for civic purposes of benefit to the whole local population.

Does the 'Wenzhou model' amount to socialism? The Chinese authors in this book all feel it does, albeit of a very different type from that espoused by Mao. Lin Zili's article, which concludes the book, is addressed entirely towards this issue. He argues that even in terms of Marx's own criteria, the 'Wenzhou model' is quite compatible with socialist values.

In addition to the translated articles, the book contains two articles by Western economists. The first, by Peter Nolan, provides an overall introduction to China's post-1978 rural reforms. The second, by

Christopher Bramall, sets the Wenzhou experience in national perspective, assessing, especially, the degree to which Wenzhou's extraordinary success is attributable to special factors of timing or location.

2. Petty Commodity Production in a Socialist Economy: Chinese Rural Development post-Mao[1]

Peter Nolan

Following the death of Mao Zedong in 1976, a sea change took place in Chinese political economy. The most important event in signalling these changes was the Third Plenum of the 11th Central Committee of the Chinese Communist Party (CCP), held at the end of 1978. This meeting set in motion a massive programme of reform in the late 1970s and early 1980s which, step by step, was to transform China's rural institutions which, for over two decades, had been based on a species of collective farm – the rural people's commune. This, in its turn, laid the basis for wide-ranging reforms in other areas of the economy. Within an astonishingly short period, the whole edifice of Maoist political economy was demolished. A major new epoch in the political economy not just of China but of all the 'socialist' countries had begun.

The contents of this chapter are as follows. Section 1 outlines the enormous changes which occurred in rural institutions, as well as identifying certain continuities. Performance of the rural economy is not, simply, a product of rural institutions, but is affected powerfully by the external environment in which these institutions operate. Accordingly, Section 1 also identifies the main changes and continuities in this respect. Section 2 analyses the consequences of these changes (and continuities) for the rural economy in relation to farm output, farm sector productivity, growth of the rural non-farm economy, rural incomes and living standards, and poverty in the countryside. As is stressed throughout this book, however, the new rural policies brought important new problems: the key question is where the net balance of advantage lies between two 'second best' situations. Section 3 analyses these problems, suggesting that some are real, but that some have been greatly exaggerated, and that, while others do exist, they cannot be attributed to the new policies. Section 4 draws together the threads of the preceding sections, arguing that current Chinese rural policies are best viewed in the context of an argument between two contrasting visions of rural development which goes back to the 1920s in the USSR. Broadly speaking, China has returned to the 'Bukharinist' path, and away from the 'Stalinist-Maoist' path which dominated rural policy in the 'socialist' countries from the late 1920s through to the 1980s. This shift is of the greatest historical significance, not

7

just for China's vast peasant masses, but also in terms of its impact on policy formation in a large number of other countries.

THE REFORM

Institutions and policies within the villages

Changes
Contracting work to the household: Beginning in the late 1970s, and accelerating into the early 1980s, there occurred a dramatic transformation of China's rural institutions and policies.[2] Its centrepiece was the splitting up of production teams (sub-units within the rural people's communes) and the establishment of different forms of 'contract' system: either 'contracting output to the group' (*bao chan dao zu*), 'contracting output to the household' (*bao chan dao hu*), or 'contracting work to the household' (*bao gan dao hu*). These systems spread rapidly. By the end of 1980 almost half the basic accounting units were employing some kind of 'contract' system:

Table 2.1
Proportion of China's basic accounting units in people's communes employing different types of contract system prior to 1983

	1980		1981		1982
	Jan.	*Dec.*	*June*	*Oct.*	*Dec.*
Bao chan dao zu	24.9	23.6	13.8	10.8	13.3
Bao chan dao hu	4.1	18.5	31.3	26.6	8.7
Bao gan dao hu	0.02	5.0	11.3	38.0	70.0
Total	*29.02*	*47.1*	*56.4*	*75.4*	*92.0*

Source: Kueh, 1984: 357

Under the *bao chan* systems, the group (*zu*) or household (*hu*) contracted with the production team to fulfil a specified amount of farm output (to be handed over to the team) for a fixed land area, with current inputs fixed and provided by the team. In return for fulfilling the contracted task the group or household was given an agreed workpoint entitlement (with proportionate reductions in workpoints for underfulfilment of the contract). Any output in excess of the contract could be retained by the group or the household (Nolan, 1983(b)).

In 1982–83 there occurred a full-scale return to family farming. 'Contracting work to the household' (*bao gan dao hu*) became almost universal practice, and by the end of 1983, over 94 per cent of peasant households in China operated under this system (ZGTJNJ, 1984: 131). In its speed and importance, the 'decollectivization' of Chinese agriculture in 1982–83 directly parallels 'collectivization' in 1955–56. The post-1978 reforms brought a profound transformation to daily life for China's 800 million peasants.

The role of the party: Before 1978 the CCP intervened deeply in all aspects of rural political, economic and social life. An important part of the post-Mao rural reforms was an attempt to increase rural economic efficiency by separating formally party from both government and economic administration in the villages. The party was now supposed to confine itself to ideological work, namely 'guaranteeing the two civilizations' (cultural and spiritual) (Nolan, 1983(b)).

It is difficult to assess the degree to which party control over village life had changed (White, 1985). Undoubtedly, the number of village cadres (both party and non-party) fell sharply in the 1980s, perhaps by as much as a half,[3] paralleling the decline in their control over daily peasant life (Nolan, 1983(b)).[4] Also, the prestige of party members who formerly administered Maoist policies suffered severely with the about-turn in party policy after 1978. For years, rural party cadres had been urging peasants to 'serve the people' and shun 'material incentive'. Suddenly, they were told to encourage 'take the lead in getting rich'. The psychological disorientation was profound. The party's influence had waned as new, more complex village power relations emerged. One commentator argued: 'In contrast to the former "fusion" of political and economic power within the collectives, there has been a process of separation into two power systems, one based on formal institutionalised authority and one on control over economic resources (including scarce skills)' (White, 1985).

In fact, the decline in party authority and its separation from administration in rural economic affairs in the 1980s was far from complete. Despite the upheavals of the late 1970s and early 1980s there still were a number of key economic channels through which the CCP exercised power in the villages, including the allocation of grain purchase quotas, of petrol and chemical fertilizer, power supply, administration of the 'birth plan', mediation in economic disputes, allocation of licences to set up new businesses, and access to health and educational facilities.

Contracts: Before 1978 most decisions on rural production and distribution were administered directly by the state or indirectly by the state's representatives in collectives. The 1980s witnessed an explosion of independent economic decision-making by individuals and groups. Integral to this process was a massive expansion of economic contracts, so that by the mid-1980s a single *xian* could have up to half a million legally binding contracts ('Handling economic disputes', 1985). A massive new edifice of economic law began to be constructed to facilitate the workings of the mushrooming markets.

Land division: By 1983, virtually all collectively owned farmland had been divided up for operation by individual farm households. Initially, the period of the land contract was unspecified, but it quickly became obvious that the uncertainty thereby produced led to a shortening of peasants' time horizons and problems in respect to investment in the land for long-term returns. Accordingly, in 1984 (Central Committee, 1984: Article 3(i)) the contracted period for most types of land was fixed at 15 years. Early in 1987, it seems likely that the important decision was taken by the State Council to extend the land contract period to 50 years and to permit land contracts to be inherited by children.[5] Land division was the heart of the 'contract system', with decisions over the multiple aspects of farm work taken out of the hands of collective cadres and returned to individual farm households: the rural 'labour process' was transformed fundamentally by this.

'Parcellization' of holdings was integral to the process of land division. Not only did each household receive a small plot, but these plots generally were sub-divided into still smaller units to enable each household to receive its share of good and bad land (Nolan, 1983(a)).

Land contracts were transferable from one household to another, where the transferring-out household was short of labour or wished to change occupation. Indeed, the process quickly became actively encouraged by the state in the interests of 'concentrating land in the hands of farming experts' (Central Committee, 1984: Article 3(i)). The household which ceased to cultivate the land was permitted legally to require the new cultivator to supply his household with a certain amount of grain at the parity (state) price (Central Committee, 1984: Article 3(i)) and, in many areas, the local authorities permitted rent payments for the use of the contracted land.

Agricultural means of production other than land: Prior to 1978 virtually all means of production in the countryside had been 'collectively' owned. In 1982–83, small 'traditional' means of production (e.g., farm tools), draft animals and most small modern means of production (including walking tractors, small sprayers, threshers, etc.,) were sold off to peasants (Nolan, 1983(b)). Peasants then became legally entitled to own individually, and to bequeath to children, both large and small means of agricultural production (Nolan, 1983(b)). Many larger collective means of production (e.g., tractors, large sprayers, trucks) also were sold off to individuals or groups of households in 1982–83. A large number (probably the majority) of them remained, however, in the ownership of the *cun* ('village')[6] or the *hezuoshe* ('co-operative'), since they were almost always beyond the financial means of individual peasants (Nolan, 1983(b); Oi, 1986(a)). Under the contract system individual households had to pay fees for the use of collective means of production. Collectively owned large means of farm production generally were operated under a contract between their drivers and the collective; often the price paid for the right to use collective assets was established through a collectively run auction among prospective operators. The operators of these assets were typically rewarded or penalized in relation to the degree of over- or under-fulfilment of contracts that they struck with the peasants (Nolan, 1983(b)), in sharp contrast to the pre-1978 system.

Technical services: Both the nature and the extent of technical service work altered in the 1980s. Alongside the rapid rise in rural incomes in the 1980s (see below) went a considerable expansion of rural technical services provision, though there were big regional differences depending on the level of development in the local economy (Nolan, 1983(b)). In well-located areas, by the early 1980s, a comprehensive system of technical services, from the *xian* down to the *cun* had become established (Nolan, 1983(b)). Pre-1978 the remuneration of technical service workers was unrelated to the quality of their work. By the early 1960s nearly all such workers had shifted to a 'contract' system with variable remuneration, depending on how well work was done.

Specialized households: In the early 1980s the state actively encouraged the development of a group of 'specialized households' who could concentrate on a narrow range of farm or non-farm production and develop their efficiency in these lines. They could sit state-run exams and obtain formal registration as 'specialized households' and thereby gain access to various benefits (Nolan, 1983(b); and Oi, 1986(a)). The state laid down that the specialized households should be 'cherished and supported' and provided with the necessary services, and that their needs should be met in respect to information, supply and marketing, and technical progress (Central Committee, 1984: Article 3(iv)). According to the criteria adopted in the 1984–85 national peasants' survey, just 3.5 per cent of households surveyed were categorized as 'specialized households' (Rural Survey Group, 1986: 11).

The rural non-agricultural economy: In the 1960s and 1970s, China's rural industries expanded quite rapidly. Though their share of total industrial output was small (in 1980, commune-run industry still produced just seven per cent of China's total gross value of industrial output – State Statistical Bureau, 1982: 212), in certain sectors they produced a large share of total output, e.g., by the early 1970s almost half of China's cement, and over two-fifths of her nitrogenous fertilizer output, came from small rural plants (Byres and Nolan, 1976: 69).

Most Western observers considered that this was a sensible strategy to pursue.[7] Small rural plants had a short gestation period; they could make use of dispersed raw material deposits; they made use of local workers who could continue to live in the villages, and the economy thereby saved on urban overhead costs, and, above all, they economized on transport costs – of materials, workers, food (to feed urban workers) and final products. Given that, in common with most less developed countries, China's transport and distribution were extremely backward, and in view, also, of the fact that this sector was neglected under Maoist policies of regional self-sufficiency, the quite rapid development of certain rural small-scale industries made good sense. In the 1980s, however, output of rural small-scale enterprises expanded dramatically. Few outside observers anticipated such an acceleration in the pace of growth of a sector that, from some standpoints, already appeared to be performing quite well. What factors explain this?

Major changes took place in respect of the collectively run (*xiangcun* – former commune and brigade) enterprises[8] which, despite the massive expansion of non-collective rural enterprises in the 1980s, were still the dominant form of rural non-farm enterprise in the mid-1980s, in terms both of employment and total output. Instead of being run directly by the collective authorities, virtually all such enterprises by the mid-1980s operated under some form of contract arrangement with the collective, so that 'collective enterprises' encompassed a wide variety of production relationships. Certain generalizations can, however, be made compared to pre-1978.

First, the position of managers altered. Instead of having a lifetime tenure, by the mid-1980s they were commonly appointed for a fixed term (say three years) often by the *xiang* authorities (see below) and the criteria for appointing collective enterprise managers shifted decisively away from the political and towards the technical. Generally, managers had become solely responsible for their enterprise's profit and loss. The manager's income was now determined by the enterprise's economic performance, with a bonus depending on the degree to which the enterprise over-fulfilled contracted targets. Bonuses could be very high by the standards of rural China (under-fulfilment of targets resulted in a financial penalty).

Within the enterprise, managers generally had much-increased freedom to organize the production process without party intervention, and profit-seeking behaviour was encouraged strongly under the new ethos. Moreover, managers were still (as pre-1978) unencumbered by the necessity of having to deal with trade unions, since there generally still were none in *xiangcun* enterprises. In external relationships, there occurred a considerable increase in enterprise independence, so that collective enterprise managers came to behave in a manner much closer to genuine entrepreneurs.

For workers too, there were dramatic changes post-1978. In the 1960s and 1970s workers in commune enterprises generally were paid in work-points allocated through their production team. Though they might earn rather more than ordinary peasants, there was no relationship between their enterprise's performance and their income, and wages were paid as time rates (Nolan and White, 1980: 30–31). For most *xiangcun* enterprises, the 1980s saw a shift to piece rates, with basic rates and bonuses related to the enterprise's performance (in the medium- and short-term respectively). Work intensity increased sharply: the prospect of extra income for workers whose living standard was low and had been unchanged for many years led them to accept greatly increased labour input for relatively small increases in personal income.[9]

The external setting of the former commune enterprises altered sharply, too, in the 1980s. Under the former system most material inputs were provided by the state at state-fixed prices and most of the final product was sold to the state at state-fixed prices.[10] Relaxation of state controls in these areas began to take effect much earlier in the collective than in state enterprises. By the mid-1980s collective enterprises had greatly increased their freedom, compared to pre-1978, to negotiate supply sources, prices, and outlets. In the early and mid-1980s not only were rural non-farm enterprises given greatly increased freedom to purchase inputs, but they had much greater freedom than state enterprises to fix prices (Xue, 1985: 20).

Among other external forces assisting the expansion of *xiangcun* enterprises were 1. the sharp increase in average incomes (see below) fuelling demand for their products (most conspicuously, this stimulated a massive rural housing boom); 2. the rapid growth in output of 'economic' crops which are inputs for many of these enterprises; 3. the rapid rise in output from large-scale urban consumer durables enterprises, which frequently sub-contract to local rural enterprises; 4. the continued backwardness of China's transport system which helped give many otherwise uncompetitive rural enterprises a cost advantage over urban enterprises.

It is a misnomer to call China's *xiangcun* enterprises of the mid-1980s 'collectives' or 'co-operatives', since they were not generally owned and/or run by employees. Rather, they were owned by the *xiang* or the *cun*. Their success was very much dependent on co-operation, however. Standing above each enterprise was a multi-layered structure to assist the enterprises in whose success the higher structures had a strong financial stake (see below). Each province had a *xiangzhen* enterprise bureau[11] which was linked to corresponding bureaux at the *xian* and *xiang* level. A *xian* bureau in an advanced area might have 1,000 or more enterprises within its territory. It had important functions in providing credit, approving relatively large new projects, researching market opportunities, etc. The key level in strategic planning, however, was the *xiang*. The relevant *xiang* department oversaw all the *xiangcun* enterprises owned by the *xiang* or *cun*. It often negotiated the purchase of inputs for enterprises; it took the decision about setting up new *xiang*-owned enterprises; held examinations for recruitment of new workers; raised capital for new *xiang* investments through issuing shares; re-arranged the employment of workers in enterprises which close down; decided the level of 'basic wages' in different enterprises, and determined the conditions under which bonuses are awarded. It also sought out new market opportunities and provided information on up-grading technical skills.[12]

The changes in the 1980s in the way *xiangcun* enterprises operated were clearly extremely important. Even more striking in qualitative terms, however (and, increasingly, in quantitative terms) was the rise of non-collective, non-farm enterprises in the mid-1980s, and it is this which is the focus of this book. Under Mao, it was impossible legally for an individual or a group of co-operators to set up an independent enterprise. Indeed, anyone leaving agriculture to work in outside activity was liable to be seriously criticized. In the early 1980s such prohibitions were removed completely. Peasants were strongly encouraged to seek non-farm employment in the villages or small towns, so as to absorb some of the agricultural labour surplus, and leave higher productivity 'farming experts' to do the farming. Rural non-farm enterprises with a multiplicity of ownership and operating structures mushroomed. These included industrial self-employed individuals, genuine, self-employing co-operatives, small groups of owner-managers, employing other workers, individual owner-operators employing workers, individuals and/or groups of peasants co-operating with *xiangcun* enterprises, individuals and/or groups of peasants leasing enterprises from the *xiang* or *cun*, and so on (see, especially, Watson, 1984/85). By 1985, these diverse forms of non-farm, non-collective enterprises were accounting for two-fifths of total employment and 27 per cent of the gross value of output in 'township' (i.e., rural non-farm) enterprises (ZGJJNJ, 1986: v, 42).

The regional pattern in terms of the relative importance of the collective and non-collective sectors in the non-farm rural economy in the mid-1980s was striking. The collectively-owned sector generally was strong in areas where the rural non-farm economy was most advanced, especially those in close proximity to large urban centres such as Southern Jiangsu: indeed, by 1986–87 this being referred to as the '*Sunan*' (Southern Jiangsu) model. In less well-located areas, with less opportunities to undertake sub-contracting from large factories, where technical skills were weaker, and where brigade and commune enterprises were weakly developed pre-1978, the private (and genuinely co-operative) sector was relatively much more important in the non-farm sector. In some areas, such as Wenzhou in southern Zhejiang province, the individual non-farm rural economy expanded very rapidly indeed in the mid-1980s. This alternative path of development was, by 1986–87, being referred to as the 'Wenzhou' model, and was becoming the characteristic form in poorer parts of the Chinese countryside. It is this model upon which this book focuses.

Hired labour: Given the central role of the exploitation of wage labour in Marx's writings, this has been a delicate issue for the Chinese leadership. In the early 1980s private rural labour hiring started to re-emerge after a long prohibition. The party's response was a 1982 national regulation which limited a peasant to hiring two 'apprentices' and five hired labourers (Nolan, 1983(b)). This was shortly followed, however, by Premier Zhao Ziyang's statement that if a person hired more than the regulations permitted, they should not be stopped. The appropriate policy was to 'wait and see' (Nolan, 1983(b)). After this, there was little direct restriction of individual labour hiring, and rural privately hired labour expanded rapidly (from a negligible base). This development has been of immense qualitative significance, and has prompted a great deal of debate within the party.

Given the huge extent of rural surplus labour, however, and the problems of labour supervision, there was quite limited expansion of hired labour in farming proper. In the rural non-farm sector the number of hired workers in individually run enterprises was growing rapidly in the mid-1980s, but the average enterprise size was minuscule. In 1985, they had an average of just two people (including the employer) per enterprise, compared to an average of 50 staff and workers per *xiang*-run, and 18 per *cun*-run, enterprise (ZGJJNJ, 1986: v, 42). Even the *xiang*-run and *cun*-run enterprises were very small by international criteria.

Income ceilings: Under Mao there were strict limits on income differentials both within any given village and at the spatial level. The change in approach after 1978 was dramatic. The idea that peasants should improve their income levels at a roughly similar pace ('the boat rises with the water level') was rejected firmly as inhibiting peasants' 'production enthusiasm'. Instead, the key slogan became 'take the lead in getting rich':

> It is only through people 'taking the lead in becoming rich' becoming examples of prosperity, creating experience of becoming well-off through hard labour, arousing other people's enthusiasm and creativity, promoting human competition, that more and more people can be led to take the path to common prosperity. (Hu and Yu, 1986)

Continuities

The changes in the early and mid-1980s outlined on the preceding pages amount to a revolution in daily life for China's vast peasant population. Not everything changed, however, and in the mid-1980s there were still some important continuities with pre-1978.

China's leading policy-makers and rural economists did not shift to the view that market forces solve all economic problems. On the contrary, they emphasized that many activities necessary to the success of the farm economy exhibit 'lumpiness' and/or economies of scale. Intervention with the market was recognized as being needed frequently to ensure that they were provided (see, e.g., Lin, 1982; Du, 1983):

> [T]he implementation of the household contract system has eliminated the drawbacks of the rural co-operative system, and only its drawbacks, *not the system itself. China will hold fast to the co-operative system.* With the development of production and the transition from a rural natural economy to a commodity economy ... *many things cannot be accomplished by one family or a household alone.* (Dai, 1986: 4) (My emphases: P.N.)

In the Chinese countryside after de-collectivization these activities principally were provided by the *hezuoshe* (former 'team'), *cun* (former 'brigade'), *xiang* (former 'commune') or *xian* (county), rather than by intervention through the price mechanism.

The most important such activity is irrigation and drainage. It was acknowledged explicitly that the free market currently would meet only a small portion of water conservation requirements, and the collectives remained massively the dominant organizer of this facility. Indeed, an important aspect of peasants' obligations to the collective was the requirement to pay either in labour time or in cash for collective water conservation (Sang, 1983: 137–39). Another important aspect of farming in which the market often works imperfectly is in the provision of a wide variety of technical services, including accounting, seed selection and supply, planting techniques, and plant protection. Although the methods by which they were provided had changed, far from being dismantled, these vital activities were greatly enhanced after 1978. Other activities critical to the success of the rural economy, but beyond the scope of individual households, are power and road construction. In the countryside in the mid-1980s these activities were still primarily organized either by the *xiang* or by the *xian. Xiang* members were still required to provide contributions in cash or kind to ensure that these activities were undertaken (Nolan, 1983(b); Hinton, 1983: 9); collectives also raised revenue for these activities with resources from the non-farm economy. In addition, the *xian* authorities contributed to these activites with revenues from the local economy.

The continued importance of collective activity is shown by the fact that in the mid-1980s it was the collective that was still the most important sector in total rural accumulation. In 1984, of the total funds invested in rural 'production' activities, just 1 per cent came from state support funds, compared to 6 per cent from the 'new economic associations' and 40 per cent from peasant households, while 54 per cent still came from collective investment (Present situation..., 1986: 2).[13]

Much admired under Mao by many outside observers was the contribution made to rural living standards by collective welfare institutions. Accident and old-age insurance is generally hard to operate in a poor, rural environment, so the collective has a potentially important role to play in this sphere. Education and health both often involve lumpy expenditures, are characterized by externalities, and are often beyond the incomes of poor people if the full cost-covering price is charged for services. Again, collectives played an important role in organizing these activities under Mao. Post-1978 there were major changes in each of these areas, most strikingly in education (where teaching methods, exam methods, the balance between different sectors, etc., altered sharply) and in health (the incomes of doctors were related to 'success' indicators, and the subsidy element in the pricing of services was much reduced)[14] (Nolan, 1983(b)). Despite these changes national policy remained strongly committed to collective organization and provision of welfare activities. This was reflected in the contributions peasants in most areas were required to make to the 'collective welfare fund' (though in some extremely rich areas with exceptionally high income from collective enterprises, the contribution was often waived).

The villages' external environment

Changes
Supply of industrial 'incentive' goods: For more than two decades in China the rate of growth of heavy industry was considerably faster than that of light industry. A sharp reversal occurred after 1978:

Table 2.2
Compound annual growth rate of different industrial sectors in China, at 'comparable' prices (%)

	1957–78	1978–85
Heavy industry (gross value)	11.0	8.2
Light industry (gross value)	8.2	12.6

Source: ZGTJZY, 1985: 309.

Note: By at 'comparable' prices the Chinese mean a linked index using different sets of constant prices for different parts of the index.

For a wide range of industrial consumer goods (especially consumer durables) extremely fast growth rates were achieved post-1978. A number of new industries were set up (e.g., colour TVs, cassette recorders, household refrigerators) and grew rapidly to high levels of output. The range and quality of consumer goods increased quickly compared to pre-1978. In only a few years, the consumption of consumer durables attained high levels for the peasant population of a low income country:

Table 2.3
Stocks of industrial 'incentive' goods per 100 peasant households in China

	1978	1985
Bicycles	30.7	80.6
Sewing machines	19.8	43.2
Radios	17.4	54.2
Clocks	51.8	163.6
of which: wrist-watches	27.4	126.3
TV sets	0.4 (1980)	11.7

Source: ZGTJZY, 1986: 112.

Farm marketing: Pre-1978 there was an almost complete state monopoly of farm purchases (in 1978 a mere 4 per cent of farm sector marketing to the non-farm sector went through non-state channels (Duan, 1983)) and over

90 per cent of the non-farm sector's purchases of farm produce were one form or another of compulsory sale (ZGTJNJ, 1985: 479). At the prices paid by the state there was, for most farm products, a higher income to be earned by selling to the 'free' market than to the state. To stimulate farm output, after 1978 the state reduced the range of compulsorily purchased produce[15] and peasants were allowed freely to dispose of produce once they had fulfilled state sales targets (Nolan, 1983). The proportion of farm output sold by peasants at state-fixed prices fell in the 1980s. Moreover, the state rapidly raised the proportion of compulsory purchases made at the higher 'premium' price for 'above quota' sales.

A crisis in agricultural marketing emerged quickly in the mid-1980s. The state was caught in a vice that was tightening with the very success of the agricultural reform in stimulating output. The state was still the principal purchaser of farm output and the main seller to urban consumers, but in its desire to maintain urban price stability,[16] it allowed a gap to open up between the purchase and sale price. This contributed to the emergence of both local and national budgetary deficits.

Following the cautious measures to reform the agricultural marketing set-up in the early 1980s, the state responded to the crisis by announcing drastic changes to the compulsory procurement which had been in operation since the early 1950s (Central Committee, 1985). The old system of state compulsory purchase[17] of grain and cotton was to be abolished and replaced by contracts[18] and open market purchases.[19] The contract was to be concluded between the peasants and the commercial departments 'after discussion prior to the planting season' (Central Committee, 1985). For products other than grain and cotton which were still compulsorily procured in one form or another, the old system was to be 'gradually abolished' at different speeds for different products and in different areas, and replaced by a system under which products were 'freely brought to the market, freely exchanged and quality is reflected in price'. It was declared emphatically: 'No unit is any longer permitted to send mandatory production plans down to the peasants' (Central Committee, 1985).

Agricultural-industrial terms of trade: In its attempt to stimulate the growth of agricultural production after 1978, the government raised substantially the purchase price of farm produce: the state purchase price index increased by no less than two-fifths from 1978 to 1981.[20] At the same time, the price at which the state sold industrial products to the villages rose very little. Consequently, this period saw a sharp improvement for the peasants in the relative prices they encountered.

Continuities
Taxation: China's rural tax system in the early 1980s was quite unprepared for the sudden emergence of a relatively small number of rich peasants, such as those in Wenzhou. China's personal income tax law was not intended to apply to peasants for whom there was no formal system of

personal income tax. It is true that peasants were supposed to pay the 'agricultural tax', but this had been unchanged for many years and, of course, was of no relevance to the rapidly growing non-farm sector. Collective enterprises were required to pay over a substantial portion (on average around one-third of profits) of their profits to higher authorities. By and large this system seems to have worked well. The biggest problem was in relation to individual enterprises where the very high incomes of some individuals caused much dissatisfaction ('red eye disease'). There is good reason to think that market forces might eventually reduce these incomes, but there are, clearly, great resentments that some extremely rich people (by Chinese standards) should be virtually free of taxation. As is described in Lin Zili's chapter (which draws this volume to a close) the government responded by introducing a set of temporary regulations to deal with the situation. They involved steep progressive taxation of rural individual industrial and commercial income. Although far from perfect, this was of more than symbolic significance: even an imperfect (though, hopefully, improving) business tax may raise more revenue in an expanding economy than a perfectly effective one in a stagnant economy.

Compulsory procurement and state price fixing: Despite the massive shift in policy which began in the early 1980s and accelerated rapidly in 1985, it remained the case that the state continued to purchase a large part of agricultural marketings. Even after the reforms, 83 per cent of agricultural and sideline sales in 1985 were to state departments of one kind or another (ZGTJZY, 1986: 93). Moreover, there is ample evidence that a large portion of state grain purchase contracts after the reform retained their compulsory character.

While the purchase prices of a large number of farm products, indeed, were allowed to fluctuate freely with market forces, this was not true in practice for the most important ones. The state contract purchases not only of grain and cotton, but also of 'several other important products' still had 'state fixed prices' (ZGJJNJ, 1986: v, 49). By 1987, the number of farm products purchased by the state at state-fixed ('unified') prices had fallen from 113 to 25, and these were reported still to account for 30 per cent of the total value of farm sales (Gao, 1987). Moreover, a considerable proportion of remaining sales was at 'floating' prices with the state fixing the limits of the float.

While ration tickets were abolished for all types of food products except grain and edible oil, most urban food produce continued to be sold through state outlets[21] with either basically state-fixed prices or 'floating prices'. Even in the 'free markets', in large cities the prices of 'several important subsidiary foodstuffs' had a state-fixed price ceiling (ZGJJNJ, 1986: v, 49).

The Chinese leadership in the mid-1980s was deeply concerned to maintain grain marketings at an adequate level and to control food prices in cities. It was reluctant to allow market forces to become the principal determinant of farm output and urban food prices for fear of the political de-stabilization that might follow from accompanying price rises:[22] the 'Polish problem' was never far from their minds. Even the relatively cautious urban food price rises for 1985 (14.4 per cent) and 1986 (7.4 per cent) (State Statistical Bureau, 1987) caused great popular dissatisfaction in a society used to a long period of price stability.

The system of supply of industrial inputs to agriculture: Changes took place in the early and mid-1980s in the nature of the supply of agricultural inputs. A large part of the supply of agricultural inputs did, however, continue to take place through state channels at state-fixed prices. Access to these was strictly rationed. A three-tiered market for certain key inputs such as chemical fertilizers and gasoline developed. The state supplied a large portion of these inputs at relatively low prices. At these prices demand in most areas still greatly exceeded supply. A second portion was supplied by the state at higher, market-influenced prices. A third, still higher, price existed on the free market, to which supplies came from a variety of channels.[23] Indeed, an integral part of the state's post-reform capacity to influence peasants to sign contracts voluntarily was its position as supplier of priority-priced farm inputs (Oi, 1986(b): 240).

PERFORMANCE OF THE RURAL ECONOMY POST-1978

The preceding section outlined the dramatic changes that occurred in China's rural institutions after 1978. From early on in this reform a fairly clear 'reform' model could be perceived, in sharp contrast to reforms in the large-scale industrial sector, where the problems were much more complex and the reform model was not clear.[24] The essence of the rural reform model was individual operation of farmland supplemented by extensive co-operation and state action to provide an effective framework for households' productive endeavours. This still left a wide array of important issues in rural policy about which there could be dispute (e.g., the degree of state intervention in farm marketing, farm price policy, hired labour, the permitted dimensions of income inequality, international trade in food products) but at the core of the reforms there was a solid base upon which virtually all Chinese leaders, in so far as one can tell, and most Chinese people were in agreement.

Important non-institutional changes also occurred after 1978, including major changes in the relative prices of farm and non-farm products, urban demand for farm produce and the supply of industrial 'incentive' goods to peasants. These would, however, have been insufficient to produce a dramatic improvement in the performance of the rural economy. Moreover, these changes were not unconnected with the transformation in rural institutions. For example, growth of output of industrial incentive goods was assisted by the rapid expansion of the rural non-farm sector both in relation to sub-contracting and direct supply of finished products.

This section outlines the extraordinary progress in China's rural economy after 1978 in relation to farm output, farm productivity, the non-

Table 2.4
Index of gross value of agricultural output (at 'comparable' prices)[a]

Index		*compound annual growth rate (%)*
1955–57	58	
		2.8
1975–77	100	
		8.4
1983–85	190	

Sources: ZGTJNJ, 1985: 238; ZGTJZY, 1986: 32.

Note:
a. A linked index using different sets of constant prices for different parts of the index.

Table 2.5
Chinese agricultural output, 1950s–1980s

	Average annual output (million metric tons)			Compound annual growth rate (%)	
	1955–57	*1975–77*	*1984–86*	*1955–57 to 1975–77*	*1975–77 to 1984–86*
Grain	191	285	392	2.0	3.6
Cotton	1.54	2.16	4.65	1.7	8.9
Oilseeds	4.71	4.18	14.14	–0.6	14.5
Jute and hemp	0.279	0.764	2.11	5.2	12.0
Sugar cane	9.05	17.02	47.09	3.2	12.0
Beetroots	1.58	2.61	8.50	2.5	14.0
Silk cocoons	0.126	0.201	0.366	2.4	6.9
Tea	0.114	0.232	0.439	3.6	7.3
Cured tobacco	0.256[a]	0.836	1.668	6.1	8.0
Fruits	2.79	5.49	11.63	3.1	8.7
Meat (pork, beef, mutton	3.99[a]	7.86	17.38	3.5	9.2
Aquatic products[b]	2.76	4.53	7.1	2.1	5.1

Notes:
a. 1957 only.
b. It is hard to disentangle the proportion included in farm production.

Sources: Luo, 1985: 186, 190, 194; ZGTJNJ, 1985: 255–6, 267, 270; State Statistical Bureau, 1986; ZGTJZY, 1986: 38; State Statistical Bureau, 1987.

farm sector, living standards and the decline in poverty. This immense change, affecting a vast number of people, is of the greatest historical importance, and provokes deep reflection among anyone concerned with rural policy in developing countries.

Farm output

There are few, if any, examples in modern economic history of such a sustained break in trend growth rates of agricultural output as that achieved in China from the late 1970s to the mid-1980s. The gross value of farm output at 'comparable' prices reportedly increased its compound annual average growth rate from under 3 per cent from the mid-1950s to mid-1979s, to over 8 per cent from the mid-1970s to mid-1980s:[25]

The acceleration was broadly-based, with a wide range of farm products reportedly experiencing unprecedentedly rapid growth (see table 2.5).

Farm sector productivity

The sharp acceleration in farm output in the late 1970s and early 1980s was produced by a farm labour force growing much more slowly than in the preceding period and than the total workforce. The reported growth of farm labour productivity is perhaps the most striking of all the data on the farm sector after 1978. After long years of stagnation under Maoist policies, farm output per worker (in real terms) reportedly grew by almost 60 per cent from 1978 to 1984, and by almost 80 per cent from 1975 to 1984.[26]

Some Western analysts expressed the fear that de-collectivization would lead to a collapse of rural capital formation in Chinese agriculture. This was not the case. Given that by the late 1970s China had already established an extremely high level of irrigation (the leading 'input' in the Asian 'Green Revolution') the most important single agricultural input for increasing farm output was chemical fertilizer. Far from stagnating, the consumption of chemical fertilizer more than doubled from 1978 to 1986 (see table below). Moreover, the quality of chemical fertilizers increased due to 1. a reduction in the proportion supplied by low-quality small plants, 2. improvement in quality in large plants, and 3. more sophisticated fertilizer handling and application (Stone, 1985: 118). The data on agricultural machinery in the following table superficially show the same story, with the total horsepower used in 'agriculture' almost doubling from 1978 to 1986.

Although technically categorized for 'agricultural' use, much of this was, however, used wholly or partly for non-agricultural purposes. A truck might carry grain to market at harvest time, but carry other products during the rest of the year. Large and small tractors are commonly used only part of the time in the fields; for much of the time they transport goods on the roads. In fact, in certain important respects, mechanized inputs into agriculture proper stagnated or declined. From 1978 to 1985, the power-irrigated area hardly altered and the mechanically ploughed area fell by over 15 per cent (despite a large increase in tractor stocks).

The remarkable growth of farm output after 1978 was achieved with a relatively small addition to the stock of fixed capital for use in agriculture proper,[27] so that there must have been a sharp fall in the agricultural fixed capital to output ratio. The main technical basis for the growth of output

Table 2.6
Changes in supply of farm inputs, 1978–86

	Unit	1978[1]	1980[1]	1983[1]	1984[1]	1985[1]	1986[2]
Stocks of:							
1. Total motive	million	159.8	200.5	245.0	265.1	284.3	(310) a
2. Large and medium-sized tractors used in agriculture	million	0.56	0.74	0.84	0.85	0.85	0.87
3. Small-sized and walking tractors used in agriculture	million	1.37	1.87	2.75	3.30	3.82	–
4. Large- and medium-sized tractor-pulled agricultural implements	million	1.19	1.37	1.31	1.24	1.13	–
5. Motors for drainage and h.p. irrigation in agriculture	million	65.6	74.6	78.5	78.5	78.2	(82) a
6. Combine harvesters	thousand	19.0	27.0	35.7	35.9	34.6	–
7. Trucks for agricultural use	thousand	73.8	137.7	274.8	349.3	427.6	494.0
8. Animal-drawn carts with rubber tyres							
1. Large	million	2.49	2.40	2.59	2.85	2.88	–
2. Small	million	29.6	35.2	55.6	59.5	61.1	–
9. Motorized fishing boats	million h.p.	2.91	3.51	4.44	4.56	4.99	–
Mechanically ploughed area	million ha.	40.7	41.0	33.6	34.9	34.4	–
Irrigated area of which:	million ha.	45.0	44.9	44.6	44.5	44.0	–
power-irrigated area	million ha.	24.9	25.3	25.3	25.1	24.6	–
Consumption fertilizers (nutrient weight)	million tons	8.8	12.7	16.6	17.4	17.8	19.5
Electricity consumed in the rural areas	billion kwh	25.3	32.1	42.8	46.4	50.9	57.5

Sources: 1. ZGTJZY, 1986: 43–44; 2. State Statistical Bureau, 1987.
Note: a. approximate figures

was the huge increase in the quantity of chemical fertilizer together with the improvements in its quality (Stone, 1985: 118).

The rural non-farm economy
Impressive as the growth of farm output was, growth of the non-farm rural economy was even more dramatic. The total value of output of this sector in real terms probably rose more than fourfold from 1979 to 1985:

Table 2.7
Growth of the rural non-farm economy

	1979	1984	1985	1985 as % of 1979
Value of output (billion yuan at current prices)	45.3	138.1	201.1	444
Employment (million)	23.8	42.6	45.8	192

Source: Research Department, 1986: 13.

Note: I have not been able to obtain an index of rural non-farm prices. The overall index of retail prices of consumption goods reportedly rose 28.1 per cent from 1978 to 1985, but much the fastest growth was in foodstuffs which reportedly rose 49.4 per cent. For clothing the index fell 3.3 per cent, and for 'daily use goods' rose just 6.3 per cent (ZGTJZY, 1986: 100). Also, it should be remembered that rural non-farm enterprises had obtained much more independence in price-setting than state enterprises, which they frequently undercut. It seems most likely that the price index for rural non-farm enterprises rose by as much as the overall retail price index; therefore, the vast bulk of the reported increase in output value probably was 'real'.

Employment also grew very quickly. By 1986 the 12.2 billion 'rural enterprises' were reportedly employing 76 million workers, amounting to 20 per cent of the rural workforce (Han, 1987(b)). The sharp rise in the importance of the rural non-farm sector employment in the mid-1980s is reflected in the rapidly changing composition of total rural production. The reported share of the rural non-farm economy (at current prices) in total rural social product rose from 37 per cent in 1984 to 47 per cent in 1986 (ZGTJZY, 1986: 33; State Statistical Bureau, 1987). By 1985 *xiang*- and *cun*-run industry was producing over 18 per cent of national industrial output value (ZGTJZY, 1986: 50). In certain sectors of the economy their contribution by the mid-1980s had become extremely important. In 1985, *xiangzhen* (township) enterprises produced 29 per cent of China's coal, 50 per cent of its clothes, and 53 per cent of the value of building materials (Han, 1987(b)).

Incomes and living standards
The rapid growth of farm output after 1978 brought about a revolution in the diet of the whole Chinese population:

Table 2.8
Food intake of the Chinese population (average per person per day)

	1952	1978	1983
Calories (number)			
Whole population	2,270	2,311	2,877
of which:			
Urban dwellers	–	2,715	3,183
Rural dwellers	–	2,224	2,806

Source: ZGTJNJ, 1985: 480.

In just a few years the Chinese population pulled sharply away from average levels of food intake that had probably changed little over many centuries. Sample survey data (see following table) reveals a dramatic and broadly based transformation of peasant living standards from 1978 to 1985.

Poverty

After 1978 new possibilities opened up for improving the lot of poor peasants. The relatively small number of poor peasants who lived in advanced areas generally benefited from the extremely rapid growth of output in those areas. Moreover, the rapid increase in funds available to collectives and local state authorities in well-located areas created the possibility to tackle effectively the problems of local poverty (Nolan, 1983(a): 70–71). The 'poor' people receiving assistance at the local level in rich areas were, however, often well-off by the standards of poor areas (Nolan, 1983(a): 70–71).

Much more important is the question of broader geographical concentrations of poverty. The issue of large spatial concentrations of poverty in the 1980s was taken very seriously by theoreticians as well as by the central and provincial leaderships. As early as 1979 the State Council decided to remit the agricultural tax on poor areas for three successive years (Nolan, 1983(a): 72). In 1984 it was decided that poor areas would be exempted from both the agricultural tax and the enterprise income tax (Lu, 1984: 26). Although, in the mid-1980s, there still were tight controls on peasants' place of residence, poor localities often benefited from the increased freedom granted to peasants to do 'outside work' (Nolan, 1983(a)). The end of rationing for most foodstuffs and the easy availability of grain coupons (and grain outside the ration) made it easy for peasants to leave their technical 'place of residence' to work and live elsewhere. The degree of labour mobility increased dramatically compared to the 1970s. There is plenty of evidence that rich areas with agricultural labour shortages were attracting workers from distant parts (Kung, 1986: 25; Kung and Chan, 1987; and there are many press reports of peasants coming from poor areas to take over contracts on land in suburban areas of big cities in the east of China. If remittances were sent back, this 'trickle down'

Table 2.9
Changes in peasant living standards as revealed by sample surveys[a]

	1978	1985	1985 as % of 1978
Average per capita consumption of:			
Grain (unhusked) (kg)	248	257	104
of which: fine grain (kg)	123	209	170
Vegetables (kg)	141	131	93
Edible oils (kg)	1.96	4.04	206
Meat (beef, pork, mutton) (kg)	5.76	10.97	190
Poultry (kg)	0.25	1.03	412
Eggs (kg)	0.80	2.05	256
Fish and shrimps (kg)	0.84	1.64	195
Sugar (kg)	0.73	1.46	200
Alcoholic drink (kg)	1.22	4.37	358
Cotton cloth (metres)	5.63	2.54	45
Cotton (kg)	0.40	0.43	108
Chemical fibre cloth (metres)	0.41	2.50	610
Silk and satin (metres)	0.02	0.07	350
Shoes (rubber, leather and canvas) (pairs)	0.32	0.55	172
Average amount of housing space per caput:			
Total (square metres)	10.2	17.34	170
of which: living space (square metres)	8.1	14.70	181
Stocks of consumer durables per 100 households:			
Bicycles	30.7	80.6	263
Sewing machines	19.8	43.2	218
Radios	17.4	54.2	311
Clocks and watches	51.8	163.6	316
of which: watches	27.4	126.3	461
Television sets	negligible	11.7	–

Source: ZGTJZY, 1986: 110–12.

Note: a. The number of peasant households surveyed was 6,095 in 1978, and 66,642 in 1985.

mechanism could have been helping poor areas, though the net benefits of migration for any particular region are complex and one should be wary of drawing over-simplistic conclusions.

The dynamism of the rural economy increased the funds available to the state which might be used to assist poor areas. There was a sharp rise in total tax payments from rural non-farm enterprises, a part of which was passed on to authorities above the *xian* level. A variety of measures were taken in the 1980s by special state organizations at different levels to help poor areas. For example, special low interest and interest-free funds were allocated to help poor areas expand profitable lines of production. Special funds were established to help road-building in poor areas (Central Committee, 1985).[28] Purchasing departments were set up to buy mountainous areas' special products, such as medicinal materials, which might otherwise be hard to market (Central Committee 1985). Relevant departments formed 'volunteer service brigades' to go to the poor areas to supply scientific, educational and medical services, with special state bonuses being given to those who volunteered (Central Committee, 1985).[29] Poor areas were encouraged to 'take the initiative in establishing lateral ties with economically and technologically advanced areas and regions, so as to import financial and human resources from other areas to develop their own' (Song, 1986).[30]

A great variety of sources, both Chinese and Western, suggest that the absolute numbers and the proportion of the rural population in poverty fell sharply after 1978. The World Bank (1986: 30) concludes: '[Using] a poverty line based on food intake requirements of 2185 Kilocalories per day, it is estimated that the proportion of the rural population in poverty declined from 31% in 1979 to 13% in 1982'... *'the speed and scale of the improvement is probably unprecedented in human history'* (my emphasis – P.N.). It seems most unlikely, in view of the range of measures taken, and the seriousness with which they were pursued, that the dimensions of poverty did not decline further after 1982. This view is reinforced strongly by evidence available at the provincial and sub-provincial level. Data on China's poorest provinces, such as Gansu, shows that even here considerable advances in average living standards occurred in the late 1970s and early 1980s. Detailed analysis of Anhui province in the same period shows that every single *xian* in the province enjoyed some improvement in real living standards (Nolan, 1988: Ch. 6).

Conclusion

The period from 1978 to the mid-1980s was an extraordinary one in China's history. Exceptionally rapid growth of farm output laid the basis for a transformation of the Chinese people's diet. The growth of agricultural output was not due to a sudden surge in the supply of fixed capital inputs. Rather, it occurred mainly because of an extremely rapid growth of farm labour productivity, which suggests tremendous 'slack' in the pre-1978 rural economy. China's package of rural reforms unleashed an extra-ordinary change in the intensity and quality of rural labour. The rapid growth of rural labour productivity was assisted increasingly by the sharp acceleration in output in the rural non-farm economy. The growth of rural productivity in turn underpinned the extremely rapid growth of average incomes. Perhaps the most striking accompaniment of the acceleration in the growth of the rural economy was the sharp decline in the numbers in poverty.

PROBLEMS

The story outlined in section 2 is one of unmitigated success for the Chinese post-1978 rural reforms. In fact, a wide array of new problems emerged. Collective farms have serious shortcomings but they do simplify life for planners and policymakers. Trying to cope with hundreds of millions of independent decision makers and accept a substantial role for market forces makes their life vastly more complex. It is undoubtedly much easier in most respects to plan a small number of large enterprises than a myriad of small ones. A wide array of criticisms have been levelled at China's rural reforms of the 1980s. They range from dire predictions of an imminent collapse of agricultural production to concerns that 'capitalism' has been 'restored' in the villages. If one is to criticize the pre-1976 system and argue in favour of the principal features of the post-Mao rural reforms, it is vital to do so with one's eyes open, recognizing frankly the difficulties and problems emerging in their wake. Accordingly, this section examines a number of the most important criticisms that have been made. It concludes that many of the problems have been exaggerated but that some important difficulties do exist. Nevertheless, it is quite possible to argue strongly, as this article does, in favour of the reforms on balance, and to hope that the Chinese leadership will take steps to tackle the most serious of the new problems. There are eight areas in which it is argued by different Western observers that the rural reforms have produced serious problems, and the arguments in respect of each of these is now examined briefly in turn.

Faltering agricultural growth rates

Chinese agriculture enjoyed a period of extraordinary dynamism from the late 1970s to the mid-1980s. This formed the basis of a major improvement in the Chinese population's diet. I have argued that the institutional changes of the late 1970s and early 1980s were the main cause of this. Over the long-term, in a country of China's size and given reasonable assumptions about the income elasticity of demand, it would be unlikely that per caput farm output growth would continue at the high rate of this period. Indeed, in 1984–86 growth slowed down, though it was still quite fast compared to other developing countries. Predicting the likely future growth rate of farm output is extremely difficult. There are, indeed, uncertainties about rural institutions, but the main question mark hangs over farm price policy in its multiple aspects. Without further substantial increases in the relative price of agricultural products, it is hard to see how output is going to increase rapidly in the future. This is a highly politicized issue because of the consequential effect on urban prices, and it is impossible to predict the outcome. Should the Chinese leadership take the path of substantially raising farm purchase prices it is essential that the poorest urban groups are, at least partially, protected from the effects.

Structure of the rural economy

There are two main issues here. The first is that of the balance between the farm and the non-farm economy. Unquestionably, the fastest rural growth rates in the mid-1980s were in the non-farm sector. There is not necessarily a contradiction between growth in the rural farm and non-farm sectors, however. Indeed, there is often a positive, symbiotic relationship between them; as labour moves out of agriculture it opens up the possibility for raising agricultural labour productivity more rapidly. The second issue is grain production. Undeniably, grain output grew much less rapidly than other parts of the farm economy in the 1980s. Direct human consumption of grain was, however, relatively high by the mid-1980s. Across the whole spectrum of the Chinese leadership there was a deep commitment at least to sustain this level of per caput grain output. In the mid-1980s this was being attained by a combination of administrative measures (the 'fixed contract purchase system') and price policy. In so far as it was possible to judge, it seemed likely that 'administrative' methods in this vital area would remain important for many areas. Given the fundamental importance of grain it was, surely, correct that this should be so. Even the 'pro-price reform' Chinese Academy of Social Sciences' Price Reform Group argued that this ought to be so:

> In China, the conditions needed for completely regulating [grain] output through the market have very far from matured (*hai yuan yuan mei you chengshou*)... Thus, within agricultural commodity prices, the system of market prices and state unified prices with fixed contract prices as the principal form cannot but co-exist for a relatively long period of time. (Chinese Academy, 1987: 20)

Despite 'de-collectivization' the state still possessed a wide array of administrative powers to enforce the desired level of grain output and marketings should 'economic' (i.e., price) measures fail to do so. Indeed, it is worth remembering that the Chinese state was able to influence deeply the structure of farm output and marketings in the 1950s prior to the collectivization of agriculture through a combination of price policy and administrative measures (Perkins, 1966: ch. 3). The main question concerned the degree to which there would be growth of grain output in order to raise meat consumption. If the state allowed meat prices fully to reflect costs of production then it is not likely that demand would be such as to stimulate a rapid growth of grain output for this purpose. On the other hand, if the state continued to use administrative means to suppress the grain price and profitability, then the supply response from peasants would be unlikely either to be such as to produce a rapid growth of grain output to be used as animal feed.[31]

Village class relations

In the absence of detailed studies of the kind available for most developing countries, only superficial analysis of this issue is possible. It is surprising that in a country in which Marx and Lenin are taken so seriously, their methodology for the analysis of class relations is not applied in conducting village studies in China in the 1980s. Judgements must be tempered, also, by awareness of the great diversity of class relations that one would expect to find in a country of China's huge land area and population, though I shall try to draw some tentative general conclusions.

The number of rural wage labourers certainly rose rapidly after 1978, mostly employed in non-farm work. Wage labourers still constituted a small proportion of the rural workforce, however, working for collective enterprises – though neither small size nor collective employment implies good working conditions. The removal of income ceilings, combined with the increased impact of market forces, unquestionably led to a much wider range of income and consumption differentials within any given village, especially in certain areas. Although the rural tax system is far from perfect, the Chinese state quickly introduced measures to attempt to control the incomes of the highest rural income earners via a progressive income tax on individual enterprises. The operation of the credit system, however, gives cause for concern in relation to its class impact (see, for example, Hu and Yu, 1986).

Already, by the mid-1980s, there were signs that some permanent 'congealing' of class relations within villages was beginning to occur, reducing the high degree of flexibility in socio-economic structure characteristic of the Maoist period. There were, however, some important factors tending to sustain mobility between stratificational positions. Compared to most poor countries, access to education and health facilities was, in most areas, relatively easy for all social strata, so that permanent stratified inequalities in human capital were likely to be relatively small. Access to land was guaranteed to all rural dwellers by the egalitarian redistribution of farmland in the early 1980s, and changing future requirements (as worker-dependent ratios alter, for example) should be able to be met via a competitive market for rented land. Access to necessary lumpy inputs (such as crop spraying, processing and irrigation) was still open to all villagers via the collective ownership of many of these facilities (irrigation, in particular). Easily divisible inputs (especially chemical fertilizer) were mainly allocated through state administrative channels rather than market forces. Whilst this meant that local political processes played an important role in their distribution, state control of the allocation of some inputs could enable it to influence the rural economy in socially desirable ways.[32] The rapid expansion of employment opportunities in rural non-farm enterprises in the 1980s almost certainly had an equalizing effect on intra-village income differentials. Most important, perhaps, for a wide range of rural economic activities (both agricultural and non-agricultural) start-up costs were low, there was ease of entry and few scale economies. These characteristics of 'petty capitalist commodity production' should ensure in the foreseeable future a reasonable degree of fluidity in the village class structure.

Spatial inequality

Areas with locational advantages were held back under Maoist policies. The reforms of the late 1970s and early 1980s enabled well-placed areas to achieve relatively large increases in labour productivity and income per person. Poorly located (often mountainous) districts, with inferior natural conditions, poor transport and, often, with weaker human capital resources, generally experienced much smaller absolute (and, often, relative) increases in labour productivity and incomes. Both at the end of the Maoist period and in the mid-1980s, poverty was highly concentrated spatially. In the mid-1980s, the range of spatial income and consumption differentials was very wide, in most respects much wider than at the end of the Maoist period. Many policies in this period, however, either intentionally or unintentionally, helped poorer areas to achieve absolute growth (even though their relative position frequently became worse): de-collectivization, increased freedom to determine the production structure, and improvement in the agricultural–industrial terms of trade benefited these areas in addition to well-located ones, while the rapid growth of the whole rural economy made possible an increase in state assistance to poor regions and provided opportunities through the market for poor areas to increase their prosperity (e.g., via remittances from migrants, and by producing specialist products to meet growing demands as incomes rose in other areas). Even though growth was uneven, it was deeply rooted, and virtually all *xian*s experienced at least some increase in average real incomes from the late 1970s to the mid-1980s.

Indicators of inequality for the rural population combine local and spatial processes. Overall indicators of inequality show a clear increase.

Table 2.10
Share of rural income taken by different sections of the rural population, 1979 and 1984

Segment of rural population	Proportion of total rural income in:	
	1978	*1984*
Top 25% of income earners	47.7	51.7
Middle 50% of income earners	43	40.1
Bottom 25% of income earners	9.3	8.2

Source: Rural Survey Group, 1986:7.

Note: National sample survey of over 37,000 rural households.

The spatial range of productive conditions and incomes in rural China is now enormous. The Maoist path of tightly holding back rich areas was deeply unsatisfactory, stifling the growth from which could come the resources to help resolve poverty. The state has done much in the 1980s to assist poor areas. It must, however, be stressed that, despite huge achievements, a large number of Chinese peasants still live in abysmal conditions. Looking at the enormous disparities in rural incomes between different areas, one cannot help feeling that still more should be done to transfer resources from rich to poor areas, and that it could be done intelligently, through, for example, a well-constructed tax system without adverse effects on rich areas' 'production enthusiasm'.

Welfare and human capital

Problems with maintaining individual contributions to collective welfare funds certainly were encountered after de-collectivization. Increases in funding did, however, occur from other sources: increased revenue from collective enterprises, increased fees (paid by a much better off peasantry), and increased state (especially *xian*) outlays. The increased funding was made possible by a more prosperous rural economy, albeit that a smaller proportion of total income may now have been allocated to these purposes. In education, peasants' demands shifted sharply, with a rapid decline in numbers attending secondary schools. Attendance at primary school was still at a high level, however, compared with other poor countries. Moreover, there was a massive increase in rural education obtained via informal channels such as TV, radio and magazines. In the health system, there also was a big structural shift, with a decline in part-time health workers, and a big increase in the provision of professional health care. Help for the locally poor in aggregate expanded considerably in the 1980s, based mainly on increased provision by collectives, which, in turn, rested on increased rural prosperity stimulated by the reforms. In welfare provision, as in personal income, the regional disparities in the mid-1980s were still extremely wide, but the simple fact that much more information is now available about the low quality of welfare in poor areas should not mislead one into thinking that conditions have deteriorated.

Accumulation and physical capital

Far from declining, as many commentators feared, total rural investment grew rapidly after 1978. Naturally, given the nature of the rural reforms, a large increase occurred in the share of private investment, and in poorer areas where the non-farm economy was weak, the collective's share in total investment was very small indeed by the mid-1980s (the 'Wenzhou' path). In addition, a substantial shift took place in the structure of fixed investment away from agriculture towards the rural non-farm economy, and, within agricultural investment, away from fixed investment towards current inputs. Fragmentation of holdings reappeared with many accompanying problems. The worst of these was the inhibitions this provided to mechanization of field work, though this was to some degree found to be self-resolving, in that the areas where such mechanization was economically desirable were those in which the process of land consolidation was most advanced. The possibility of severe deterioration in land quality due to privatization was greatly reduced by the establishment of long tenures on land contracted from the collective and by the granting of inheritance rights to land contracts. In addition, changed methods of organizing care of forestry resources probably resulted in a net decline in soil loss through deforestation. Total resources allocated to water conservation probably fell in the 1980s. This was not necessarily a problem, however, since China had already achieved, by the 1980s, an extremely high irrigation ratio, and it was probably rational to allocate fewer resources to this activity than in the past, and to concentrate those resources on improving the quality of water control work.

Population growth

A renewed upward movement in birth rates occurred in the mid-1980s. To a considerable degree this was attributable to an exceptionally large population cohort entering the marriage age rather than to an increased motivation to peasants to have children after 'de-collectivization'. The motivation to have children may well have been just as strong in people's communes as in the mid-1980s, since in the communes the family's income from the collective was directly related to the number of workers it contained. The severity of the 'One Child Family' campaign in the early 1980s, and its temporary success in forcing down birth rates, does not support the notion that the party's capacity to influence peasants' birth plans had been greatly weakened. Moreover, it lends support to the view that, despite considerable problems in the rural party apparatus in the early 1980s as policies changed violently from 'serve the people' to 'take the lead in getting rich', the party still wielded considerable power in the villages. The party's back-tracking in 1985/6 in the face of great popular discontent helped allow the birth rate to rise again, but the rate was still low compared to other developing countries.

Obsession with money-making

The main change in this respect has been in official ideology and in what constitutes legitimate behaviour. Under Mao it may have been illegal for peasants to produce, buy and sell at a profit for themselves and their families, but it is quite improbable in the light of what happened before and after Mao (and, indeed, under him) that this drive ever was transformed. Moreover, this is a productive, useful drive, that was central in impelling the advance of China's rural productive forces after 1978, just as it had been in often disadvantageous circumstances, pre-1955.[33] Furthermore, this force was not wholly uncontrolled; rather, the parameters within which it operated were powerfully influenced by state action in the interest of socially desirable goals at different levels.

CONCLUSIONS

Bukharinism and petty commodity production

In the 'socialist' countries, from the time of the Soviet debates in the 1920s through to the present day, there have been two fundamentally opposed visions of rural development. The 'Bukharinist' vision is sympathetic to individual farming, and to the positive role of market forces, while recognizing the crucial function both of co-operation and appropriate state action. The 'Stalinist' vision is hostile to individual entrepreneurship and to 'petty capitalistic' production, and confident in the state's ability to control directly the rural production process in the broader social interest. Even over the long periods in the 'socialist' countries when Stalinist collective farms were the only permitted form of rural institution, the appeal of an alternative approach remained alive, if only as an unpublished, stigmatized sub-culture in political life. Indeed, the very virulence with which the 'capitalist' road in the countryside has been attacked in the 'socialist' countries is eloquent testimony to the enduring presence of Bukharinist, 'NEP' ideas. This can be easily seen by the rapidity with which these ideas surfaced on the occasions when ideological controls were lifted. In China, the most vivid examples of this were the 'Hundred Flowers' in 1957, the relaxation in the early 1960s prior to the 'Socialist Education Movement', and, finally, in the late 1970s after the death of Mao. In the Soviet Union, the 'NEP model' re-emerged as an explicit rallying point for market socialist ideas in the post-Stalinist period (Lewin, 1975).

Even in advanced economies with huge accumulations of capital, petty commodity production can perform a useful role in certain sectors. In poor developing countries, with limited development of transport and modern industry, 'petty commodity production' carried on in small units of production (not just in the villages, but in the cities, too) is an immensely powerful force. It rests generally on intense self- (or family) exploitation, or exploitation of a small number of wage labourers. The principal motivation for the hard labour of the myriads of entrepreneurs involved is, simply, to improve the living conditions of their families, but it can prove a powerful engine for the development of the productive forces, unleashing the physical and intellectual activity of large numbers of people in response to widening market opportunities. The stimulation of this force requires a reasonable degree of security for the 'petty commodity producers', in terms of their property rights and the inheritance of those rights, and rights to retain a certain proportion (not necessarily all) of the income deriving from their efforts. The crushing of that force, in the Soviet Union under Stalin and in China under Mao, placed a severe constraint on overall growth and helped reduce the efficiency of resource use since 'petty commodity producers' tend to squeeze out the last drop of output from capital goods. The liberation of that long-suppressed force in rural China after 1978 was a major factor in the explosion of productivity that occurred in that period.

Collective farms and China's agricultural performance

The contrast in China's rural economic performance pre- and post-reforms is extraordinary. Whether one looks at growth of output per caput, or at productivity of land, labour and capital, a massive change took place that provided the basis for a major leap forward in the standard of living in both town and countryside. Most important of all, this growth provided the basis for an extraordinary reduction in (though it must be emphasized, not the elimination of) absolute poverty. By any criterion, this was an event of major historical importance. Unfortunately, it is impossible to reach unambiguous conclusions about this phenomenon. Other factors intervened in producing the results observed, notably a whole set of both demand- and supply-side interactions between the urban and rural economies. An important part of the explanation for the observed results lies, however, with the nature of collective farms.

In most circumstances, there generally are high costs involved in attempting to organize agricultural labour in large centrally directed units. These costs affect not just the rural economy's output with given resources, but also its capacity to grow: the peasants' drive to improve their skills, to seek better ways of producing output, to branch into producing new types of output, is reduced; also, of course, if at each period of time less is produced from given resources, then the potential surplus available for investment for growth at each point is reduced. Only under quite exceptional conditions is it likely that collective cultivation will work well. Indeed, it is this small number of exceptions (e.g., Israeli *kibbutzim*) in which peasants' mutual trust is established that sheds so much light on what generally is absent in 'socialist' countries' collectives. It is not a coincidence that under private agriculture one rarely encounters farms with a large number of hired workers; nor is it a coincidence that it is rare for peasants voluntarily to form producer co-operatives.

Although collective cultivation of the soil and collective income distribution are formidable barriers to good farm performance, co-operation of one kind or another is generally essential. The state (central or local) often has acted as the agency (more or less voluntarily) to ensure that activities vital to the farm economy, but which the market fails to provide, are carried out. The most striking instances of this are state-directed irrigation and drainage projects using conscripted peasant labour. They also include, however, a wide array of state funded (or partially state funded) schemes: research institutions (whose potential contribution to growth is enormous), rural transport networks, provision of information, organization of food stores, support for rural education and health, insurance schemes, marketing agencies, provision of credit, etc. These vital activities rarely take the form of a free transfer from the non-farm sector, but are more generally financed directly or indirectly by peasant contributions, and can be regarded as a form of state-led co-operation. It should be noted that such 'state' directed activity has by no means always been organized by the central government. In China in the 1980s, the most important level at which the state organized such activities was the *xian*, i.e., the 'local' state apparatus embracing up to around one million people (mostly peasants).

Throughout history peasants have also, to different degrees in different types of political, social and ecological environments, and under different degrees of population pressure, themselves devised co-operative arrangements of one kind or another. These do not necessarily enable villagers to benefit equally, nor are they necessarily democratically run, but they are locally evolved, non-state institutions which do permit a higher level of rural productivity to be achieved. These range from the widespread practice in Asian rice agriculture of labour exchange at peak times in the agricultural season, to co-operative purchase of lumpy inputs both traditional (e.g., draft animals) and modern (e.g., tractors) to locally run institutions to control water supply, and, of course, include a myriad organizations found in the agricultural sector of the advanced capitalist countries.

Getting the correct solutions to questions of lumpiness and economies of scale in the rural economy is complex, and there are few general rules that apply. The desirable outcome in each case is likely to be a different blend of individual provision, state-organized co-operation and co-operation organized independently by groups of peasants. Only if these problems are solved, however, and a suitable framework established can the dynamic force of rural petty commodity production be released to full effect.

The rural reforms of the 1980s and inequality

A major attraction of collective farms in the eyes of many people is their elimination of exploitation through land rent, usury and wage labour, which frequently combine in a set of 'inter-locked' markets in non-'socialist' poor economies. Not only is this form of socio-economic relationship abolished in collective farms but the prospect is held out, too, for personal income distribution to be conducted on fair principles ('to each according to their work') and with due consideration for the needs of the least well-endowed section of the village (a portion of personal income distributed 'according to need').

No slogan has attracted more ire in the 'socialist' countries than that which Bukharin enunciated as the basis of Soviet NEP in the 1920s:

> Our policy in relation to the countryside should develop in the direction of removing, and in part abolishing, many restrictions which put the brake on the growth of the well-to-do and kulak farm. To the peasants, to all the peasants, we must say: Enrich yourselves, develop your farms, and do not fear that constraint will be put on you ... However paradoxical it may appear, we must develop the well-to-do farm in order to help the poor peasant and the middle peasant. (Quoted in Carr, 1958: 280)

Similar slogans were at the basis of China's brief periods of 'NEP' in the early 1950s and early 1960s. Faced with the desperate need to raise rural production, the party leadership appealed to individual peasant incentives, with calls to 'expand the household and become rich' (*fa jia zhi fu*) and 'become rich through hard labour' (*qin dong zhi fu*). In the Chinese countryside of the early 1980s no set of slogans better symbolized the sea-change in leadership philosophy than the switch from the Maoist 'serve the people' (*we renmin fuwu*) to 'take the lead in getting rich' (*xian fu qilai*).

For a long time, it was accepted by most commentators in the 'socialist' countries that encouraging individual peasants to become well-off was inseparable from intra-village class polarization. Two major points can be made about this issue. The first is that the 'cost' of the development of unequal class relations has to be set against the 'benefit' of a possible stimulus to rural production with potentially beneficial consequences for the whole economy, and for the reduction of absolute poverty. The second is that the degree to which intra-village inequality is likely to develop under such circumstances is likely to be less than many critics (both inside and outside the 'socialist' countries) of the Bukharinist 'take the lead in getting rich' approach imagine, especially if appropriate action is taken by the state. There are a number of reasons why this is so. First, the possibility of cumulative development of intra-village inequality is greatly reduced if farm modernization takes place in the wake of a reasonably egalitarian land reform, especially if the state effectively prohibits the development of a market in land ownership (as distinct from rights to rent land). Secondly, many important modern farm inputs are non-lumpy, and can be purchased by all farm strata, giving them all a possibility to benefit from new technology, albeit to different degrees. Third, as long as the state doesn't attempt to stifle it, and especially if suitable policies are taken to encourage it, it is likely that as incomes rise in a poor country there will be a lengthy period during which output and employment in small-scale rural non-farm enterprises expand rapidly. This generally has an equalizing effect on intra-village income distribution. Fourth, the possibility for all village strata to benefit from rural growth is increased greatly if the state apparatus (frequently locally) and/or peasants themselves co-operatively, is able to provide an array of public goods, including health, education, transport, information, irrigation, credit, processing facilities, marketing, insurance, research, crop spraying, and so on. The more that such provisions are made, the more powerful, too, is likely to be the operation of inter-temporal movements in positions in the village class structure, attributable to changes in worker-dependent ratios over the course of the family cycle (i.e., 'Chayanovian' elements in rural differentiation). Finally, although taxing rural wealth and/or incomes is not easy, it is not beyond the wit of a well-motivated state to devise methods to tax extremely high rural incomes should these emerge. One obvious and relatively straightforward method is a rates levy on the size or value of domestic housing. But since most rural economic activities, given reasonable state policies in the respects outlined above, are characterized by relatively easy entry, low economies of scale and very competitive product and factor markets, it is unlikely that exceptionally high incomes would remain for any length of time. In the case of Wenzhou, for example, the extraordinarily high incomes of button traders were unlikely to remain without attracting a host of new entrants, in turn driving down the income from this activity.

Encouraging 'petty capitalist commodity production' is, indeed, likely to encourage intra-village inequality in a modernizing poor economy. This has been seen clearly in post-1978 China. 'Unequal growth' and 'polarization' are quite distinct phenomena, however. Even in the absence of appropriate state action, the alarmist Leninist 'polarization' thesis seems to be based on a misconception about economies of scale in agriculture. If suitable state action is taken then there are real possibilities for making use of the market mechanism in the rural areas to stimulate growth in an unequal but not polarizing fashion, with considerable fluidity over time in peasant households' positions in the village class structure.

Collective farms and peasant consciousness

Inequality of asset ownership and incomes is not the only meaningful kind of inequality. Although collective farms are able to perform well in terms of these aspects of economic inequality, in respect of other kinds of inequality there is reason to be deeply concerned. A central impulse behind the formation of collective farms in the 'socialist' countries was a desire on the part of the party leadership to remould peasant consciousness. One can question this as being plain unrealistic. It was far-fetched to imagine that the frequently impoverished, individualistic peasant populations of Russia, Eastern Europe, China, South East Asia and Africa could develop a 'collectivist' mentality of the kind exhibited by a tiny number of highly committed (mostly intellectual) Jewish refugees. To persuade them to build on traditional forms of co-operation was feasible and sensible, but to attempt to create a fully collective rural society was, with hindsight, utterly unrealistic. Not only was such a project unrealistic, it was also highly questionable from the simplest moral standpoint. This was a gigantic exercise in social engineering: an extraordinarily arrogant, undemocratic attempt by a tiny minority massively to transform the thinking of the vast majority of the populations of these countries. Such a revolutionary change involved enormous risks, even more so when one recognizes the essential economic role of the agricultural sector (in the simplest sense, the producer of food) in a poor economy.

Notes

1. The issues examined in this chapter are developed in greater length in Nolan, 1988.
2. See, especially, the careful accounts in Watson, 1983, and 1984/5.
3. For example, following the 'de-collectivization' in Xindu *xian* in Sichuan province the

number of village accountants fell from 2,700 to 700 (Nolan, 1983(b)).

4. Though this decline has been far from complete.

5. Han (1987 (a)) refers to these changes, but at the time of writing the author has not seen them officially confirmed.

6. Formerly the 'brigade' (*dui*).

7. See, e.g., Riskin, 1971, and Perkins, 1977.

8. Unless otherwise indicated, the information in the remainder of this subsection is taken from the author's field work in 1983 (Nolan, 1983c). Gaunghan *xian*, where the author researched, was extremely advanced in the reforms undertaken and had already put into practice policies that were to be adopted later in other areas.

9. Despite considerable growth in the 1980s of *xiangcun* enterprises' staff and workers' average wages (though at a much slower rate than their productivity), their average wages in 1985 still amounted to just 60 per cent of the level of those in state enterprises (ZGTJNJ, 1986: 100 and 105). Due to differences in the cost of living between town and countryside the difference in the real value of wages probably was somewhat less than this figure suggests.

10. The 'state' in this case usually meant local authorities, notably the *xian*.

11. In the case of Sichuan, for example, this was set up in 1977 (Nolan, 1983(b)).

12. Kung and Chan in their interesting (1987) account of rural export industries in Guangdong's Dongguan *xian* provide a similar view. The 'entrepreneurial spirit' of *xian* and *xiang* cadres was vital in establishing the framework within which small rural enterprises can expand successfully.

13. From a survey of 272 villages (*cun*) in 71 *xian*.

14. The main argument being that if peasants pay closer to the real cost of providing health care they will insist on a higher level of service.

15. Already, by 1980, the number had fallen to 132 (at the peak, 230 types of farm produce were compulsorily purchased) (Duan, 1983).

16. *Index of retail prices in state-run trade*

	1952	1957	1978	1984
Grain	100	107	129	145
Subsidiary foodstuffs	100	126	152	207
Clothing	100	100	101	97
Daily-use goods	100	98	107	111
All consumer goods	*100*	*109*	*119*	*138*

Source: ZGTJNJ, 1985: 532.

17. 'unified' (*tong gou*) and 'allocated' purchase (*pai gou*).

18. 'fixed contract purchases' (*hetong ding gou*).

19. 'market purchase' (*shichang shou gou*).

20. This was a major contributory factor to the substantial government budget deficits in the 1980s (ZGTJNJ, 1985: 523).

21. It was reported that the proportion of urban residents' food expenditure in free markets rose from 17 per cent in 1984 to 36 per cent in 1986 ('Free markets...', 1987).

22. Prices would, presumably, settle at somewhere between the state and 'free market' prices.

23. Oi (1986(b): 234) gives data for parts of three provinces in 1984 indicating that for chemical fertilizer the ratio between the state quota price, the state 'negotiated' price and the free market price was in the order of 1:2:3.

24. That was still the case in mid-1987 as this chapter was being written.

25. Indeed, the growth rate from 1978 (a year of above-average natural disasters) to 1985 (at 1980 prices) was reported to be no less than 10.2 per cent (average annual compound growth rate) (ZGTJZY, 1986: 32).

26. It must be stressed that these data are rough indications only. Apart from the statistical problems discussed above, measuring changes in gross value of agricultural output in the late 1970s and early 1980s was complicated by the big changes in the composition of output, and the usefulness of any particular year's prices as the basis for constructing an index of output at

constant prices is reduced by the large changes that occurred in relative prices.

27. Discussed in detail in Nolan, 1988, Ch. 6.

28. For example, in Sichuan, the state in 1983 was providing poor areas with 3,000 *yuan* for the purchase of materials (e.g., explosives) for every kilometre of road constructed (Nolan, 1983).

29. In Sichuan in 1984 teachers who worked in poor areas (defined for this purpose to include 20.9 per cent of the province's total population) were allocated to one grade higher than they would have been in the normal plain areas (equivalent to a 10 per cent increase in income) (Nolan, 1983(b)).

30. See, for example, the account in Han (1986(c)) of the co-operation established in Shandong province between the economically advanced cities and the most backward areas in the province.

31. There is, of course, a variety of intermediary possibilities.

32. In Taiwan, in the 1960s and 1970s the state maintained a monopoly over chemical fertilizer sales, which had important consequences for the state's ability to influence the rural economy: 'A monopoly over fertilizers made every peasant – without discrimination – beholden to the state. Such a monopoly also allowed the state to determine the crucial equation in economic development: the transfer of surplus from agriculture to industry' (Amsden, 1979: 357).

33. The brief Chinese 'NEP' period came to an abrupt halt in the autumn of 1953 with the announcement of the 'general line' on the transition to socialism. 'NEP' conditions were to return again briefly in the early 1960s.

References

Amsden, A., (1979) 'Taiwan's economic history', *Modern China*, July.

Byres, T. J., and Nolan, P., (1976), *Inequality: India and China Compared, 1950–1970*, Milton Keynes, Open University.

Carr, E. H., (1958) *Socialism in One Country, 1925–26*, Harmondsworth, Penguin Books.

Central Committee of the Chinese Communist Party, (1958) 'Resolution on Establishment of People's Communes in the Rural Areas', 9 August in Selden, 1979.

————(1984) 'Circular on Rural Work in 1984' ('Document Number One') 1 January 1984, published in *People's Daily* (*Renmin Ribao*), 12 June.

Chinese Academy of Social Sciences, Price Reform Group, (1987) 'Prices: Questions and thoughts on pressing ahead with the reform', *Economic Research* (*Jingji Yanjiu*), No. 4.

Chinese Economic Yearbook, 1986 (ZGJJNJ, 1986) (*Zhongguo jingji nianjian*) Beijing, Jingji guanli chubanshe.

Chinese Statistical Summary, (1985) (ZGTJZY, 1985) (*Zhongguo tongji zhaiyao*) Beijing, Zhongguo tongji chubanshe.

———— (1986) (ZGTJZY, 1986) (*Zhongguo tongji zhaiyao*) Beijing, Zhongguo tongji chubanshe.

Chinese Statistical Yearbook (1984) (ZGTJNJ, 1984) (*Zhungguo tongji nianjian*) Beijing, Zhongguo tongji chubanshe.

———— (1985) (ZGTJNJ, 1985) (*Zhongguo tongji nianjian*) Beijing, Zhongguo tongji chubanshe.

———— (1986) (ZGTJNJ, 1986) (*Zhongguo tongji nianjian*) Beijing, Zhongguo tongji chubanshe.

Dai, Y. N., (1986) 'Beefing up Rural Co-operative System', *Beijing Review*, No. 25, 23 June.

Du, R. S. (1983) 'The contract system, which links remuneration with output, and the new development of co-operative economy in the rural areas', *People's Daily (Renmin Ribao)* 7 March.

Duan, Y. B., (1983) 'Some situations in and opinions on farm production procurement', *Economics for Agricultural Production Technology (Nongye jishu jingji)* No. 7, July, translated in *Joint Publications Research Service, China Report, Agriculture*, 26 January 1984.

'Free markets in China's cities and towns', 1987, *Beijing Review*, No. 20, 18 May.

Gao, S. Q., (1987) 'Progress in economic reform, 1979–86', *Beijing Review*, No. 27, 6 July.

Han, B. C., (1987(a)), 'Grain production and diversified economy', *Beijing Review*, No. 22, 1 June.

_____ (1987(b)) 'Industry becomes important in countryside', *Beijing Review*, No. 23, 8 June.

_____ (1987(c)) 'Farmers active in commercial sector', *Beijing Review*, No. 19, No. 11.

'Handling economic disputes', (1985), *Beijing Review*, No. 11, 18 March.

Hinton, W., (1983), 'A trip to Fengyang county', *Monthly Review*, Vol. 6, November.

Hu, W., and Yu, Z., (1986) 'Differentials in peasant income and the goal of becoming well-off together', *People's Daily (Renmin Ribao)*, 11 April.

Kueh, Y. Y., (1984) 'China's new agricultural policy program: major economic consequences, 1979–1983', *Journal of Comparative Economics*, Vol. 8, No. 4, December.

Kung, J., (1986) 'Beyond subsistence: the role of collectivisations in rural economic development in post-Mao China', unpublished paper.

Kung, J. S., and Chan, T. M. H., (1987) 'Export-led industrialisation: the case of Dongguan in the Pearl River Delta in China', unpublished mss.

Lewin, M., (1975) *Political Undercurrents in Soviet Economic Debates*, London, Pluto Press.

Lin, Z. L., (1982) 'New forms in China's rural socialist co-operative economy', *Wen Hui Bao* (Shanghai), 29 October, translated in *Joint Publications Research Service*, No. 82, 958, *China Report, Agriculture*, 28 February 1983.

Lu, Y., (1984) 'Gap between rich and poor is bridged', *Beijing Review*, No. 46, 11 November.

_____ (1986) 'Communists work for collective prosperity', *Beijing Review*, No. 26, 30 June.

Luo, H. S., (1985) *Economic Changes in Rural China*, Beijing, New World Press.

Nolan, P., (1983(a)) *Growth Processes and Distributional Change in a South Chinese Province: The Case of Guandong*, London, Contemporary China Institute.

_____ (1983(b)) Author's notes from a two-month field trip (July–August) to investigate rural reform in Sichuan Province.

_____ (1988) *The Political Economy of Collective Farms: An Analysis of China's Rural Reforms since Mao*, Cambridge, Polity Press.

_____ and White, D. G., (1980) 'Socialist development and rural inequality: the Chinese countryside in the 1970s', *Journal of Peasant Studies*, Vol. 7, No. 1, October.

Oi, J. C., (1986(a)) 'Peasant households between plan and market – cadre control over agricultural inputs', *Modern China*, Vol. 12, No. 2, April.

_____ (1986(b)) 'Peasant grain marketing and state procurement: China's grain contracting system', *China Quarterly*, No. 106, June.

Perkins, D. H., (1966) *Market Control and Planning in Communist China*, Cambridge, Mass., Harvard University Press.

———— (ed.) (1977) *Rural Small-Scale Industry in the People's Republic of China*, London, University of California Press.

'Present situation and trends in the rural reform', (1986) *People's Daily (Renmin Ribao)*, 30 April.

Research department on industry and enterprises of the Development Institute, (1986) 'On the expansion of rural non-agricultural production', *Economic Research (Jingji Yanjiu)*, No. 8, August.

Riskin, R., (1971) 'Small industry and the Chinese model of development', *China Quarterly*, No. 46, April–June.

Rural Survey Group, (1986) 'The situation and trends in rural reform', *Problems of Agricultural Economics (Nongye Jingji Wenti)* 1986, No. 6.

Sang, J., (1983) *Everyday knowledge on rural economic contracts (Nongcun jingji hetong changshi)*, Taiyuan, Shanxi renmin chubanshe.

Selden, M., (1979) (ed.) *The People's Republic of China: A Documentary History of Revolutionary Change*, New York, Monthly Review Press.

Song, P., (1986) 'Report on the 1986 plan for national economic and social development', *Beijing Review*, No. 20, 19 May.

State Statistical Bureau, (1982) 'Communiqué on fulfilment of China's 1981 national economic plan', *Beijing Review*, 17 May.

———— (1986) 'Communiqué on the statistics of 1985 economic and social development', *Beijing Review*, 24 March.

———— (1987) 'Communiqué on the statistics of 1986 economic and social development', *Beijing Review*, No. 9, 2 March.

Stone, B., (1985) 'The basis for Chinese agricultural growth in the 1980s and 1990s', *China Quarterly*, No. 101, March.

Watson, A., (1983), 'Agriculture looks for shoes that fit', *World Development*, Vol. 11, No. 8, August.

———— (1984/85) 'New structures in the organisation of Chinese agriculture: A variable model', *Pacific Affairs*, Vol. 57, No. 4, Winter.

White, G., (1985) 'The impact of economic reforms in the Chinese countryside: towards the politics of social capitalism?', manuscript.

World Bank, (1986) *China: Long-term Development Issues and Options*, Washington D.C., World Bank.

Xue, M. Q., (1985) 'Rural industry advances amidst problems', *Beijing Review*, No. 50, 16 December.

3. The Wenzhou 'Miracle': an Assessment[1]

Chris Bramall

Introduction

Wenzhou is a coastal *shi* (municipality) located in the extreme south east of Zhejiang province, bordered to the south by the province of Fujian and to the west by the mountainous hinterland of central Zhejiang. Its surface area is 11,783 square kilometres of which 76 per cent is classified as mountain and hills, the highest of these rising to 1,611 metres above sea level. Wenzhou's flatlands are found almost entirely along the coast while one of its *xian* (Dongtou) is composed entirely of islands. The *shi*'s 1984 population was 6.21 million, giving her a population density comparable to that of Taiwan. The population is distributed amongst the nine *xian* (counties) of Leqing, Yongjia, Rui'an, Dongtou, Taishun, Wencheng, Cangnan, Pingyang and Ouhai and the two *qu* (districts) of Wenzhou city (Lucheng and Longwan) (Tao *et al.*, 1986: 97).

In the 1980s, this apparently unremarkable *shi* has acquired national prominence because of its impressive economic performance since 1978. Some data on this are to be found in the Appendix below; they show a rate of growth of output that is startling. As measured by the gross value of agricultural and industrial output (GVIAO), real output grew at an average annual rate of 16.6 per cent (calculated using OLS) between 1978 and 1986. Moreover, over the 1979–86 period, total *shi* revenue increased more than sixfold. Whether measured against the performance of other regions and countries, or against Wenzhou's historical performance, such growth is dramatic.

It is, however, the increase in incomes per head of more than threefold, or more than 18 per cent per annum on average between 1980 and 1986, that is most remarkable. Of course, such income data need to be interpreted carefully. For example, they are taken from two different sources and may not be based on comparable definitions of income. Moreover, they are measured in current prices and there are no data available on inflation rates during this period. Even so, one cannot fail to compare this trend favourably with the low level income stagnation experienced by both *shi* and country over the 1957–78 period. Moreover, if such growth had occurred in an independent economy of comparable population, and even more so if it had occurred in a low-income country of a comparable population, such as Haiti, Somalia or Burundi, it would have aroused extraordinary international interest.

Accompanying this growth of incomes, output and revenue – the question of causality is more complicated as will be seen below – was a proliferation of organizational forms in rural industry and commerce. Many of these new forms were based upon rural households which increasingly used their surplus labour time for industrial and sideline production whilst maintaining their involvement in farming; these households are called *jianye nonghu* or non-specialized peasant households. More specialized forms of organization soon developed, however, such as households specializing in non-farm production (*jiating gongchang*), labour-hiring enterprises (*siren gugong qiye*), joint household enterprises (*lianhe qiye*) and even share-issuing enterprises (*gufen qiye*). By 1986, there were already 15,400 enterprises of the latter type in the rural part of Wenzhou *shi* (He (ed.), 1987: 23) while the total number of individual households engaged in industrial and commercial activities (*geti gongshangye*) had increased from a mere 1,844 in 1979 to 138,000 by 1986. Between 1980 and 1985, the gross industrial output value (GVIO) of the 'household' sector (individual and joint household enterprises) grew at an annual average rate of almost 72 per cent (ibid: 97) to reach the level of 1,707 million *yuan* by 1986 (ibid: 20).

As important as the growth of the 'household' sector is its diversification into commerce and services which also was occurring during the early 1980s. One indication of this is the share of the sector in retail sales throughout the entire *shi*, as shown in Table 3.1.

Table 3.1
The composition of retail sales by sector, 1980–85

	State	Supply & marketing co-ops	Collective	Household	Total
1980	38.6	35.4	23.9	2.1	881
1982	35.2	31.1	26.4	7.3	1,043
1985	27.5	18.0	27.0	27.5	1,925

Source: Wang and Li, 1986(b): 23.

Note: 'Total' is social retail sales in million *yuan*. The other figures are percentage shares.

The rise in the share of the household sector parallels a decline in those of the state-owned sector and, strikingly, the supply and marketing co-operative sectors. That the household sector's share was the same as the state sector's in 1985 represents a phenomenal rate of growth of retail sales, from 18.5 million *yuan* in 1980 to 529.4 million in 1985, a 29-fold increase in a mere five years. Clearly, then, it is misleading to describe the Wenzhou pattern of economic growth as one of rural industrialization.

But whilst many aspects of Wenzhou's rate and type of growth are

Table 3.2
The range of incomes in Wenzhou in the mid-1980s

Occupation	Location	Income per head	Source
Poorest farmers	Dingbao *cun*, Cangnan *xian*: 1985	50	Wang and Li 1986a: 21
Poor farmers	Wuyi *cun*: 1984	105	Zhao Renwei, below
Average farmers	Wenzhou: 1984	417	Zhao Renwei, below
Rich farmers	Jinxiang, Cangnan *xian*: 1984	574	Li Shi, below
Hired workers	Wenzhou: 1985(?)	800	Zhao Renwei, below
Richest farmers	5 *cun* in Yishan *qu*, Cangnan: 1984	1,000+	Dong Fureng, below
State workers	Wenzhou: 1985	1,260	Zhao Renwei, below
Household industry	Yishan *qu*, Cangnan *xian*: 1985	3,000	Zhao Renwei, below
Household commerce	Yishan *qu*, Cangnan *xian*: 1985	7,000	Zhao Renwei, below
Average labour hirers	Wenzhou: 1985(?)	35,000	Zhao Renwei, below
Richest traders	Wenzhou: 1985(?)	51-100,000	Zhao Renwei, below
Richest labour hirer	Wenzhou: 1985(?)	150,000	Zhao Renwei, below

Notes: All data are of annual net income per head in current *yuan*, except in the cases of state and hired workers where they refer to annual wages plus bonuses. The occupational categories above are generally self-explanatory. State workers are workers in state-owned enterprises and the term 'farmer' is a translation of *nongmin*. The term *gouxiaoyuan* (literally, a buyer and seller) is translated as trader.

clearly positive, there have been others that have attracted strongly negative comment within China. This is particularly true of the growing income differentials that have emerged. The range of incomes in Wenzhou by the mid-1980s is summarized in Table 3.2.

Although these data are incomplete and not precisely comparable – because of different years and also because wages and incomes are not identical, with the latter being very sensitive to labour participation rates – an astonishing range of differentials is apparent from this table. The farmers of poor *cun* like Dingbao had incomes per head in 1985 that were lower than the *shi*'s average collective distributed income in 1978, more than half a decade earlier; in 1985, too, some 80,000 rural households were still dependent upon state aid and loans (Wang and Li, 1986(a): 21) although growing tax revenue from the more prosperous localities ensured that such aid was much more generous than hitherto. Moreover, the ratio of the income of the richest labour hirer to that of the poorest farmer is about 3,000:1 and thus certainly compatible with differentials in even relatively stratified OECD capitalist countries such as the USA. This is remarkable enough in itself; even more so is the emergence of this pattern after barely half a decade has elapsed.

The purpose of this chapter, however, is not to repeat at length the various positive and negative features of Wenzhou's economic performance during the 1980s, which are considered in detail in the chapters that follow. Instead, it tries to accomplish two tasks, the first of which is the isolation of the causes of the 'miracle'. Are these essentially macro-economic, local or institutional? The second task is to consider whether this pattern of growth can be replicated in other backward areas of China (it has already been introduced into parts of Anhui, for example) and, much more importantly, to assess whether it is desirable. Are there other substantive economic and social costs overlooked in the chapters that follow? Does the rate of growth of income per head justify the income differentials that have emerged and, if not, can these differentials be restricted by government policy without sacrificing the growth dynamic?

Explaining the 'miracle'

That the economy of Wenzhou experienced extremely rapid rates of growth of output and income per head is not in doubt. Much more debatable are the reasons for this growth. Although Chinese writers give the credit to institutional change in the form of the introduction of small, private, family-based enterprises, this argument is not self-evidently true. A number of other factors need also to be considered and this is the object of the following section.

The role of macro-economic change

One possible explanation of Wenzhou's rapid growth might be macro-economic. The package of macro-economic policy changes introduced throughout China after 1978, involving institutional reform, relative price changes and shifts in the allocation of investment, has undoubtedly generated rapid growth. It is not inconceivable in principle that Wenzhou's growth is simply one consequence of this transformation. For example, the combined impact of the all-China package might have been to bring about 'take-off' in areas such as Wenzhou by raising the profitability of the farming sector above some critical level. This in turn could have produced an increased demand for industrial products and the retained profits necessary to finance non-farm investment. Both demand and supply-side impulses would have combined to stimulate the growth of rural industry and commerce.

This proposition can be evaluated by considering the two consequences that one would expect if it were true. First, one would expect to see output and income growing at a rate little different from the national average over the 1980–86 period, and certainly no better than in areas where geography and inherited industrial and transport infrastructure are comparable. Second, one would expect a rate of growth of *xiangzhen* enterprise output at least equivalent to that of household industry; for if both are subject to the same macro-economic impulses, there is nothing to explain growth disparities except organizational form. There is an element of truth in the argument that profits from farming were directly available to households for investment in industry and only indirectly available for *xiangzhen* enterprises, either via the *xian* bureau or via household saving, but little

Table 3.3
Comparative growth rates of GVIAO in China and Wenzhou, 1981–86

	China	*Wenzhou*
1981–82	8.8	8.5
1982–83	10.2	13.9
1983–84	15.0	34.6
1984–85	16.4	32.9
1985–86	9.3	12.4

Sources:

China: The growth rates for 1981–82, 1982–83 and 1983–84 are derived by summing estimates of gross agricultural output (*Zhongguo jingji nianjian* 1985: III-14) and gross industrial output value (ibid: III-20) to estimate GVIAO and then calculating a growth rate from this. The rates of 1984–85 and 1985–86 are taken from State Statistical Bureau, 1986(b): 27 and *ibid.*, 1987(a): 20, respectively.

Wenzhou: growth rates given in He (ed.), 1987: 152.

Note: Annual growth rates of GVIAO in 1980 constant prices.

more than that; as Kueh points out, available private finance for *xiangzhen* enterprises was both absolutely large and growing quickly (Kueh, 1984: 30).

Considering the second question initially, the evidence is not conclusive. It is true that *xiangzhen* enterprise gross output value grew at an annual average rate of 30 per cent over the 1980–85 period, whilst that of household and joint enterprises grew by 72 per cent (He (ed.), 1987: 97). The problem with this comparison, however, is that the time period is much too short. It is plausible, for example, that because *xiangzhen* enterprises started from a much higher base, their growth rate was inevitably slower than that of the household sector in the short-term. In the longer term, however, a convergence of growth rates might occur.

But the answer to the first question posed above is far more definite. This is reached by simply comparing the growth rates of the gross value of industrial and agricultural output (GVIAO) in China and in Wenzhou over the 1981–86 period. GVIAO is chosen in preference to GVIO alone because of the inter-dependence of agriculture and industry; the growth of rural industry may, in principle, assist or hinder the growth of agriculture but it is unlikely to be neutral. The findings are shown in Table 3.3.

It is evident from this table that the Wenzhou growth rates have been consistently higher than the China average; this is particularly true of 1983–85 when the *shi* achieved incredibly rapid rates of growth.

Even more telling is a comparison of trends in peasant incomes per head. In 1978, rural collective distributed income per head in Wenzhou was substantially below the all-China average; the same is true of net peasant incomes in 1980. By 1985, however, the picture had changed dramatically:

Table 3.4
Trends in peasant incomes per head in Wenzhou and China, 1980–86

	1978	1980	1985	1986
Wenzhou	56	165	417	505
China	77	191	355	424
Wenzhou as % of China	73	86	117	119

Sources: Wenzhou – 1978: Zhejian tongjiju (ed.) 1984: 86–103; 1980: Zhao Renwei, below; 1985: ibid; 1986: He (ed.) 1987: 7.
China – 1978: Zhonggong Sichuan sheng wei yanjiushi (ed.) 1984: 225; 1980: State Statistical Bureau, 1986(a): 586; 1985: Zhao Renwei, below; 1986: State Statistical Bureau, 1987(a): 26.

Note: 1978: distributed collective income per head in current *yuan*. 1980–86: net peasant incomes per head in current *yuan*.

Even allowing for an inflation rate in Wenzhou that was higher than the China average, the extent of the transformation is remarkable. This previously poor *shi* had not only caught up with but surpassed the Chinese average.

Therefore, although caution is needed before concluding that differentials in rates of both GVIAO and peasant income growth must persist in the long run, this evidence does suggest that the Wenzhou experience can hardly be explained by purely macro-economic factors. That favourable macro-economic factors played a role in allowing Wenzhou to grow rapidly is not in doubt, but this does not show why her growth rate was relatively faster than that of China as a whole.

Local factors
If macro-economic change in the Chinese economy offers only a partial explanation for Wenzhou's impressive achievement compared to other areas of China, how important was local geography and the base from which the experiment started in the late 1970s?

The role of the farm sector: In principle, a healthy farm sector could have played a critical role in providing the dynamic for the growth of the non-farm rural sector. On the demand side, high incomes per head and a high income elasticity of demand for industrial products amongst peasant farmers would encourage industrial production. On the supply side, a highly profitable farming sector can provide the finance for investment in industrial capacity and for modern farming inputs, including machinery and fertilizers, which raises the profitability of farming yet further and hence establishes a virtuous circle. How dynamic in practice, then, was Wenzhou's farming sector? Did it provide the market and the finance that fuelled the growth of rural industry and commerce? More precisely, was Wenzhou's farming sector in the early 1980s very close to reaching some critical threshold of farm sector income which, if exceeded due to the influence of macro-economic stimuli, would trigger a process of non-farm rural development?

In terms of its environment, Wenzhou enjoys something of an intermediate position in Chinese terms. Consider weather first of all. Its sub-tropical climate provides annual rainfall of 1,800 mm, 1,830 hours of sunlight and an average air temperature of 18 degrees Celsius. This is far more conducive to the development of the farming sector than the climate in areas such as Gansu, Ningxia and Shaanxi where wind-blown sand, drought, and the enormous variation in temperature across the year that is a feature of desert areas provide an exceptionally inhospitable environment. Moreover, Wenzhou's elevation is far less than that of Qinghai, Tibet and western Sichuan where snow is frequent and the growing season extremely short. Even in January, the thermometer registers an average temperature of above 7° in Wenzhou and the *shi* is one of the wettest places in China. Nevertheless, the fields of Wenzhou are no Elysium. Annual rainfall is heavily concentrated in the summer months and flooding is a persistent problem. Moreover, cumulative annual hours of sunlight, whilst much higher than the 1,228 of misty Chengdu in the Sichuan basin, are significantly less than in Shanghai (2,014) and Nanjing (2,155). In aggregate and recognizing that the environmental determinants of crop growth are sunlight, rainfall and mean air temperature, it is evident that Wenzhou is reasonably well-favoured but not exceptionally so.

Another key determinant of crop yields, perhaps the key in rice-growing areas, is irrigation. Again, Wenzhou is immensely privileged compared to the provinces of the Loess, the Gobi desert and the Tibetan plateau, being crossed by four considerable rivers: the Ou, Ao, Feiyun and Qingshui. But relative to Sunan (southern Jiangsu), the area located within the triangle Nanjing–Hangzhou–Shanghai, Wenzhou's poverty is plain to see. There is no Changjiang (Yangzi) and no Lake Tai; nor is there the extensive canal network, based around the Grand Canal, that extends across the entire area. The reasons for this have everything to do with topography because irrigation is extremely difficult and expensive in mountainous areas even when rainfall is considerable. In the case of Wenzhou, in sharp contrast to Sunan, almost 76 per cent of total surface area is hill or mountain. As a result, rice-based farming is difficult except on the coastal plain and the valley floors; in all, only 2 per cent of total area is used for farming.

It is not clear, however, that population density is an important constraint. Although it has been pointed out in the chapters that follow that cultivated area per capita by the mid-1980s was only around 0.45 *mu*, and this is far lower than the national average of 1.4 *mu*, it is not clear that this means a great deal. As has already been said, Wenzhou's growing conditions – while inferior to those of Sunan – were markedly superior to many areas of northern and western China; in other words, the comparison ignores land quality. Additionally, it is increasingly accepted that the extent of economies of scale in farming where mechanization is almost nonexistent (and Wenzhou certainly falls into that category) is limited. In short, it is not obvious that 0.45 *mu* per capita is a holding size of less than the optimum.

Wenzhou's other major problem is that there is no large urban concentration within, or even adjacent to, its boundaries. The presence of such an urban centre is crucial in the Chinese context for two reasons. First, it is a source of demand for crop output; rural areas enjoying excess demand clearly will attain much higher rates of profitability than those that do not and these retained profits will tend to exacerbate spatial differentials by allowing high levels of reinvestment in modern inputs. Second, urban centres are a source of human nightsoil, the significance of which to the Chinese rural economy, even in the 1980s, is enormous. If this nightsoil can be transported by boat – by far the most profitable mode of transport – then the rural hinterland is doubly privileged. In this sense, the contrast between Wenzhou and Sunan is enormous, the latter enjoying the presence of the metropolis of Shanghai and Sunan's own extensive canal network.

Thus, local climate, topography, population density and urbanization were relatively favourable for farming in Wenzhou in the early 1980s. Nevertheless, local factors were much less conducive to a prosperous farming sector than in many other areas of China, such as the Chengdu plain, the Dongting basin, the Pearl river delta and the verdant and rolling countryside of Sunan. Indeed, one of the areas of China where heavy grain procurements and rapid collectivization during the 1950s came close to precipitating a crisis was Wenzhou's Pingyang *xian* (Lardy, 1987: 167).

This interpretation is confirmed by available data on relative per capita

Table 3.5
Distributed collective income in Wenzhou relative to other provinces, 1978–81

	1978	1979	1981	Average, 1978–81
Wenzhou	56	66	71	64
Guizhou	46	46	66	53
Sichuan	72	80	75	76
Zhejiang	91	104	112	102
Jiangsu	85	95	121	100
All-China	75	84	101	87

Sources: Wenzhou – Zhejiang tongjiju (ed.) 1984: 86–103; Others – 1978 and 1979: Vermeer, 1982: 20; 1981: *Zhongguo guojia tongjiju* (ed.), 1982: 198.

Notes: Incomes are measured in current *yuan*. This table is not as helpful as it might be because collective distributed income is a much narrower concept than net peasant income. No data on the latter measure are available for Wenzhou, however, except for 1980 and to invoke a single year comparison is dangerous because of the impact of harvest fluctuations at a provincial level; Sichuan's 1981 floods and their impact upon incomes are an example of this.

incomes at the beginning of the 1980s (Table 3.5.).

On the basis of Table 3.5 – and 1980 data on comparative net peasant incomes do not contradict it – Wenzhou appears as a low income *shi*. Nevertheless, it is clear that it was by no means one of the poorest places in China. Firstly, its relatively low income status is exaggerated by the unit of aggregation; the dispersion of incomes at the level of the *shi/diqu* (prefecture) is considerably more than that of the province because of the disproportionate effect of high income *shi* and *diqu* on provincial averages. Secondly, even if this is ignored, peasant collective distributed incomes per head in Wenzhou were certainly higher than in provinces such as Guizhou, Gansu, and Xizang; the last two almost certainly experienced lower peasant incomes per head than Guizhou in the late 1970s (net peasant income per head in Gansu in 1978 is given as 98 *yuan* compared to 108 *yuan* in Guizhou. (See Zhongguo guojia tongjiju, 1985: 574.)

Nevertheless, if the Wenzhou average was higher than that for other provinces, peasant incomes in some of its *xian* were still very low. The existence of low income localities is evident in Table 3.6 below.

Table 3.6
National income per head by *xian*, 1980–81

	1980	1981	Average, 1980–81	As % of Wenzhou average
Dongtou	174	210	192	72
Leqing	265	235	250	94
Yongjia	177	189	183	69
Rui'an	269	283	276	104
Pingyang	188	207	197	74
Wencheng	165	191	178	67
Taishun	172	217	195	73
Wenzhou city	503	508	506	190
Wenzhou	261	271	266	100

Source: Zhejiang tongjiju (ed.), 1984: 86–103.

Notes: National income (*guomin shouru*) per head measured in 1980 constant *yuan*. The weighting used in the original source to obtain the *shi* average is unclear. It has therefore been re-calculated by using *xian* population weights. Median national income per head – 196.5 *yuan*, 1980–81, for all-Wenzhou – here gives a very much better indication of the *shi*'s prosperity than the mean.

Table 3.6 shows clearly that the poorest *xian* in Wenzhou were far behind the *shi* mean, with only Leqing and Rui'an being close to, or exceeding, it. Moreover, the gulf between them and Wenzhou city is understated by these data because the figures for Wenzhou city include a substantial rural area which in 1982 was formally separated from the city and re-named Ouhai *xian*. In that year, the national income per head of the latter was only 306 *yuan* compared to 800 *yuan* for the city proper (Zhejiang tongjiju (ed.), 1984: 86–103).

The backwardness of Wenzhou in the early 1980s thus has two dimensions. First, the *shi* as a whole was a low-income area by Chinese standards, although incomes per head were higher than in many parts of western China. Second, there was an immense gap between the city of Wenzhou and its rural hinterland. It is thus hard to believe that the extraordinary growth of the *shi* in the 1980s can be attributed to the prosperity of its farming sector. Even if there is some critical minimum level of farming income per head which must be reached in order to trigger 'take-off' in China, it is difficult to see how an area starting from Wenzhou's degree of backwardness could have reached it before other, more prosperous, regions.

The inheritance: To what extent, though, was Wenzhou a suitable choice for a rural strategy based firmly upon rural industry and commerce? Did it, in 1980, have the infrastructure necessary to allow the operation of a market economy? Did it have any tradition of industrial production and commerce?

At first glance, the answer would seem to be rather pessimistic. In terms of infrastructure, there was no railway within its boundaries; the completion of the first such, linking Wenzhou city with Jinhua in central Zhejiang and hence connecting it with Hangzhou to the north and Fuzhou to the south, is scheduled for the late 1980s. Moreover, though more extensive than the national average, the network of navigable waterways within the *shi* compared poorly with that of Zhejiang as a whole; in 1984 there were 4,379 persons per kilometre of navigable waterway in Wenzhou compared to the provincial average of 3,760. The road network was similarly underdeveloped with a density of 2,869 persons per km in 1984, substantially higher than the Zhejiang mean of 1,776, and vastly greater than the national average of 1,117. Nevertheless, one should not underestimate the importance of Wenzhou's location on the coast in facilitating the growth of industry and commerce after 1980 as the chapter on the construction of the town of Longgang in Cangnan *xian* makes clear. Port facilities on the *shi*'s four main rivers were extensive and enabled her to trade with other Chinese ports and gain access to export markets; moreover, the cost of coastal transportation of goods was much lower than alternative forms.

Furthermore, it would be a mistake to conclude that Wenzhou had been ill-served by her history. This is particularly apparent from the extent of industrial development pre-1949. The long coastline and natural harbours of the *shi* were largely responsible for the development of a considerable commercial maritime tradition. The city of Wenzhou itself boasted extensive port facilities by the early twentieth century. It had been designated a Treaty Port in 1876 and its development was so swift that it was handling 19 per cent of all provincial exports by 1932 (Ministry of

Industry, 1935: 63); the percentage of imports was much smaller however, with 96 per cent of these (by value) going through Ningbo. Its export products included matting, matches and forest products such as timber, tea and paper.

Wenzhou also has a strong industrial tradition. The city proper, and the adjacent Yongjia *xian*, was an important centre for handicraft and industrial products by the 1930s. For example, this sub-region was the leading producer of umbrellas in the province, boasting 107 of Zhejiang's 200 umbrella manufacturers in the early years of that decade. More significantly, in view of development trends in the 1980s, only 13 of these 107 enterprises employed more than 5 workers (Ministry of Industry, 1935: 708–11). Another Wenzhou/Yongjia speciality in the 1930s was mat weaving; some 70,000 workers were so employed and the first factory of the province to be equipped with modern mat weaving machinery was established there in 1918, although fierce Japanese competition was beginning to have adverse effects by the late 1930s (ibid: 684–85). Nor was handicraft and emergent modern industry confined merely to the area around Wenzhou city. Rice milling, brewing, tea firing and umbrella manufacture were to be found throughout the rural parts of the municipality. Moreover, there were other *xian* specialities; Leqing was known for its lace manufacture (ibid: 539), Rui'an for establishing the first condensed milk factory in China (ibid: 612) and even the relatively low income *xian* of Pingyang and Taishun were involved in the production of hand-made paper and pottery (ibid: 480–81).

Of course, the process of industrialization was not without its problems, mainly because of the partial integration of Wenzhou into the world economy; this made it vulnerable to Japanese competition and to the world depression of the 1930s. On balance, however, the gains outweighed the costs especially in the long term in respect of technology transfer and the growth of a trained pool of labour. In part the concentration of handicraft and modern industry along China's eastern coast was a simple reflection of it being owned by foreigners; but on the other hand, the backward and forward linkages that this created were a definite spur to indigenous industrial development.

The industrial tradition was expanded upon after 1949. Industrial diversification into areas such as chemicals and engineering occurred but traditional skills were also developed within modern industry; according to the municipality's government:

> Wenzhou is among China's leading suppliers of dairy products.... Known as the 'home of ceramics' in China, it has played an important role in the growth of China's building ceramic industry. (Cited in Zhao Shengwu *et al.*, 1986: 98)

Much of this new growth was within the state sector of the economy rather than under the direction of rural collectives but, as with Sunan, technology transfer and co-operation between the two undoubtedly facilitated the growth of the latter's *shedui* enterprises.

As in the pre-1949 period, macro-economic trends imposed some constraints. This was particularly the case with persistent Maoist emphasis on the need to develop the industry of the interior rather than of the coastal areas which led to nationally determined state enterprise wage levels and the consequent need to subsidize inland provinces using the tax revenues collected in Zhejiang, Jiangsu and other coastal areas. This undoubtedly had some effect, as is shown by the fall in the share of coastal provinces in gross industrial output value from 69 per cent in 1952 to 62 per cent by 1980 (Zhongguo guojia tongjiju, 1985(b): 139). Nevertheless, the extent was not so great as markedly to restrict industrial development.

But if Wenzhou's inheritance was considerably more favourable than that of Guizhou or Gansu, how does it compare to other parts of eastern China? For if its inheritance were as favourable as that of Sunan, Wenzhou's development in the 1980s would not be at all surprising. Rather, the question would be, why was Wenzhou's rural economy so backward before 1978?

When comparisons are made between Wenzhou and Sunan, however, it quickly becomes clear that the latter enjoyed massive advantages. Of critical importance here was Shanghai itself. For, of course, the great port was not merely the centre of the lower Changjiang region, but the industrial and commercial focus of the entire national economy dwarfing the contribution of any other province, let alone city; even in 1978, and despite having barely 1 per cent of national population, Shanghai contributed almost 13 per cent of China's gross industrial output value.

Indeed, it is difficult to exaggerate the beneficial impact of Shanghai on the entire rural economy of Sunan, both before and after 1949. In particular, it played a crucial role in promoting the development of *shedui* enterprises (known as *xiangzhen* enterprises after the weakening of the commune in 1982–83). One important component of this was the importance of the city as a source of demand for industrial products; in 1978, per capita peasant incomes within the *shi* averaged 290 *yuan*, much higher than the all-China average of 134 *yuan* (Zhongguo guojia tongjiju, 1985(a): 574) and urban incomes were higher still. Given a high income, elasticity of demand for non-food products and land scarcity within Shanghai itself, the demand for industrial products could only be met by the rural non-farm economy of Sunan. Another key element was technology transfer. According to Fei Xiaotong:

> ... most rural industry in the four *diqu* had developed economic and technical cooperation with Shanghai.... This indicates that the economic development of Shanghai had a great impact on the economy of rural industries and the whole surrounding area, playing the part of an economic centre. Among the more than 2,000 rural factories in Wuxi *xian*, 709 were linked up with major plants in large and medium-sized cities such as Shanghai and Wuxi. They cooperated in a total of 895 items, most of them involving plants in the two cities.... [This

represents] . . . a new pattern of industrialization in China where 'big fish help small fish and small fish help shrimps'. (Fei Xiaotong *et al.*, 1986: 73–4)

Whether Sunan benefited relative to Wenzhou from its absence of mountains, and the presence of good transport linkages, is more controversial because the result was relatively greater foreign involvement in the local economy. In the case of silk (see Eng, 1986, passim), the presence of the foreigner encouraged the development of towns specializing in silk cocoon production and allowed access to foreign markets. During the last decades of the 19th and the early decades of the 20th century, the impact on the rural economy was unquestionably favourable. World depression and Japanese competition, however, had disastrous effects, leading to starvation in some areas of Sunan where silk had become the key means of raising revenue to purchase foodstuffs (Fei, 1983: 19; Eng, 1986: 157–62). Nevertheless, for the 1861–1932 period, Eng concludes that the contribution of the West was neither obviously constructive nor destructive:

> Western capital and the foreign-run Maritime Customs played a minimal role in the development of silk reeling. . . . At the same time, the neo-Marxist paradigm has overemphasized the immiseration of peasants. For a period, export growth did promote economic welfare. (ibid: 188).

Moreover, considering also the post-1949 implications, the long-run net effects of foreign involvement were probably positive both because of the impact of technology transfer and the development of a pool of skilled labour. Even the destructive effects of war with Japan after 1937 did not eliminate this legacy.

By 1980, Sunan's industrial development had proceeded even further in this respect, albeit along collective (*shedui*) lines; moreover, there is little doubt that the profits generated by its farm sector played a significant role in accelerating the process in that they were readily mobilized for investment at the levels of team, brigade and commune alike. By 1983, *xiangzhen* enterprise gross income totalled 475 *yuan* per head in Sunan, compared to the all-China average of 74 *yuan* and a figure of 121 *yuan* in northern Jiangsu.[2]

Industrial development in rural Wenzhou was by comparison paltry. As a percentage of total industrial output value, the contribution of *xiangzhen* enterprises in some *xian* was considerable; in Yongjia in 1980 it was 40 per cent, for example (Pan, 1984: 1022). But the development of *xiangzhen* industry was limited even as late as 1984. For example, *xiangzhen* gross output value per head at 1980 constant prices in 11 *xian* in northern Zhejiang usually included in Sunan was 265 *yuan* compared to only 74 *yuan* in the *xian* of Wenzhou.[3]

In summary, Wenzhou was not especially advantaged or disadvantaged relative to the China norm. It did not enjoy the combination of factors that gave Sunan a place in the sun, far in advance of the rest of the Chinese economy but nor did it suffer from the immense difficulties that hampered development in the Chinese hinterland.

Institutional change

We have therefore seen that neither macro-economic nor local factors can adequately explain the Wenzhou phenomenon. Instead, the dynamism of its economy seems attributable to institutional changes and, specifically, to the removal of restrictions on the economic operations of small, privately owned rural enterprises. Still, one question remains: does the economic dynamism of the small, family-run enterprise stem from its size or from its ownership type?

The only evidence we have on this in the case of Wenzhou is the comparison of the relative growth rates of collectively owned *xiangzhen* enterprises and private family enterprises, cited earlier, which shows the annual output growth rate of the former to be only around half that of the latter. A superficial interpretation of this would be that size is the key factor because both family and *xiangzhen* enterprises are privately managed following the growth of leasing of *xiangzhen* enterprises to groups and individuals in both China and Wenzhou in the early 1980s. This interpretation is rather suspect, however, because *xiangzhen* and family enterprises are not treated equally. First, the managers of *xiangzhen* enterprises are circumscribed in their freedom of action by very restrictive leases. For example, the contract between the enterprise manager(s) and its owners (usually the village management committee) is a short term one of perhaps one to three years. Further, the manager(s) only retains the percentage of enterprise profits stipulated in the contract; his/her control over the use of retained profits is therefore very much less than absolute. Moreover, although the manager is allowed to link wages in the enterprise to employee performance, the size of bonuses in relation to the basic wage is usually fixed in the lease contract.

Second, the fiscal treatment of household and *xiangzhen* enterprises is unequal; effective rates of taxation for the latter are much greater than for the former, although this is partly because newly established household enterprises qualify for short-term profit tax exemptions which older *xiangzhen* enterprises enjoyed earlier. In addition to *xiangzhen* enterprise income taxation, a part of profits is used to subsidize poor teams by the *xian* authority and also to promote agricultural mechanization. Furthermore, *xiangzhen* enterprises are forced to spend more on workers' welfare and although managers are able to dismiss workers, the pressures to avoid doing so on anything other than a very small-scale are formidable. The result is undoubtedly to raise unit labour costs.

Nevertheless, even though the above does suggest that ownership type is an important explanatory variable for rapid household enterprise growth, size seems also to be important. The survival of a small-scale, privately owned industrial sector in OECD economies throws some light on the issue. Particularly interesting is the case of Japan where the share of small businesses in industrial output and retail sales is a good deal higher than the OECD average as Table 3.7 indicates.

Table 3.7
The share of small businesses in OECD retail and industrial sectors

	Industry share	Retail sales share
Japan	58 (1978)	79 (1979)
USA	37 (1972)	71 (1972)
West Germany	44 (1967)	n.a.
UK	25 (1977)	39 (1977)

Source: Kosai and Ogino, 1984: 71.

Notes: Industry share is the percentage of industrial value-added contributed by small businesses. The retail sales share is the percentage of all retail industry sales attributable to the small retail sector. Definition of small: Industry – Japan: 1–299 employees; USA: 1–249; UK and West Germany: 1–499; Retailing – all: 1–49 employees.

This, of course, does not mean that the importance of small businesses is necessarily an important factor in explaining Japan's 'economic miracle' – but it hardly suggests they are unprofitable either. The reasons for the continuing vitality of the Japanese small business sector put forward by native economists is that large companies continue to find it cost effective to sub-contract parts of the productive process to them. This, in turn, reflects their relatively lower labour costs and their ability to specialize in one particular area of production, with the resulting product being of high quality. Significantly, it has little to do with the particular type of goods being produced; the traditional Japanese small company certainly specialized in textiles and labour-intensive production processes, and many still do, but the 1970s has seen diversification into heavy industry such as chemicals, precision instruments and electronics (Kosai and Ogino, 1984: 70).

This, therefore, implies that, if the ownership type is held constant, there is room for an extensive small business sector provided that its products can be produced at low cost, are specialized and are of a competitive quality. In the case of Wenzhou, there is little to suggest that differences in labour costs are significant in explaining performance differentials between household and *xiangzhen* enterprises; this is much more important in explaining why *state* enterprises fare particularly badly in relative terms for they are required to play a welfare as well as a productive role, such as the responsibility for paying pensions to retired former employees, even though reforms during the 1980s have tried to emphasize the latter at the expense of the former (Wang and Li, 1986(b)). In terms of product quality, there is no doubt that this is generally low in the household sector, and that it has an adverse effect upon the sector's growth. But where household industry in Wenzhou derives advantage is from its lower unit costs in certain areas of production where product variety is at a premium (e.g., buttons, clothing). In such areas, the post-1978 period has seen a reaction to the conformity in dress of the Maoist era in favour of diversity throughout China and, because there simply is not a mass market for a particular item, the minimum efficient scale of production is much smaller than it would be in the case of, say, extractive industries. As a result, household industry can compete in price terms even though it suffers from poor quality.

Yet it still remains unclear to what extent the differential performance of *xiangzhen* and household industry derives from size alone. It is not sensible to caricature the former type as subject to diseconomies of scale because they are too large precisely because their average size remains incredibly small by international standards; in China as a whole, the average *xiangzhen* enterprise employed 21 workers in 1980 and this had risen to only 26 by 1985 (Zhongguo guojia tongjiju, 1981: 190–92; State Statistical Bureau, 1987(b): 21–24). Thus, both *xiangzhen* and household industry would be included in the 'small' category in Table 3.7. Indeed, it may be that their respective growth rates differ simply because of the household sector starting from a very low base in 1980; if this is the true explanation, one would expect to see the growth rates of the two converge over time and perhaps, therefore, we must suspend judgement on this issue in the interim.

As has already been noted, it is not possible to address the specific contribution of ownership type to the Wenzhou phenomenon because household industry has never existed post-1949 except in a private form. Moreover, a comparison of pre-1978 *shedui* (collective ownership and management) with post-1978 *xiangzhen* (collective ownership and growing private management) enterprise – which would address this issue – is replete with difficulty because of the myriad macro-economic changes that occurred simultaneously, thus making it impossibly difficult to determine causality. Nevertheless, the rapid growth of *shedui* industry in Sunan during the 1970s, when both ownership and management responsibility were collective, suggests strongly that high rates of growth and profitability could be achieved without private ownership or management. The best example of this is Wuxi *xian*. Here the growth of *shedui* enterprises dates from 1974 when no less than 1,212 rural factories were established. As a result, the share of communes and brigades in total rural gross output – the sum of team, brigade and commune levels – rose from 23 per cent in 1970 to 64 per cent in 1977 and 79 per cent by 1980 (Leeming, 1985: 115). Given that all this pre-dates both leasing and post-1978 macro-economic change, it is an impressive testament to the dynamism of collective industry. Yet it still falls some way short of being conclusive proof of the proposition that 'the ownership/management type' does not matter. For it is not impossible that private control would have produced even better results; indeed, given Wuxi's long history of rural industrialization – it was known as 'little Shanghai' pre-1949 – and its excellent transport links, probably any type of attempt to develop rural industry, irrespective of ownership or management type, would have produced spectacular results.

Nevertheless, both *xiangzhen* and household enterprises have undoubtedly been the beneficiaries of a partially reformed state sector. The reform of the state sector has admittedly been going on throughout China since 1978. Attempts have been made to raise labour and capital productivity by allowing state enterprises greater control over retained profits, by granting enhanced authority to enterprise directors and by introducing employment contracts to replace life-long tenure for newly recruited workers. But although it would be too harsh to say these reforms have been a complete failure, they have certainly been no more than a partial success. For state enterprises remain handicapped by their role as social units, such that their profit and loss account may reflect, for example, the extent of their expenditure on pensions for retired workers rather than their operational efficiency. Further, because the threat of 'firm death', whether through bankruptcy or takeover, remains a distant one in the absence of a bankruptcy law (though a draft has been completed) or effective stock market, there is hardly a spur to profit maximization. Most critically of all, corporate profitability continues to be determined not by internal efficiency, but by the relative price structure of inputs and outputs. Until relative prices are re-structured to bring them closer to current long run marginal costs, the prospects for equal competition both within the state sector and between the state and other sectors remain bleak indeed.

This is very much the view of state enterprise employees and managers in Wenzhou. According to a ship fitter in a state enterprise in Wenzhou:

> Owners of private enterprises in Wenzhou are getting rich while we workers can only lead a life on the margins with just enough to eat and wear. (Wang and Li, 1986(b): 21)

The problems facing state enterprises are also reflected in their performance – 21 per cent of those in Wenzhou city were running at a loss in 1986 (Wang and Li, 1986(b): 21) – and their share in the municipality's GVIO, which fell from 31 per cent in 1980 to 18 per cent in 1985 (ibid: 23). Although further attempts have been made to grant them more autonomy, including the copying of the *xiangzhen* leasing approach, it remains to be seen how this will operate in practice.

Yet to argue that the household sector will not long survive fundamental reform of state-owned enterprises is unconvincing. It has already been seen that product market segmentation exists in both China and other OECD countries; thus, in many areas, the state sector would not be able to compete with small businesses even if reformed. Therefore, post-reform, household and *xiangzhen* growth rates are likely to be slower but there is no reason to suppose such enterprises will disappear. Moreover, it is not obvious that fundamental relative price changes are on the Chinese government's immediate agenda. The political ramifications of allowing market determination of product prices and employee earnings are so considerable that the whole issue remains in abeyance. The problem here is that there are widely *perceived* to be net social benefits from state ownership even if these are at the expense of financial losses. Until these perceptions change, 'the window of opportunity' for the household and *xiangzhen* sectors will remain open.

In summary, Wenzhou's success does not seem explicable in terms of macro-economic factors, local economic geography or a particularly favourable conjuncture of historical conditions. The failure of the Chinese government fundamentally to reform the operating environment for state enterprises, and the tight restrictions still imposed upon *xiangzhen* enterprises, does suggest that a part of the explanation must lie in the household sector's operational autonomy. Nevertheless, household (and *xiangzhen*) enterprises have benefited from their small scale of operation. Even if all controls on state and *xiangzhen* enterprises were to be removed, there would still be a profitable household sector in Wenzhou. As it is, the combination of asymmetrical operational autonomy and small scale has proved to be particularly potent.

Towards an evaluation

The significance of the Wenzhou model lies in its pioneering nature; if the results are regarded as successful by the Party, it is liable to be extended to other parts of China. A careful evaluation is therefore in order and this must have two aspects. First, do the chapters that follow adequately cover the various costs and benefits derived from the experiment? In particular, have any important costs been ignored? Second, does this revised cost-benefit analysis produce net benefits of a magnitude sufficient to justify the experiment's introduction, or ratification, in other parts of China?

Immiseration?

It is immediately obvious from even a brief look at the assessments of the model made by Chinese economists that a very wide range of issues has been discussed and a great many of the obvious costs have been carefully described. The results, broadly speaking, are that rapid rates of output growth have been achieved and these have provided the basis for substantial increases in rural incomes per head. These gains have been offset to some extent by growing spatial and intra-local income differentials, and deteriorating workplace conditions deriving from growing labour intensity.

But one important issue has not been considered: whether the fruits of growth have 'trickled down' to low income mountainous areas. The reason for being suspicious about this is twofold. First, the incredible empirical finding noted earlier that the poorest households, even in 1985, had an annual income per head of 50 *yuan* and that whole districts had incomes per head barely in excess of 100 *yuan*. This suggests that certain areas have not benefited much from the process of rural development and perhaps their living standard has even fallen. It is of course possible, however, that these 1985 levels do represent an improvement if pre-1978 incomes per head were substantially below the 50 *yuan* level. It is, therefore, essential to consider whether a process of immiserization has taken place within the *shi* and, equally importantly, within *xian* in other *diqu* bordering on Wenzhou.

The second reason is the theoretical plausibility of such an outcome. Consider a situation in which a number of low-income areas are adjacent to a high income and rapidly expanding region; in other words, a dual economy model of the type of Lewis. In the absence of widespread capital-saving technical progress in the 'modern' (high income) sector, production therein will expand by using under-employed and unemployed labour available within the sector itself in the short term. In the longer term, providing the 'modern' sector continues to grow and that population growth does not accelerate in response, this 'reserve army' will gradually be depleted. The growing labour shortage that will result will be met, assuming no significant legal or geographical barriers, by labour migration from the 'traditional' to the 'modern' sector. But what will the impact of this out-migration be on the 'traditional' sector?

One can think of various positive effects that the process might generate. Out-migration may increase average farm holding size and thus stimulate mechanization to reap the benefits of economies of scale. Alternatively, out-migrants may remit large sums of money to their originating area by virtue of obtaining relatively high income jobs in the 'modern' sector; on an international scale – for example, remittances from Sri Lankan migrants working in the Middle East – these flows may be of immense importance and the same argument applies to a dual economy model.

The problem is that as well as these favourable impulses (spread effects), there may also be unfavourable ones (backwash effects). As Myrdal points out, it is by no means obvious that the spread effects will necessarily outweigh the backwash effects (Myrdal, 1957: Ch. 3). There are two difficulties here. First, low income mountain areas may not have any 'surplus labour' at all. It is particularly important to recognize how much labour is absorbed in 'traditional' transport; in parts of mountainous southwest Sichuan, for example, labour absorbed in this way was estimated as accounting for up to 20 per cent of labour days in the 1970s (Zhongguo kexue Chengdu dili yanjiusuo, 1980: 195). Thus, although the labour may be surplus to direct farming requirements, its marginal product is not low. In a case like this, the establishment of income differentials between the 'modern' and 'traditional' sector would lead to an outflow of productive labour from the latter such that higher output in the 'modern' sector will be at least partially offset by lower output in the 'traditional' sector; the process may generate macro-economic net benefits but these will not accrue directly to the 'traditional' sector. These difficulties are resolved in the Lewis framework by the assumption of a marginal product of labour that is zero (or at best less than the subsistence real wage) in the traditional sector, so that net output gains accrue from migration.

Second, even if 'surplus labour' exists in the 'traditional sector', it does not follow that this particular type of labour will migrate; much more likely is an outflow of skilled productive labour. Not only will this group be much more aware of opportunities in the 'modern' sector but also it will be better able to meet the direct costs of migration from savings. Furthermore, this migrant labour may be much younger (and by implication more economically active) than the 'traditional' sector average, thus further compounding that sector's problems (Myrdal, 1956: 27). In the Lewis model, these problems do not arise because both transaction costs and asymmetric information sets are ignored.

Nor should it be supposed that these are merely academic objections to the process of labour migration. As the World Bank has noted:

> ... experience from northeast Brazil and certain regions of Mexico suggests that younger, more skilled and better educated population groups tend to migrate, leaving behind an older and less well-trained group. As a result, some communities of origin have lost the very resources that could stimulate their vitality and development, and total (and even per capita) output has declined. (World Bank, 1985: 94)

But has this process happened in the case of Wenzhou? Data deficiencies and an abbreviated time scale preclude any definitive conclusion; nevertheless, some analysis is possible for the 1978–84 period.

First, consider population. If a Lewis-type model is operating in Wenzhou, one would expect to see the population of high income *xian* growing more quickly than that of low income *xian*. As Table 3.8 demonstrates, however, there is little evidence of this.

Although there are substantial differences in incomes between these *xian*, they are not reflected in any clear pattern of differential population growth. Yongjia, for example, is a very low income *xian* and yet its rate of population growth over 1978–84 was the second highest. Nevertheless, these data could be more helpful. First, it is not clear in practice how severe controls on migration were during this period. It is difficult to believe that there were not very severe controls on rural–urban migration; only this can satisfactorily account for Wenzhou city's relatively slow population growth rate given the vast income differentials between it and its neighbours. How restrictive controls upon inter-*xian* migration were, especially in the early part of the period, is not clear; however, many had certainly been removed by the mid-1980s. Moreover, there is no indication of whether there was a net outflow of skilled labour from the low income *xian* which might be quantitatively small but qualitatively large. Further, it is plausible that net labour outflows from the low income *xian* have occurred but do not show up in the statistics because of a more rapid natural growth rate therein; this latter might have been a response to rising per capita incomes. But – and more alarmingly – it might be a response to improvements in health care such that population growth negates increases

Table 3.8
Population growth by *xian* 1978–84

	Total population (millions)		Growth rate, 1978–84	Income per head, 1980
	1978	1984		
Dongtou	0.108	0.117	1.36	174
Leqing	0.824	0.928	1.98	265
Yongjia	0.683	0.764	1.86	177
Rui'an	0.949	1.038	1.49	269
Pingyang	1.528	1.689	1.67	188
Wencheng	0.315	0.344	1.47	165
Taishun	0.283	0.308	1.40	172
Wenzhou city	0.923	1.018	1.66	503
All Wenzhou	*5.613*	*6.207*	*1.68*	*263*
	1980	1984	Growth rate 1980–84	
Qingtian	0.444	0.465	1.13	
Yunhe	0.253	0.275	2.14	

Sources: 1978, Zhejiang tongjiju (ed.) 1984: 86–103; 1980, Pan (ed.) 1984: 1,000–1,153; 1984, *Zhejiang jingji tongjijiu nianjian*, 1985.

Notes:
   1. These populations are calculated on the basis of the *xian* boundaries of 1978. Since that year, Pingyang has been sub-divided into Pingyang and Cangnan *xian* and Yunhe into Yunhe and Yining *zizhixian* (autonomous county). Ouhai *xian* has also been created since 1980 out of the rural areas of Wenzhou city but no data is available on the population of these areas in 1978.
   2. Both Qingtian and Yunhe were part of Lishui *diqu* in 1980–84 but have been included in the analysis as both are low income *xian* adjacent to the western edge of Wenzhou *shi*. Yunhe's income level is not known but Qingtian was the poorest *xian* in the province in 1980 with a distributed collective income of only 41 *yuan* per head (JPRS: China Report – Agriculture, No. 224, 19 September 1982). The 1980 Wenzhou average was 69 *yuan* in that year (Zhejiang tongjiju (ed.), 1984: 86–103.
   3. Growth rates are annual averages derived from end-year populations only and expressed as a percentage.
   4. Population data include both urban and rural inhabitants.
   5. Incomes per head are *guomin shouru* data at constant 1980 prices.

in total output and even induces a fall in per capita output. In that sense, high rates of population growth in low income *xian* can be viewed as damaging.

An analysis of trends in output value per head is, therefore, more useful as an indicator of the impact of the Wenzhou growth process upon low income *xian*. If the impact of rural modernization is as suggested by Lewis, one would expect to see rising output values per head in the low income *xian*, though at a slower rate than in the higher income *xian*. If a more Myrdalian process has occurred, in which migration has been mainly confined to highly skilled groups of workers, then one would expect to see stagnant or falling output values per head. Evidence on these trends is presented in Table 3.9.

Table 3.9
Growth of real GVIAO per head by *xian*, 1978–84

	GVIAO per head (yuan)		
	1978	*1984*	*Growth rate, 1978–84*
Dongtou	266	768	17.7
Leqing	269	640	14.4
Yongjia	194	414	12.7
Rui'an	335	708	12.5
Pingyang	247	499	11.7
Wencheng	167	239	6.0
Taishun	170	272	7.9
Wenzhou city	767	1,599	12.2
All Wenzhou	*337*	*704*	*12.3*
	1980	*1984*	*Growth rate, 1980–84*
Qingtian	225	346	10.8
Yunhe	241	384	11.6

Sources: 1978, Zhejiang tongjiju (ed.) 1984: 86–103; 1980, Pan (ed.) 1984: 1,000–1,158; 1984, Zhejiang tongjiju (ed.) 1985.

Notes:
1. GVIAO per head are calculated from population and figures on GVAO and GVIO; they are at constant 1980 *yuan*. Growth rates are annual averages derived from 1978 and 1984 values only.
2. The figures for Wenzhou city include Ouhai *xian*. The 1984 figure comes from summing the data in Zhongguo guojia tongjiju, 1985: 153 (city proper) and Zhejiang tongjiju (ed.), 1985 (Ouhai).

These data suggest very strongly that the lowest income *xian* of Wenzhou have benefited from the growth process, with Wencheng and Taishun achieving annual average growth rates of 6 per cent and 7.9 per cent respectively. Even allowing for a divergence between the growth of gross and net output value – and it is not necessarily the case that value-added as a proportion of gross output has fallen – these are impressive growth rates by international standards. Yet more impressive is the case of Yongjia which had the third lowest level of GVIAO per head in 1978 and yet achieved an annual average growth rate of more than 12 per cent.

Furthermore, the growth rates achieved by the neighbouring low income *xian* of Yunhe and Qingtian in Lishui *diqu* suggest either rapid growth within that prefecture itself, or extremely powerful spread effects generated by Wenzhou. Whatever the explanation, it certainly does indicate that Wenzhou's growth has not been at the expense of other regions within Zhejiang province.

A caveat to all this is the impact of rural modernization on the farming sector within Wenzhou, and particularly within its low income *xian*, for it is suggested in some of the chapters that follow that farming has suffered from migration and non-farm investment encouraged by the relatively higher incomes to be earned outside the farming sector. Now it is certainly true that the share of farming in GVAO has fallen from around 72 per cent in 1980 to some 63 per cent by 1985 (He, 1987: 98) but it is not obvious that this is a cause for concern because a falling share is quite compatible with a substantial increase in the level of output per head. This theoretical possibility receives some support from the finding that total grain output averaged 1.402 million tonnes per annum during the Fifth Five Year Plan (1976–80) and 1,702 million tonnes during the Sixth (1981–85) (ibid: 97); even allowing for population growth, that indicates a definite increase per head. Furthermore, the argument that the worst effects of rural modernization have been felt by the farming sector only after 1984 is probably correct, but says rather more about the inadequacy of the macro-economic relative price structure than it does about the growth process in Wenzhou. Problems in the farming sector are very much an all-China phenomenon (see, for example, the report of a survey in *Nongye jingji wenti*, No. 6, (1986): 4–13).

One also might interpret the above table as showing that differentials within the *shi* have narrowed rather than widened during the early 1980s. For while the poorest *xian* have grown much less rapidly than the others, the gap between some of the higher output per head *xian* and Wenzhou city has narrowed somewhat; for example, the growth rates achieved by Dongtou and Leqing were significantly higher than the 12.2 per cent achieved by Wenzhou city. This may reflect the impact of controls on state industry in the latter. Such an interpretation is probably too optimistic, however. First, the narrowing may be a statistical artefact reflecting the city's relatively high starting point. Second, the GVIAO measure excludes commerce, transport and construction, all of which probably grew much faster in Wenzhou city than either its GVIAO or the tertiary sector in other *xian*. Therefore, it would be much more helpful in answering this question to compare growth rates of national income per head; however, these are not available. In their absence, the most convincing conclusion on spatial differentials within Wenzhou must still be that they have widened over the 1978–84 period.

Nevertheless, all the evidence considered above does suggest a negative answer to the question: has immiserization occurred in the poorest *xian* in Wenzhou during the 1978–84 period? Indeed, the evidence suggests that output growth per head has been significant. Of course, one cannot be too definitive about this. The impact of backwash effects in low income areas may only be felt in the long term and arguably, an analysis of income and output trends at the sub-*xian* level is a necessary complement to analysis at the level of the *xian*. Even so, the data available so far give grounds for cautious optimism.

National applicability

The question of the national applicability of the Wenzhou model has two aspects. First, in those areas where thriving small-scale private enterprises exist (such as in Anhui and Shandong provinces as well as Wenzhou), do the social benefits outweigh the costs? Second, is the Wenzhou approach viable in all those parts of China where incomes per head are low and rural industry/commerce underdeveloped?

Consider the second question first. On the demand side, one must accept that other areas will not be able to attain the growth rates achieved by Wenzhou because the latter, along with parts of Shandong and Anhui, enjoyed exceptionally favourable demand conditions. Wenzhou was able to exploit not only the (dynamic) impact of rising national income on demand for its products, but also the existence of (static) excess demand throughout China at the end of the 1970s. This arose from the inability of large state enterprises successfully to enter those product markets where few economies of scale existed – such as those for buttons and badges (as noted in the section Institutional Change, above). Wenzhou's household sector was one of the first to penetrate these types of markets and by the mid-1980s its products were selling nationally, even reaching Tibet. According to Wang and Li:' ... even in Lhasa, the capital of the Tibet Autonomous Region, small traders from Wenzhou account for one-quarter of the city's 2,000 retailers' (Wang and Li, 1986(a): 20).

As a result, the *shi* enjoyed the position of a monopoly producer in a national market and the output value of its household sector, and the profits derived from it, grew very quickly. For 'late starters', however, much less (static) excess demand will exist; indeed competition in markets for textiles and fashion accessories is likely to be stiff.

The outlook for these 'late starters' will, however, be less bleak than this analysis suggests. First, many of them will enjoy significant locational advantages relative to Wenzhou, especially in terms of transport costs. For example, one would expect the price of the products of the Sichuan household sector to sell more cheaply in Tibet, Qinghai and Xinjiang (assuming that labour and capital costs are broadly comparable). Second, the transport costs incurred in shipping products from areas with well-developed household sectors in eastern China make it likely that (static) excess demand continues to exist in most areas of western China, the Wenzhou presence on the streets of Lhasa notwithstanding. Third the long-run outlook for the fashion accessory and textile markets throughout China (*ceteris paribus*, especially in the area of politics) must be favourable given the pattern of income elasticities of demand for such products. Thus, whilst the 'late starters' may not be able to reap the static, once-and-for-all gains enjoyed by Wenzhou, the scope for dynamic gains based on market growth remain.

On the supply side, the key factor is probably the availability of physical infrastructure, especially transport. This is true of both transport within the local economy and access to the national and international economies. Internationally, the record of land-locked countries in achieving rapid growth has been extremely poor; one can think of sub-Saharan African countries such as Botswana, Zambia and the Central African Republic, as well as southeast Asian states such as Nepal and Afghanistan. The explanation seems to have much to do with the relatively lower cost of water-borne transportation of goods relative to alternative forms, and therefore countries or regions having a high percentage of their border in the form of coastline or a major river have definite advantages. This is not to say that such constraints upon development cannot be overcome; Zimbabwe and Paraguay are examples of countries that have made at least some progress. But the experience of the Soviet Union, which is handicapped by having her major rivers running north–south and hence away from the key European population centres, and a very high proportion of her coastline impassable to shipping because of ice, is a salutary one. The limitations of her inherited geography have slowly been overcome since 1917, but only at great cost.

The same seems to be true of China and, as has been seen above, both Sunan and Wenzhou are heavily dependent upon their transport infrastructure. In the case of the former, the main deficiencies are in raw materials, particularly coal and timber, which are transported in from Shanxi province (partly by rail and partly by sea) and from abroad respectively. As for Wenzhou, transport plays a key role in distributing products outside the *shi* and hence compensating for the absence of nearby urban centres of population; for example, the button market of Qiaotou is the largest in Asia. Even so, the extent of development in Wenzhou exhibits a marked spatial dichotomy between the coastal *xian* and those located in the mountains such as Taishun and Wencheng. As Zhao points out (below), average per capita income in these two and Pingyang was only about 200 *yuan* per farmer in 1985 compared to the *shi* average of 417 and a figure of more than 1,000 *yuan* in some villages in Cangnan.

Seen from this perspective, it is evident that there is tremendous scope for the application of the Wenzhou approach to rural modernization in large areas of China, principally along the eastern coast. But it is equally evident that the challenge to be overcome in developing inland provinces such as Gansu and Shaanxi in the north and Yunnan and Guizhou in the south is daunting. These are not only handicapped by lacking coastline and navigable waterways but also by a formidably difficult mountain topography; for example, the difficulties involved in constructing rail and road links in the area of Gansu between Tianshui and Baoji in Shaanxi are desperate. Even in the Sichuan basin, the difficulties can hardly be underestimated; the existing Chengdu–Chongqing railway, for example, has been hewn out of the steep hillside rising above the Tuo river for much of its length. In Qinghai and Tibet, the problems are compounded by the vast distances involved; when Tibetan exiles bemoan the failure of the Chinese to develop the economy of their homeland, they usually ignore the province's dependence upon gigantic and perpetual convoys of trucks making the long 30-hour haul from the railhead in Golmud with essential supplies of oil and manufactures, and similar trade, through the passes of the Himalayas via Nepal, to India.

But this does not mean that the Wenzhou phenomenon is a special case and largely devoid of significance for low income regions. For the model can be introduced throughout eastern China and the revenue generated in the process can be used either directly to raise incomes per head in the hinterland, or to begin the long process of establishing the infrastructure required for indigenous development. This seems a much more plausible strategy than mechanically applying the Wenzhou model always and everywhere throughout China in expectation of immediate success.

It is, however, predicated upon the ability to design and introduce a satisfactory system of taxation in those areas, like Wenzhou and Sunan, where rural modernization is a relatively simpler undertaking. Indeed, the issue of taxation is central to an evaluation of the first question posed in this section of the wider applicability of the Wenzhou approach to rural modernization. Not only is it difficult to see how low income provinces can benefit without such a system, but also it is hard to believe that a model that generates such enormous income differentials will win general political acceptance. To recognize the need for material incentives and exhort the population to 'take the lead in getting rich' is one thing, but to accept income inequalities on the Wenzhou scale is quite another. The first two can be justified either by an appeal to Marx or to the experience of OECD countries, but the last is far more problematic.

But if the question of political feasibility is put to one side, what are the economic arguments for and against a tax system which has the twin objects of raising revenue (to aid low income areas) and imposing some constraints upon the growth of income differentials?

It is clear that relatively progressive rates of taxation on profits and personal incomes carry with them the threat of higher marginal rates and hence disincentives to productive enthusiasm and to investment. There is thus a danger that the baby of rapid income growth will be thrown out with the bath water of income inequalities. But, conversely, and given that marginal propensities to consume fall as incomes rise, a progressive tax system can ensure rapid demand expansion. If one further assumes a dynamic Verdoorn-type relationship between productivity growth generated via demand-induced technical progress, the desirability of progressive taxation becomes apparent.

The historical evidence on this issue is not very clear. At first glance that would not seem to be the case. For while it is apparent that rates of personal taxation at the upper end of the scale (that is, above 80 per cent) are counter-productive in OECD countries, it is equally clear from the experiences of West Germany and the Scandinavian countries that progressive taxation is not incompatible with rapid growth. The same is true of Japan where an acceleration of GNP growth has coincided with an increasingly progressive tax structure as Table 3.10 demonstrates.

Table 3.10
GNP growth and sources of tax revenue in Japan, 1889–1980

			Share in tax revenue of:	
	Growth rate		Income tax	Corporation tax
1889–1938	3.15	1910	10.0	9.9
1955–80	7.74	1970	36.2	32.9

Source: Minami 1986: 43 and 340

Notes:
1. The growth rate is the per annum average of GNP.
2. The years chosen for income and corporation tax shares are reasonably representative of the two growth periods being compared. The figure for corporation tax in 1910 includes the business tax.

It would, however, be foolish to interpret this table as 'proving' that a progressive tax system is conducive to rapid growth, for there is always the counter-factual proposition: would growth have been even faster if taxation had been less progressive? Moreover, the post-1945 period was a golden age for all OECD countries relative to the inter-war years, and even to the late nineteenth century, that had much to do with the expansionary role of the USA in the world economy and the Bretton Woods system of fixed exchange rates. Even so, this evidence suggests that progressive taxation is not quite so incompatible with rapid growth as much of the conventional wisdom would have one believe.

On balance, therefore, both because the negative impact on growth can easily be exaggerated and because the differentials that have already emerged in the *shi* are so enormous, there does seem to be, in principle, a case for some form of progressive taxation. But is a progressive system of taxation a feasible option for an economy like Wenzhou's?

It is certainly true that the taxation of small household enterprises has created considerable problems in the *shi* during the 1980s, mainly because of widespread evasion. In the main town of Rui'an *xian*, for example, it is estimated that the average business avoided about 4,000 *yuan* in taxation in 1985 (Wang and Li, 1986(b): 23) and some of Wenzhou's officials see the task of tax collection as near to impossible, not least because of the Tax Department's incompetence. According to one: 'They are past masters in controlling state-owned enterprises but utter idiots in dealing with private business' (ibid: 23).

But that having been said, the problem of evasion is perhaps exaggerated, at least in that it has not prevented a large volume of revenue from being raised from the rural non-farming household sector. This is demonstrated by Table 3.11 which illustrates the share of total taxation derived from various sources.

Table 3.11
Tax revenue in Wenzhou by sector of origin, 1982–86

	Revenue (million yuan)	Shares in revenue by enterprise type (%)			
		State	Collective	Individual	Other
1982	191	39.2	56.1	4.0	0.7
1983	230	33.2	60.0	5.3	1.5
1984	272	28.2	62.0	9.1	0.7
1985	393	23.7	64.9	10.7	0.7
1986	503	23.9	63.5	11.7	0.9

Source: He (ed.), 1987: 152–53.

Notes: The revenue data here are for industrial and commercial taxes only; they exclude taxation levied on farming which accounted for about 8 per cent of total revenue in 1986. Data cover both urban and rural areas.

At almost 12 per cent of total industrial and commercial tax revenue, the contribution of the individual (or household) sector was clearly non-negligible. Moreover, this comparison actually understates its true contribution because it ignores revenue contributed by registration fees; if this latter is included, the share of the household sector rises to more than 20 per cent (He (ed.), 1987: 156). It is true that the household sector was still relatively undertaxed; for although it contributed in excess of 20 per cent of revenue, its share in industrial output was 28.3 per cent in 1985 and 33.8 per cent of total retail sales (ibid: 136). Nevertheless, it is also clear that the *shi* has succeeded in designing a system of taxation well able to extract revenue from the individual sector.

Yet it had manifestly not been able to produce a design capable of controlling income differentials. The reasons for this are evident when the particular types of taxes used are considered. The tax mentioned by Zhao Renwei (below, chapter 7) on the space occupied by stalls, for example, is virtually a lump sum tax – and thus conducive to growth rather than equity – and certainly not related to income in either principle or practice. The payment of a registration fee by households to enterprises – in principle at a rate of 10–15 per cent of the former's volume of business (see Zhao Renwei) – is clearly an income tax by design, but the scope for connivance between enterprise and household is immense such that actual tax payments bear little relation to actual taxable income. As a result, revenue is raised (about 8 per cent of total revenue derived from industrial and commercial enterprises) but not in a progressive manner.

In response to this, the *shi*'s government introduced a series of 'temporary regulations on individual business incomes' in 1986 (Lin Zili, below, chapter 10). How successful, however, is such a system of progressive taxation likely to be? The evidence from other low income countries is discouraging. In India, for example, the system of taxation – based around taxes on income – is progressive in principle, but in practice very little revenue is generated. This is mainly because marginal tax rates are very high, encouraging widespread evasion which is facilitated by administrative connivance; the value of taxation evaded was estimated as Rs.14 billion in 1968–69, or over 30 per cent of the total tax revenue (Balasubramanyam, 1984: 65 and 214). As a result, the bulk of revenue is raised by a regressive system of indirect taxation levied on items of consumer expenditure. The same is largely true of Sri Lanka and, in both cases, the problem arises from both a lack of political will and the sheer difficulty of designing a suitable tax system when corruption is endemic and income extremely difficult to measure. For example, the idea of an expenditure tax, in which the tax base is 'income minus saving', has been tried following Kaldor's suggestion, but was unsuccessful not least because 'income minus saving' was as difficult to measure as income alone. It is for these reasons that most low income countries raise revenue almost entirely from indirect taxation.

Nevertheless, there are ways in which revenue could be raised in a progressive manner. In Taiwan, for example, more than 25 per cent of total tax revenue was raised by tariffs on imports, primarily of consumer goods, during the 1960s (Ho, 1978: 241). There is no reason why differential rates could not be applied to imports of durable and luxury consumer goods, thus making the tariff structure progressive. Further, there is no reason in principle why a system of progressive indirect taxation on domestic consumer goods could not be implemented, with the tax collected at the factory gate rather than from the retailer. As luxury good suppliers in China are mainly large, state-owned enterprises, this type of taxation would be more difficult to evade than if levied on a myriad small retailers. A further possibility might be to introduce some form of property tax, which is both difficult to evade and discourages the use of land for non-farming activities, an important consideration in areas like Wenzhou where population density is high and farmland per head limited in quantity. All this suggests that, even if the 1986 regulations should fail, it is far from impossible to design a system of taxation which is progressive.

That having been said, the fact remains that the tax base of such a system would be small and, while its impact might be progressive, there must be legitimate doubts about the volume of tax revenue that it could raise. Therefore, if the object is to minimize income differentials, it is at least as important to optimize the way any tax revenue is used. So far, the use of tax revenue to fund the construction of transport infrastructure in low income regions alone has been considered. But there is clearly another alternative, namely the use of revenue to enhance equality of opportunity in the fields of education and health. Precisely because this will have an immensely beneficial effect upon the distribution of *pre-tax* incomes, it will matter very little if the method of raising tax revenue itself is non-progressive, provided that it is neutral or, at worse, only slightly regressive. Further, this type of approach could be applied within the Wenzhou *shi* itself as well as to other provinces.

In short, weaknesses in the methods of *raising* revenue can be overcome by improving the manner in which that revenue is *used* in order to equalize pre-tax income. Some idea of the importance of this is clear from a consideration of the USA and Japan, as seen in Table 3.12.

Table 3.12
Pre- and post-tax differentials: some international comparisons

	Gini coefficients	
	Pre-tax	*Post-tax*
USA	0.404	0.381
Japan	0.335	0.316
OECD	0.366	0.350

Note: Data are for the mid-1970s and are taken from Kosai and Ogino, 1984: 110.

International comparisons of Gini coefficients are fraught with difficulties deriving from differences in definition and measurement; in addition, they are an ambiguous guide to changes in income distribution over time (see Fields, 1980). Nevertheless, what is striking from this table is how unimportant in market economies the impact of the tax system is compared to the pre-tax distribution of incomes; in all three cases in the table, the impact of taxation is small (although it is much more important in terms of the share of the bottom 20 per cent).

Further, the case of Taiwan is particularly instructive in suggesting how growth can be combined with equity by the use of revenue invested in the provision of infrastructure, including physical structures as well as health and education. In 1980, Taiwan's post-tax Gini coefficient has been estimated as 0.303 which is a significant fall from its 1966 level of 0.358 (Kuo, 1984: 218). This reduction in income inequality has little to do with the impact of public provision or taxation.

> The experience of Taiwan – unusually low Gini coefficients and no significant transfers through welfare payments – bears out our conviction that significant and sustained changes in income distribution equity are achievable mainly through the modification of the basic forces underlying the pattern of growth... (Kuo *et al.*, 1981: 91).

These 'modifications' include land reform, heavy investment in rural electrification, irrigation, education and transport and the growth of rural non-farm employment opportunities. Further, there is little to suggest that

Taiwan was especially favoured overall; US aid, the legacy of Japanese colonialism and the island's geography helped, as did the Guomindang's (Kuomintang's) determination not to 'fail' in Taiwan as it had on the mainland. Nevertheless, the lack of an indigenous resource base, the need for high levels of military expenditure and a large rural population relative to the area of farmland were equally important constraints (see Little, 1979, for a discussion of some of these issues).

Moreover, one should not ignore the possibility that the scale of income inequalities that has emerged in Wenzhou during the 1980s is a transient phenomenon. It is extremely likely that some individuals and households have been much slower to see the possibilities open to them in business than others and therefore, as knowledge percolates more widely, a process of income 'catch-up' will occur, not least because growing product market competition will lead to the erosion of quasi-monopolistic profits. This writer would not put too much faith in such a process, however. 'Early starters' may well be able to erect barriers to entry – not least by bribing local government officers – to deter late arrivals; nor should one ignore the impact of growing private sector wealth on income flows, or the capacity of 'early starters' to diversify into as yet untapped product areas. In short, the evolution of income differentials is just as likely to be centrifugal as centripetal.

In sum, there is no particular reason why rapid growth in the more suitable areas of eastern China cannot be accompanied by at worst modest income differentials even if it is unlikely, or at least speculative, to suggest that such differentials will disappear of their own accord. The key to achieving such an outcome lies not just in the introduction of a progressive system of taxation and an obsession with the post-tax distribution of personal incomes, but rather with a use of revenue directed towards infrastructure construction and improvements in the quality of education and health in low income areas. The Wenzhou model shows that it is undoubtedly possible to raise a substantial volume of tax revenue by a variety of means, even when accounting and tax administration are in their infancy and where the growth dynamic is provided by the establishment and growth of thousands of small family enterprises in rural areas.

Of course, this is a long term programme. Equality of opportunity in terms of education and health care lies on a distant horizon while investment in infrastructure involves long gestation periods and requires severe topographical conditions to be overcome, even in many parts of eastern China. Accordingly, there must be a willingness to tolerate large income differentials in the short term and not to respond with a highly progressive system of income taxation which is unlikely to succeed. Whether that will be politically possible is rather doubtful and, of course, the whole approach is critically dependent upon the re-distribution of tax revenue from high to low income areas. In the case of a small island like Taiwan, spatial differences between high and low income areas were much more obvious than in mainland China as was the favourable impact of re-distribution. The transfer of funds from, say, Sunan to Gansu is much more difficult in that resentment in the former will probably be considerable; certainly, Shanghai's role as a financial milch-cow before 1978 was regarded very unfavourably by her inhabitants. The result may be a degree of connivance between the various levels of government and enterprises within a given region to retain as much of the fruits of growth as possible, thus making the re-distributive task of the central government much more difficult. This, indeed, is perhaps a good reason for the national government discouraging the spread of Western-style federal government based on universal suffrage in that it may unite population and popularly-elected government in resistance to national re-distribution of tax revenue and hence lead to what is euphemistically called 'chaos'. The problems posed by regional separatism in India for national policy tend to lend support to this argument. A strong central government may therefore be a necessary price to pay if the fruits of growth in areas like Wenzhou are not to be wasted.

Appendix

Output, income and population growth in Wenzhou, 1978–86

	Population	GVIAO	GVAO	GVIO	Distributed income	Net income	Tax revenue
	(millions)	(millions of 1980 yuan)			(yuan per head at current prices	(million yuan)
1978	5.61	1,892	891	1,001	56	na	81(1977)
1979	5.72	2,116	989	1,127	66	na	na
1980	5.82	2,548	1,136	1,412	69	165	na
1981	5.93	2,615	1,167	1,448	71	na	181
1982	6.02	2,836	1,324	1,512	88	na	191
1983	na	3,230	na	na	na	na	230
1984	6.21	4,370	1,990	2,380	na	na	272
1985	na	5,775	na	na	na	417	393
1986	na	6,491	na	na	na	508	503

Sources: Population: 1978–82: Zhejiang tongjiju (ed.) 1984: 86–103; 1984: Zhongguo guojia tongjiju (ed.) 1985: 153; GVIAO, GVAO and GVIO: 1978–82: Zhejiang tongjiju (ed.) 1984: 86–103, 1983, 1985 and 1986: He Rongfei (ed.) 1987: 152; 1984: Zhongguo guojia tongjiju (ed.) 1985: 153; Distributed income: Zhejiang tongjiju (ed.) 1984: 86–103; Net incomes: 1980: Zhao Renwei, below; 1985: ibid; 1986: He Rongfei (ed.) 1987: 7; Tax revenue: He Rongfei (ed.) 1987: 151–52.

Notes:
1. 'Distributed income' is rural collective distributed income, a series discontinued throughout China after the emasculation of the commune in 1982.

2. 'Net income' is peasant net income. It is doubtful whether the 1985 and 1986 figures are exactly comparable in terms of their definition and coverage. Note also that Wang and Li, 1986(a): 15 give figures of 179 and 447 *yuan* for 1980 and 1985 respectively.

3. These data are for the entire Wenzhou municipality.

4. 'na' = not available.

Notes

1. This chapter stems from a series of discussions between the members of the Cambridge Research group on the Chinese Economy during 1986–87, to all of whom I am in debt. I am particularly grateful to the head of the group, Peter Nolan, for suggesting that I should write this chapter and for his comments on an earlier draft. I should also like to thank the Economic and Social Research Council for financial support during its writing. I am further indebted to Professor Dong Fureng and the Chengdu Economic Research Institute for an invitation to research there during November 1987; some of the data used in this article are an accidental by-product of that visit. None, however, of the above individuals or institutions bear any responsibility for the opinions expressed or mistakes contained within it.

2. These figures are calculated from data on population and *xiangzhen* enterprise gross incomes taken from Zhongguo guojia tongjiju, 1984: 84 (population) and 1988 (gross income). Data on northern Jiangsu are derived from these sources and data given in Fei (ed.), 1986: 93. Northern Jiangsu is assumed to comprise the *diqu* of Xuzhou, Lianyungang, Yancheng, Huaiyin and Yangzhou. Sunan here refers to southern Jiangsu only, therefore excluding northern Zhejiang. 'China' here is the national total less Jiangsu.

3. These eleven *xian* are Jiashan, Pinghu, Haining, Haiyan, Tongxiang, Deqing, Changxing, Anji, Yuhang, Xiaoshan and Lin'an. The estimates per head are calculated from data on *xiangzhen* gross output value and population taken from Zhejiang tongjiju (ed.), (1985).

References

Balasubramanyam, V. N., 1984, *The Economy of India*, London, Macmillan.

Eng, R. Y., 1986, *Economic Imperialism in China*, University of California: Berkeley, Institute of East Asian Studies.

Fei Xiaotong, 1983, *Chinese Village Close-Up*, Beijing, New World Press.

———— *et al.*, 1986, *Small Towns in China*, Beijing, New World Press.

Fields, G. S., 1980, *Poverty, Inequality and Development*, Cambridge University Press.

He Rongfei (ed.), 1987, *Wenzhou jingji geju*, Hangzhou, Zhejiang renmin chubanshe.

Ho, S. P. S., 1978, *Economic Development of Taiwan 1860–1970*, London, Yale UP.

JPRS: China Report-Agriculture, No. 224, 3 September 1982, 'National survey of rural production brigades having average per capita incomes of less than 300 *yuan* in 1981' (translated from *Gongshe Caiwu*, 1982, No. 7).

Kosai, Y. and Ogino, Y., 1984, *The Contemporary Japanese Economy*, London, Macmillan.

Kueh, Y. Y., 1984, *Economic Planning and Local Mobilisation in Post-Mao China*, London, Contemporary China Institute, School of Oriental and African Studies.

Kuo, S. W. Y., 1984, 'Urbanisation and Income Distribution: The Case of Taiwan 1966–80', in Syrquin, M., *et al.*, 1984, *Economic Structure and Performance*, London, Academic Press Inc.

———— *et al.*, 1981, *The Taiwan Success Story*, Boulder, Colorado, Westview Press Inc.

Lardy, N. R., 1987, 'Economic Recovery and the 1st Five Year Plan', in Fairbank, J. K., and Twitchett, D., 1987, *The Cambridge History of China*, Vol. 14.

Leeming, F., 1985, *Rural China Today*, Harlow, Essex, Longman Group Ltd.

Little, I. M. D., 1979, 'An Economic Renaissance' in Galenson, W. (ed.), 1979, *Economic Growth and Institutional Change in Taiwan*, London, Cornell UP.

Minami, R., 1986, *The Economic Development of Japan*, London, Macmillan.

Ministry of Industry (Bureau of Foreign Trade), 1935, *China Industrial Handbook–Chekiang*, Shanghai (re-printed by Ch'eng Wen Publishing Company, Taibei, 1973.

Myrdal, G., 1957, *Economic Theory and Under-developed Regions*, London, Duckworth and Co.

Nongye jingji wenti, No. 6, 1986.

Pan Yiping (ed.), 1984, *Zhejiang fenxian jianzhi*, Hangzhou, Zhejiang renmin chubanshe.

State Statistical Bureau (ed.), 1986(a) *China Statistical Yearbook, 1986*, Oxford University Press.

───── 1986(b), 'Communiqué on the fulfilment of the 1985 Plan', *Beijing Review*, Vol. 29, No. 12, 24 March 1986.

───── 1987(a), 'Communiqué on the fulfilment of the 1986 Plan', *Beijing Review*, Vol. 30, No. 9, 2 March 1987.

───── 1987(b), 'Development of Economic Sectors', *Beijing Review*, Vol. 30, No. 3, 19 January 1987.

Vermeer, E. B., 1982, 'Income differentials in rural China', *The China Quarterly*, No. 89 (March).

Wang Youfen and Li Ning, 1986(a), 'Buttons work miracles in Wenzhou', *Beijing Review*, Vol. 29, No. 42, 20 October 1986.

───── 1986(b), 'Rural changes promote urban reform', *Beijing Review*, Vol. 29, No. 43, 27 October 1986.

World Bank, 1985, *China: Long-Term Development Issues and Options*, London, John Hopkins University Press.

Zhao Shengwu *et al.*, 1986, 'Wenzhou' in Tao Li *et al.*, 1986, *China's Open Cities and Special Economic Zones*, Hong Kong, Economy and Science Press.

Zhejiang tongjiju (ed.), 1984, *Zhejiang jingji gaikuang* (part 2).

───── 1985, *Zhejiang jingji tongji nianjian*.

Zhonggong Sichuan sheng wei yanjiushi, 1984, *Sichuan sheng qing*, Chengdu, Sichuan renmin chubanshe.

Zhongguo guojia tongjiju, 1981; 1984; 1985(a) *Zhongguo tongji nianjian*, Zhongguo tongji chubanshe.

───── 1985(b), *Zhongguo gongye jingji tongji ziliao*, Zhongguo tongji chubanshe. *Zhongguo jingji nianjian 1985*.

Zhongguo kexue Chengdu dili yanjiusuo, 1980, *Sichuan nongye dili*, Chengdu, Sichuan renmin chubanshe.

Zhongguo nongye nianjian bianjibu (ed.), 1985, *Zhongguo nongye jingji gaiyao 1983* Beijing, Nongye chubanshe.

4. The Wenzhou Model for Developing the Rural Commodity Economy

Dong Fureng

Some colleagues and I recently carried out an investigation in the rural areas of Zhejiang province's Wenzhou and Jinhua cities. In the countryside, we saw an extraordinarily rapid and profound transformation taking place which was both immensely exciting and caused us to reflect deeply. Here I should just like to outline some of my impressions from that visit and from previous rural visits.[1]

The development of a commodity economy is essential to socialist modernization in China's rural areas

The task involved in modernizing China's rural areas is great but arduous. It is no exaggeration to say that national modernization depends upon its success. Since the introduction of the production responsibility system in the countryside, with *bao gan dao hu* as the main form, one major problem has been how best to develop this system in order to further the process of modernization. The experience of rural Wenzhou and other areas demonstrates that the development of a commodity economy is the requisite path for socialist modernization in rural China. Throughout most of rural China the introduction of the production responsibility system meant that the peasant household became the basic unit of production. The combination of a large population and a limited arable area necessitated extremely small-scale agricultural production. Average contracted cultivated area per rural household is no more than 8 mu^2 [i.e., 0.53 hectares]. In many villages there is still a semi-natural economy and in certain places there still is a basically natural economy. This is a severe barrier to China's modernization. Only by expanding the commodity economy, and the rural commodity economy in particular, can we fundamentally transform our backward national, and especially rural, economy. Since 1979, rural Wenzhou's commodity economy has developed at a roaring pace, like an uncontrollable torrent, sweeping along the majority of the population and the village economy in a great many districts in Wenzhou. The extraordinary speed and depth of the transformation has changed every aspect of economic and social life in the villages, and has set Wenzhou's villages on the road to modernization. A similar high-speed advance has occurred in areas with relatively advanced rural economies such as southern Jiangsu and northern Zhejiang provinces. Advances are also taking place in somewhat less developed areas, such as Zhejiang province's Jinhua and some districts of Anhui province. Over a large part of rural Wenzhou, the principal changes in village social and economic life resulting from this are the following:

Increased division of labour in the countryside has developed the forces of production

Although the emergence and development of the rural commodity economy is partially a result of an increased division of labour, it is also true that expansion of the commodity economy can promote the social division of labour, which is in turn a crucial factor in developing the productive forces and in social progress. In some parts of rural Wenzhou, the growth of household industries and the establishment of specialized markets has caused the emergence of many kinds of business activity. For example, there are more than 100,000 people working in trading in rural Wenzhou, engaged in buying raw materials from, and selling finished products to, locations throughout China. Expansion of the commodity economy has stimulated the development of transport. According to figures for June 1985, the number of goods haulage depots (excluding those below *xiang* level) in the three *zhen* of Liushi, Beibaixiang and Wengyang, had risen to 90, employing over 400 workers and carrying on average 2,500 tonnes of freight per month. Some of these firms guarantee delivery to any part of China within 16 days by express service, and within 22 days if carried by the slow delivery service. Some motor vehicle transport companies have also started up, carrying both goods and passengers. Expansion of the commodity economy has also furthered the expansion of post and telecommunications and information transmission. The post and telecommunications department has grown enormously and is extraordinarily busy; Liushi *zhen* now receives more than 25,000 telegrams per month. For many rural households, the telephone has become essential equipment for business and daily life. Specialist firms providing economic and technical consultancy information, as well as employment agencies, have appeared. A service sector, including hotels and restaurants, has also developed rapidly.

The division of labour within household industry has become progressively more elaborate. In the production of badges and labels in Jinxiang *zhen*'s villages, each household specializes in a different part of the production process, including design, writing, engraving, working up raw materials, moulding, stamping, painting, glazing, perforating, pin-making and assembly. Yishan *qu* also has a broadly based division of labour in the production of textile products from re-processed fibres. More than 600 households specialize in the sorting of waste materials, 1,200 in pulling apart the old fabrics, 6,430 in spinning, 6,490 in weaving, over 2,900 in sewing, 380 in purchasing raw materials, 200 in transport and more than

8,000 people in marketing the finished products. All the peasant households are linked together by means of 11 specialized markets. This division of labour has enabled a substantial advance in the productive forces. In Wenzhou since 1979 more than 830,000 surplus rural workers have transferred from agricultural to non-agricultural employment, causing the proportion of the total rural labour force employed in agriculture to fall from 89 per cent in 1978 to just 37 per cent in 1985, and in certain localities with advanced household industry, the figure is as low as 10 per cent.

The commodity economy's rapid expansion has tapped the population's latent productive enthusiasm. People now work hard and fully utilize their knowledge and skills. Moreover, the inter-sectoral transfer of labour has caused an increase in aggregate productivity because marginal labour productivity in industry, transport and commerce is much higher than in agriculture where marginal labour productivity is zero. Furthermore, household industry has relied upon materials discarded by state enterprises in the production process. Thus, all rural resources, whether manpower, materials or land, have been fully utilized and the productive forces have rapidly developed.

In Wenzhou, the gross value of agricultural output (including the output produced in enterprises run by *cun* and lower levels) increased by 223 per cent from 1980 to 1985, and the value of output produced by household industry increased by 42 per cent simply in 1984–85. The growth rate was even faster in some areas where the commodity economy was well-developed. For example, in Rui'an *xian*'s Jinhou *cun* income increased 33.7-fold between 1978 and 1984. Indeed, in Liushi *zhen*'s Luzhuang *cun* in 1984 the average output value per household reached no less than 100,000 *yuan*! As a result of this growth in production, peasant income increased rapidly with per capita peasant income in Wenzhou rising from 165.2 *yuan* in 1980 to 417 *yuan* in 1985, an increase of 162 per cent. In some well-developed areas the income level is even higher. In 1984, the figure was 760 *yuan* in Rui'an *xian*'s Xianjiang *xiang* and Heng *cun*, and more than 1,000 *yuan* for five *cun* in Yishan *qu*. In these areas, it is common to find households with an annual income of more than 10,000 *yuan*. Many of these households have built beautiful multi-storeyed houses; for instance, in Yongjia *xian*'s Qiantou *zhen* where households with an income of more than 10,000 *yuan* account for 80 per cent of all households, 70 per cent of households have built new houses, each with an average floor space of 101 square metres. Some of these new houses are even larger, comprising five or six storeys and a floor space of more than 200 square metres.

Changes in economic and social relations and in lifestyle
Social relations in the countryside have gradually been influenced by the growth of financial and economic ties as the commodity economy has developed. Though family relationships are still an important factor in economic relations in Wenzhou's countryside (about 90 per cent of hired

workers are directly related to their employers), their importance is declining. For example, some factories now set examinations to test the educational level, skills, health etc., of applicants for jobs as hired workers. The market, too, plays an increasingly important role in production and in people's lives. In some villages economic relations between households are mediated through exchange. People are concerned with changes in the market and pay great attention to market information. The slow and easy-going rhythms of country life are being replaced by the intensity of an urban lifestyle as the population pays increasing attention to time, efficiency, performance and business income. The difference between town and country is being reduced; because land is scarce, streets and housing are taking on an urban character. Modern household conveniences, such as running water and household appliances, become more common in peasant homes. People have even begun to pay attention to sanitation (e.g., they change their shoes when entering their houses). Income differentials between town and country are also being reduced, and some peasants now have much higher incomes than urban residents. Some families are beginning to lead a modern life.

The elimination of backward ideas and outmoded practices
The ideas associated with a market economy, such as the importance of time, the market, competition, accounting, enterprise, initiative and credit, are all taking shape and developing. The old ideology that trade was unimportant has now been cast off by the people of rural Wenzhou. 'The red eye disease' of envying the wealth of others is no longer prevalent. Instead, people consider that it is natural for higher incomes to accrue to those who have ability. People have a fairly high tolerance of growing income inequalities. Many have become less anxious to obtain political power because they have seen that its fruits can now be obtained with money instead. Moreover, the peasants have become used to competition. One trader we spoke to said, 'Competition tastes good.' An enterprise boss said, 'We do not fear competition; we welcome it.' This entrepreneurial spirit has flourished everywhere as people have acquired a thirst for risk and adventure. Furthermore, many old ideas unfavourable to the development of a commodity economy are being eroded. For example, the traditional practice of a constant interest rate immutable to changes in the demand for and supply of money has been displaced by the emergence of loans among the people with fluctuating interest rates, and some credit co-operatives, too, have changed to a floating rate of interest. Consequently, the Agricultural Bank, which has an inflexible interest rate, has lost ground, and its role in the capital market has been weakened. The growth of the commodity economy has also taught more and more cadres and peasants to adapt their thinking, work and lives to its requirements. The expansion of the rural commodity economy is training group after group of the talented people required for rural socialist modernization. They possess a modern outlook, are innovative and good at business. Of course, we must

not pretend that there are already a great many such talented people in rural Wenzhou, but the outlook is encouraging.

These developments are of great significance. Chairman Mao Zedong said, 'The law of value is a great school.' Only by developing a rural commodity economy in which China's peasants participate can we ensure that China's cadres and ordinary people understand this law and act according to its rules.

The Wenzhou model is one alternative in developing a rural commodity economy

According to the theory put forward by W. A. Lewis and others, in a developing country there usually exists a dual economy with a backward agriculture sector, in which there is a large quantity of surplus labour, a marginal labour productivity that is zero or even negative and a subsistence living standard, and a modern industrial sector, in which marginal labour productivity is a great deal higher. The task of economic development is to transfer this surplus labour from the agricultural sector to the industrial sector, so that the two sectors may develop simultaneously. This is not the place to discuss Lewis' theory in detail, but it certainly is the case that the transfer of agricultural surplus labour to the non-agricultural sector is a process through which all developing countries must pass. It is inevitable that China must also, in the course of its development, pass through this process.

China's rural population accounted for 68.1 per cent of total population in 1984 (82.1 per cent in 1978) and the agricultural population for 82.1 per cent in 1983 (84.2 per cent in 1978); the labour force employed in agriculture accounted for 70.7 per cent of the total labour force (73.8 per cent in 1978). There was no significant change in these proportions during the period from 1949 to 1978; the rural and agricultural populations accounted for 89.4 per cent and 82.6 per cent respectively of the population total in 1949, and the agricultural labour force accounted for 83.5 per cent of the total labour force in 1952. This shows that the modernization process in China was very slow during this period. So far, we have no accurate figures for surplus labour in our countryside, with estimates varying between one third and one half of the agricultural labour force. There were, in total, 325.38 million agricultural labourers in China in 1984. Therefore, if we calculate surplus labour on the basis of the latter percentage share, then even at present levels of agricultural labour productivity in agriculture, there are more than 160 million labourers who could be transferred from the agricultural to the non-agricultural sector. This figure is greater than the current non-agricultural workforce of 150 million. In comparison, Wenzhou's 1984 rural labour force totalled 1.8 million, of which 1.6 million were employed in agriculture cultivating an average per capita area of 0.46 *mu*, implying a surplus of about 0.8 million. If either agricultural labour productivity or population increases during the transfer process, however, more agricultural labourers will have to be transferred. This task must be accomplished, otherwise neither agricultural nor national modernization will be possible. But how should such a transfer be effected? If we exclude the possibility of international migration of labour, the experiences of China and other countries suggest that there are two alternatives.

One is to develop industry and other activities in the urban sector, and thereby transfer agricultural surplus labour from the countryside and employ it in non-agricultural activities. Quite a number of developing countries (even some developed countries in the course of their history) have followed this road. We also believed that this was the only possibility during the 1950s and thought that it had to be persevered with, even if its precise form had to vary from country to country. Nevertheless, this approach has encountered a series of common problems. For example, a great amount of investment is needed in industry, housing and infrastructure in the urban sector; the labour from the countryside needs to be thoroughly educated and trained, and so on. None of these can be accomplished quickly and, in fact, it takes a very long time to complete the transfer process in this way. This approach results either in the situation found in some developing countries, like India, where too many people have moved into the cities from the countryside (about 300 families move into Bombay every day) causing tremendous social problems (slums, vagrants, beggars, disease and disorder), or the imposition of restrictions on labour migration as in China. Though these restrictions have avoided the social problems that have occurred in India, much of the agricultural surplus labour is tied to limited land as a result. In this situation it is very difficult to increase labour productivity, spread advanced technology and improve peasant living standards. At the same time, agriculture has to be squeezed in order to accumulate capital funds to support industrial and commercial development in the cities. This exacerbates the backwardness of agriculture.

The other possibility is to develop industry and other non-agricultural activities in *xiangzhen* (small towns) in rural areas and thereby transfer surplus labour from the agricultural to the non-agricultural sector gradually without much geographical movement. Some developing countries have taken this road, and since the late 1950s China has also done so. By taking this road, we can avoid some of the difficulties mentioned above. The industrial and other enterprises which develop in the villages and small towns are generally small scale and technologically backward, and so do not need huge amounts of capital nor well-educated or highly skilled workers; moreover, workers can be recruited from nearby, so that their families need not migrate. Thus, surplus labour can be more easily absorbed by taking this road than by taking the first one. However, these enterprises also generally have certain disadvantages, such as a backward technology, a low level of productivity, poor product quality and a high level of consumption of material inputs.

Within this approach to the problem of surplus labour, there are a number of possibilities, though they can be broadly categorized into two types. The first (the Sunan Model) is to develop public enterprises, including those owned by collectives, by *xiangzhen* government, or jointly by *xiangzhen* government and state enterprises. Within this category, enterprises operate in different ways. Some co-operate with city-based enterprises in producing complete products, or spare parts, or components; some of these products are not easily produced in an urban environment (because, for example, production causes serious pollution, or is very labour intensive, or the costs of production are too high in cities), or have limited possibilities to increase output (for example, because of a scarcity of urban land). Sometimes, urban enterprises provide financial and technical assistance to the former. Some rural enterprises, however, have no direct production links with the urban enterprises.

The rapid development of public enterprises in China's *xiangzhen* has attracted much attention in recent years. According to a report published in *Guangming Ribao* (29 September 1985), the total number of *xiangzhen* enterprises[3] was in excess of 6 million by 1984, employing more than 50 million workers; of these enterprises, only 15 per cent were agricultural.[4] The gross industrial output value of all *xiangzhen* enterprises accounted for 12.7 per cent of the national total.[5] Their development greatly impressed me during the course of my visits to the cities of Suzhou (Jiangsu province), Zhengzhou (Henan province), Wenzhou and Jinhua (both in Zhejiang province). They have great dynamism and innovative spirit. Many were producing goods of high quality; for example, the woollen sweater factory in Suzhou city's Bixi *xiang*, the sewing machines of the Leqing factory in Wenzhou city's Hongqia *zhen* and the leisure shoes produced by Menghu *xiang*'s Shaolin number 4 shoe factory, a *xiangzhen* enterprise controlled by the state-owned Lanxi rubber-soled shoe factory located in Jinhua city. Plenty of the products rival those from large urban enterprises and many of them are exported.

The rapid expansion of publicly owned *xiangzhen* enterprises has enabled them to absorb a huge amount of rural surplus labour. In Suzhou city, the share of agricultural workers in the total workforce was only 57 per cent by 1984, while in its Jin *xiang*, the share was just 44 per cent.[6] Jinhua city's *xiangzhen* public enterprises have already absorbed some 260,000 surplus agricultural workers over the last four years at an annual rate of around 60,000. The growth of non-agricultural *xiangzhen* enterprises has also boosted agricultural production, promoted the growth of rural towns and increased rural (principally agriculturalists') incomes. Although certain problems have also resulted, such as increasing competition with urban enterprises for scarce raw materials and energy supplies, excessive credit expansion and some products of poor quality, there can be no doubt that this approach has an important role to play in China's rural modernization, and that is one path to the development of a rural commodity economy. Some villages in Wenzhou city have adopted the path of developing *xiangzhen* public enterprises to promote rural modernization, expansion of the rural commodity economy and absorption of agricultural surplus labour.

The second alternative (the Wenzhou model), which is very widespread in Wenzhou and also in some parts of Anhui province, is to develop privately owned enterprises (individual household or co-operative), especially peasant household industry, commerce and transportation. This combination of household enterprise and specialized markets based mainly on peasant individual commerce has produced an exceptionally rapid development of the commodity economy and has led to an extraordinarily swift and thoroughgoing transformation of every aspect of social and economic life in Wenzhou.

As a path for absorbing agricultural surplus labour, the development of private enterprises in the rural areas has some similarities with *xiangzhen* public enterprises in comparison with the expansion of big industries in urban areas. For example, they do not need state investment, can avoid the various social problems created by over-rapid urbanization, can help to reduce urban–rural income differentials, facilitate the co-ordinated development of industry and agriculture, and promote the development of a commodity economy and rural modernization.

Compared with the Sunan model of rural development (public ownership), the Wenzhou model (private ownership) has a number of important advantages:

- It is easier to raise funds for the development of industry and other non-agricultural activities. Apart from a very small amount of investment by state enterprises, most of the fund used by the *xiangzhen* public enterprises either came from the accumulation fund administered by the people's communes, or, after the introduction of the household contract system, from the established or expanded *xiangzhen* public enterprises themselves (other funds are raised in the form of bank loans and loans by individuals). This kind of financing is somewhat easier than depending on state investment, but it is less convenient than raising funds from the peasants themselves, whether individually or jointly. As we have seen already, in some villages in Wenzhou, nearly every household has bought various items of mechanized and semi-mechanized equipment to produce buttons, electrical appliances, clothes, labels, zips, etc. This type of machinery costs from a few tens to a few thousand *yuan* and is not, therefore, beyond the scope of ordinary households. Some equipment, however, may cost over a hundred thousand *yuan* but although no single household can afford to buy it, several in combination can buy it easily. These financial advantages of the Wenzhou model go a long way towards explaining the extremely lively state of manufacturing and commercial activity in many villages in the city.

- The surplus labour is more rapidly transferred from agriculture to the non-agricultural sector. Thousands of households have bought equipment and engage in industrial and commercial activity, so that in some villages anybody who is capable of doing something has been involved in some form of activity, such as old women and children employed in assembly work. Thus, in these areas there is not only full employment but even a labour shortage and so some workers have been recruited from outside, especially from mountain areas. For example, plastic shoe production in Rui'an *xian*'s Xiangjiang *xiang* has absorbed not only the whole surplus labour force in its own area, but also, at peak seasons, more than 3,000 workers from other areas. Farming has become a sideline occupation in these areas, with the people stopping work in the factories for a short time in busy farming periods, or hiring peasants from mountain areas to do the farming if there is too much work for them. In this way, surplus labour has been absorbed much more quickly by the non-agricultural sector in Wenzhou than by large urban-based enterprises or by *xiangzhen* public enterprises. In 1978, there were about 1.8 million workers in rural Wenzhou of whom 1.6 million, or 89 per cent, were engaged in agriculture and 0.2 million or 11 per cent in non-agricultural activities. Of these agricultural workers, about 0.83 million have moved into the non-agricultural sector since 1979. In 1985, 0.6 million, or 28.5 per cent of the total labour force of 2.1 million, were engaged in crop production and 1.32 million, or 63 per cent, in industrial and sideline activities. Of the 0.83 million recently transferred from agriculture, 0.33 million were employed in industry, 0.22 in commerce and 0.28 million in various types of business outside Wenzhou.

● The techniques and skills required by industrial production are more quickly disseminated in the countryside. One of the difficulties affecting industrial development in developing countries is a shortage of skilled workers; the same is true of China where the techniques and skills of industrial production are unfamiliar and even mysterious to peasants who have long been accustomed to traditional farm tools. But by developing *xiangzhen* public enterprises, peasants can master the necessary skills and techniques after only a short period of training. The development of household industry in some of Wenzhou's villages, however, shows that modern industry breaks down certain industrial skills into many relatively simple operations. As long as they have suitable equipment, peasants can relatively quickly acquire non-complex industrial techniques. For example, in Leqing *xian*'s Liushi *zhen* and the neighbouring villages, practically every household is producing electrical equipment of one kind or another. Altogether, they make more than 1,200 different types. The extent and rate of spread of these skills and techniques has, therefore, been quicker in peasant household industry than through *xiangzhen* public enterprises.

● It leads to a rapid and widely dispersed increase in peasant incomes. In Sunan, peasant incomes have increased in recent years reflecting increases in agricultural purchasing prices, output growth and, increasingly, the incomes earned by workers in public *xiangzhen* enterprises. In Wenzhou, however, the growth and dispersion of income increases has been greater because almost all households are participating in industrial or commercial enterprises and, of course, some households have members engaged in trading and other activities. Apart from those households hit by disasters, such as the death of workers, there are no extremely poor families to be seen. In my view, taking the Wenzhou path leads to a faster and more widespread growth of peasant income (though, naturally, an imperfect tax system also plays a role in this).

• The Wenzhou model can easily be introduced in other parts of China, which is not the case with the Sunan approach, where *xiangzhen* public enterprises are invariably found in areas close to large cities and often benefit from the technological assistance of urban enterprises. It is relatively difficult to take this path in areas which don't have these conditions. As I concluded from my investigations in Sunan and in Zhengzhou *shi*: '*Xiangzhen* industry should first be established on firm industrial bases around cities and then set up in other areas.'[7] Perhaps this view of the path for expanding rural *xiangzhen* industries is still correct. After investigating the deviation from this path in Wenzhou, however, this conclusion is in need of some revision. The experience of Wenzhou city shows clearly that the path of utilizing peasant household industry, that is, not relying on villages which are close to cities with advanced industry, can expand industry which doesn't have high technical requirements. Thus, this path is easier to promote in the vast areas of the countryside. Over the past few years, the exceptionally rapid expansion of village household industry in Anhui province proves this point.

• Expansion of the commodity economy enables China to transfer its agricultural surplus labour to the non-farm sector and enables it to attain rural modernization, but it should be noted that there are two different paths. It is still necessary to expand large-scale industry and other branches of production in cities. It is also both necessary and practical to expand public enterprise in *xiangzhen*. The path of some of Wenzhou's villages, however, of developing rural household industry, commerce and other activities is also a path that can be adopted. Naturally, the two different paths outlined above may also be considered. This is the sort of path we saw being taken in Jinhua city.

The Wenzhou model for developing the rural commodity economy: some issues requiring research

The feasibility of the Wenzhou model has been debated for some time, and a number of different views have emerged. In the following, I put forward some of my own views on the more important issues involved.

The issue of public ownership as the dominant feature of the economy
We must maintain public ownership as the dominant feature of the national economy because the modernization process is a socialist one in China. There is no question about this. Because the expansion of rural *xiangzhen* public enterprises supports the principle of keeping public ownership in the dominant position, it puts the cadres' and masses' minds at rest. In some areas of Wenzhou, however, rural household industries and commerce play the leading role and co-operative enterprises are developing. Here the public sector is relegated to a secondary role, and in some cases, as the result of severe competition, public enterprises have become private enterprises, remaining public only in name. It seems that private/co-operative enterprises will continue to develop so long as government policies allow them to do so. People often ask, however: 'Is this development in keeping with the socialist principle of keeping public ownership in the dominant position? What are the features of a socialist economy and what direction should socialist modernization take?' I think that the questions should be answered in this way: by maintaining public ownership as the dominant sector, we mean for the national economy as a whole, but not necessarily for every village or area (e.g., *xian*, city etc.). Moreover, the question is not simply one of absolute size (e.g., a certain proportion of total social output value) but one of whether public enterprises control the commanding heights of the Chinese economy and are able to direct its development along socialist lines. Indeed, the issues involved in developing household industry are similar to those involved in the expansion of peasant household agriculture; even if the household sector (including agriculture, industry and commerce) continues to increase, in terms of size and its share in total social output value, this cannot change the socialist direction of our economy. On the contrary, its development is subordinated to the public sector which has many powerful measures of regulation that it can apply (e.g., financial and fiscal measures). Moreover, when rural co-operative enterprises are fully developed, they too will be controlled and regulated by the public sector, e.g., by having some shares held by the state.

The problem of competition for energy, raw materials and markets
It is inappropriate to criticize rural household enterprises in Wenzhou and *xiangzhen* enterprises in other areas for competing for scarce inputs and markets with urban industries. There are some problems, however. If we do encourage the development of rural industries and allow market forces to play their role, the problem of mis allocation cannot be completely avoided even under a centrally planned system; frequent overstocking of some products and shortages of others, over-investment, and duplication in construction are some examples. Of course, this problem will become more serious as rural household enterprises develop and is undesirable because it causes a waste of resources. Misallocation will occur when producers have

inadequate information on the market and miscalculate, or when they pursue their own short-term interests. Misallocation is often linked with impulsiveness. Generally speaking, impulsiveness is undesirable because it results in misallocation, but impulsiveness is not always undesirable because often it cannot be separated from the allocative signals of the market. Some peasants in Wenzhou are very anxious to acquire market information in order to respond to market signals by swiftly producing the goods required. For example, many households in Yishan *xian* produce nylon clothes with left-over bits and pieces because first, they see that they can make use of the materials and second, they see that there is a demand for this kind of cheap clothing amongst the peasants. Here impulsiveness in responding to market signals has played a desirable role. But this impulsiveness may lead to misallocation because the demand for this kind of clothing will become smaller as peasants' income increases. If they continue to produce or expand their production, this clothing will be over-produced. Misallocation of resources can be avoided by various means, e.g., by developing an economic information service which the peasants need badly. Therefore, *xiangzhen* public enterprises and particularly rural household enterprises should not be rejected because of the misallocation that sometimes results.

The problem of competing with large urban industry for energy, raw materials and markets also exists, though it naturally isn't all competition. The development of coal mines run by collectives or individuals in Shanxi province, for example, has played an important role in mitigating China's coal shortage. In some cases in Wenzhou, too, these problems don't exist because enterprises make use of large industry's waste materials, or produce spare parts for large urban industries, or make small daily-use items for households. Furthermore, in some cases, the problem of competing with big urban enterprises for energy and raw materials can be solved by consultation and co-operation; for example, some factories in Jinhua fight for peaches to make canned products and this has reduced the production of canned export products in a certain urban state factory. The state-run factory and the *xiangzhen* food enterprise reached an agreement whereby each would use different grades of peach to produce different qualities of canned peach. The problem of fighting with large urban enterprises for markets also exists, but rural enterprises can hardly be blamed for having large market shares merely because their products are cheap and of high quality. The solution is for the large urban industries to improve their production methods and management. If the success of the rural enterprises is because they enjoy preferential treatment, however, (e.g., exemption from taxation for three years), or are involved in illicit activities (such as tax evasion or bribery) then some policy measures should be imposed. It should also be pointed out that rural industries (whether public or private) have a wide range of production possibilities and a great many of these do not involve competing with large urban industry for materials and markets. Sometimes the competition from rural enterprises arises from irrationally priced products and materials. The solution to this lies in reforming the price structure.

Poor quality products and fraud

Rural enterprises, particularly household industries, are often blamed for manufacturing poor quality, and fraudulent products. But we must recognize that both public enterprises in Sunan and private enterprises in Wenzhou have produced some high quality products. It is certainly true, however, that there are many more problems of product quality in Wenzhou's rural household industries than in *xiangzhen* public enterprises. There are two categories of problems with low quality. The first category is that in which low quality is due to deficient materials and this doesn't warrant criticism, especially as the price is often very low. The second category is where quality is low due to low levels of technique, absence of strict testing, or even intentionally producing shoddy produce. Though the problem cannot be avoided, it can be gradually reduced by strengthening regulations. Its existence also reflects the absence of a fully competitive market, however; for when the market is fully developed, producers of low quality, high price products will not be able to hold their ground and will find it impossible to practise fraud. Moreover, as one peasant in Wenzhou argued:

> It would not be so difficult to solve the quality problem if we had some advanced equipment. But we are afraid of policy changes, and dare not buy equipment the cost of which requires several years to recoup. We only want to buy the equipment which is not so advanced but cheap, and which will recoup our investment in only one or two years.

Growing income differentials

Although accurate statistics are lacking, there can be no doubt that peasant income differentials have widened in Wenzhou over the last four years. This is one important reason why some people favour *xiangzhen* public enterprises and oppose peasant household enterprises. There are several different aspects of income disparities. The first is the growing income disparity between developed and under-developed areas (particularly mountainous areas). In some *xian* in Wenzhou, such as Wencheng and Taishun, some peasants still do not have enough food to eat or enough clothes to wear; they are extremely poor. But this situation is not a result of exploitation by more developed areas, but of factors such as a poor transport system, low levels of education, and difficult natural conditions. Indeed, developed areas have helped to absorb increasing amounts of labour from these poor areas and hence have helped these peasants to increase their incomes greatly; the experience of the developed areas in developing commodity economy has also been passed on to the poor areas. The best way to resolve these income disparities is to develop the commodity economy in poor areas, doing the best we can to disseminate the lessons to be learned from the advanced areas.

The second case concerns growing income disparities within a given village. This should be regarded as an inevitable phenomenon and a price that has to be paid at a certain stage of economic development. In the long run it may play an active role in stimulating economic growth and thereby gradually reducing income disparities. At present, widening income differentials in Wenzhou are accompanied by large absolute increases for nearly every peasant, unlike the situation that existed in the early stage of capitalism, in which a small number of people accumulated more and more wealth, while the majority suffered the abject poverty and misery of wage labour. Of course, in some areas of Wenzhou, income disparities have become too large; the assets owned by some individuals are worth over 100,000 *yuan* or even several hundred thousand *yuan*. This problem should be tackled through a strict tax system and by imposing a progressive income tax.

The third case concerns income disparities between cadres and workers employed in state industries or institutions on the one hand, and peasants working in rural household enterprises on the other. These have persuaded some cadres and workers either to find additional part-time employment or to take more drastic action. For example, many cadres have a second occupation in the evening (e.g., some doctors and teachers glue together paper boxes or make wooden crates) and the families of some have established household commercial or industrial enterprises of their own to make more money. A small number of workers have even left state enterprises. It is difficult to deal with this problem, although it may be mitigated by imposing a severely progressive income tax.

Another problem is hired labour. This arises in different situations. In Wenzhou's peasant household industry, the great majority of the workers are from within the household. Some households hire one or two or even more workers who work together with their employers as apprentices. After the hired workers have learned certain skills and saved some money, they may leave to open their own businesses. Very few enterprises have hired more than 20 or 30 workers, and even fewer have hired more than 100. Many hired workers have family or social ties with their employers and work not only to earn money but also to learn skills; many current employers were previously hired workers. Some of the hired workers are from poor mountain areas or from economically backward neighbouring areas but unlike those peasants who lost their land during the early stage of capitalism or in some present developing countries, those workers still maintain contracts to farm the land. They come to work in a household industry in developed areas and their incomes have greatly increased. The lowest wage rate is 2 *yuan* per day and the highest is 20–30 *yuan* per day. At the agricultural busy season the average daily wage in agriculture is 14–18 *yuan* plus five free meals and two packets of cigarettes, and 6–7 *yuan* at other times. At the same time, they can study industrial production and management skills in the process and will later play an important role in transforming the backwardness of the poor areas. As for those enterprises hiring more than 20, 30 or even 100 workers, they do, after all, operate within a socialist country, and their owners have lived under a socialist system for more than 30 years. Therefore, they know how to treat their hired workers with due consideration. For example, some employers discriminate in favour of poor families when they hire workers and some of the enterprises run various welfare, labour protection and insurance systems similar to those in state enterprises. Though exploitative relations do exist in these enterprises, we have not seen the intense class confrontation or the abject suffering of hired workers that we saw in the early stage of capitalism or before 1949 in China. We should not simplistically reject the present hiring of labour on moral grounds, or on those of socialist ethics. The extremely limited scale of labour hiring that is normally the case in Wenzhou has unquestionably helped to develop the economy, to increase peasant incomes and to spread new technology. This is not to say that we should allow the scale of labour hiring to expand limitlessly; some controls on the number of hired workers and wages must be introduced as must measures for the protection of labour. In China, the private economy and the hiring of labour in the countryside can be controlled and because the public sector is in the leading position, our socialist system will not be endangered.

Declining agricultural production

Various measures have been taken to subsidize agriculture by developing *xiangzhen* public enterprises in Sunan. These are designed, on the one hand, to reassure peasants who have not yet moved out of agriculture and to encourage agricultural investment on the other. These measures help to stimulate agricultural production and co-ordinate the development of agriculture and industry under circumstances in which the relative prices of agricultural and industrial products cannot be substantially changed. But the case of some villages in Wenzhou is different. In these areas it is peasants' individual household industry and commerce and certain peasants' co-operative enterprises that are expanding. Consequently, the *xiangzhen* generally doesn't transfer profits from industry to peasants and agricultural matters, since practically every household farms contracted land, as well as undertaking industrial and other non-agricultural activities, and, in this way, industry and agriculture are united within a single peasant household. So long as leadership and management are strengthened, industry and agriculture can develop in a co-ordinated fashion. There are villages in some areas of Wenzhou in which the co-ordination of industry and agriculture has gone relatively well. The peasants obtain a lot of income from industry and commerce, and then have more capital to use for expanding agriculture. In these places the peasants run their own agricultural service organizations with very good results. There are some areas, however, where agricultural production has been damaged because peasants obtain very high incomes from industry and commerce, while from their very small arable area they obtain only an insignificant income. Therefore, agricultural production is not held in high esteem. They work on contracted land for only a few days during busy seasons or do not work themselves but hire peasants from the mountain areas to work for them. Even so, most of the peasants do not want to give up their contracted land, since they wish to ensure their grain supply and to have a fallback position to retreat to (which perhaps explains why the development of a commodity economy in agriculture has been very slow and has fallen far behind the development of industry and commerce in Wenzhou). In some villages, agricultural production is declining; only a small amount of land is used to grow green fertilizer, ploughing is done relatively crudely and farmland irrigation facilities are falling into disrepair. This is a serious problem. The experience of Yishan *xian* suggests that this problem can be partially solved by strengthening leadership and management. But to eliminate it fundamentally, we must further adjust the relative prices of agricultural and industrial products, and try to concentrate land holdings in the hands of a few specialized farming households so as to expand the scale of production and to speed up the expansion of an agricultural commodity economy. But the problem of how the land can be gradually concentrated exists not only in Wenzhou but also in other areas where the commodity economy is relatively developed. At the moment, land concentration in the hands of specialized farming households is in contradiction with the household contract system. In Wenzhou, some households do subcontract their land to other households and collect 400 *jin* of rice per *mu* as remuneration (in economic terms, this is a rent); in addition, the subcontractors have to pay the agricultural tax. The subcontractors will only agree to subcontract if they consider it to be to their economic advantage. The reasons discussed above mean that, in practice, there are not a great many people who wish to subcontract land.

Xiangzhen (small town) construction
Local government in Sunan has made great progress in small town construction by using part of the income generated by rural public enterprises. Many new *xiangzhen* with various modern facilities have been constructed. The same has been done in Wenzhou. For example, in Baixiang, an old town in Yishan *xian*, the sight of new multi-storeyed houses replacing old houses and broad paved streets leaves a deep impression. The capital for the construction came entirely from the masses themselves, with the *zhen* government playing an important role in planning and leadership. Longgang in Cangnan *xian*, a newly established modern town, is another example. About 133 million *yuan* investment has been put into the development within less than two years; over 0.6 million square metres of building space have been constructed; 11 roads, totalling 21 kilometres, have been built, all with three or four storey buildings with running water. Most of the investors are local peasants and a few are from outside. The funds for the various public projects are collected by means of

different levies related to the location of buildings and different fees for public facilities. For example, in the case of a vegetable market, within three days 220 people contributed 76,400 *yuan*, and the market was built in 28 days. At the moment, we need to investigate the question of whether or not a large amount of capital should be used for urban construction and whether the construction standards should be very high. It can be seen that Wenzhou's path to expanding the rural commodity economy can simultaneously promote *xiangzhen* construction. Moreover, the speed of construction is very fast. Naturally, the construction can be even quicker and even better if, like Baixiang *zhen* and Longgang *zhen*, the *xiangzhen* government provides unified planning and unified leadership. As the peasants become well-off, are there difficulties in *xiangzhen* construction? In Linshi *zhen* the people wanted to set up a TV broadcasting station. The masses themselves raised the capital, with one peasant at one go contributing 5,000 *yuan*, and the station was constructed rapidly. At the very least, *xiangzhen* construction in Wenzhou's villages is not inferior to that in certain villages in Sunan where there is an advanced commodity economy. Of course, if *xiangzhen* governments had their own funds, town construction would be achieved better and more quickly. But the problem is that formerly they did not have their own budget; they handed over all their income to higher authorities and received a specified allocation from it. The Zhejiang provincial government is preparing to establish a budget at the *xiangzhen* government level and, in this way, the problem may be solved.

The long-term prospects for household enterprises

This is another issue that is worth investigating. It is true that household enterprises are not advanced industrial organizations. Generally speaking, in terms of capital, technology, product quality, labour productivity, economic returns, etc., they are inferior to large urban industry, and even to certain *xiangzhen* public industries operating modern equipment. From the long-term point of view, most household enterprises will become larger-scale units in various ways (it should be noted that some family industries still exist even in the advanced capitalist countries). This is shown by the fact that different forms of co-operative enterprises are developing in Wenzhou. But the process will take a very long time. Under conditions in which the economy, especially the modern industrial sector, is undeveloped, household enterprises will continue to exist well into the future in China. Though they have plenty of disadvantages compared with big urban industries or even *xiangzhen* public enterprises, they also have some advantages, e.g., labour is cheap, production is flexible, management expenses are extremely small, the enterprises are fully independent and there is no problem of 'eating from the big pot'. It is true that technology in these enterprises is backward. High technology is not required to manufacture all products, however. We should not expect that a great amount of new technology will be developed within household enterprises, but it is possible that a limited amount will be developed. For example, plastic shoe manufacture in Rui'an *xian*'s Xianjiang *xiang* was converted from hand production to using machinery for mould processing within four years and, in the next year, its household enterprises began to install machinery for plastic injection. During the nine-month period ending in September 1985, more than 1.22 million *yuan* was invested in technological transformation and 22 sets of plastic injection machinery were bought. Technological transformation has not only raised labour productivity, but has improved product quality. Moreover, the technological progress and improvement in product quality has enabled Wenzhou's rural household industry to become more competitive. Furthermore, it should be noted that, as large-scale industry develops, there will be some products which it is unwilling or which it finds difficult to produce, but which are needed on the market. Rural household industry can plug these gaps, of which a great many exist. Hence, even after a long period of development, some new opportunities will still exist for rural household industry. Here I do not want to defend the backwardness of household enterprises. The point remains, however, that, given China's undeveloped economy and massive agricultural labour surplus, labour productivity in backward household industry is vastly higher than in agriculture where marginal labour productivity is zero, or even negative. Thus, in comparison with the surplus rural labour remaining in agriculture, their transfer into household industry is a step in the right direction, facilitating China's modernization in farming. It is absolutely impossible in a short space of time for us to transfer such a huge surplus labour force from agriculture into modern industries.

Wenzhou's specialized commodity markets

It is difficult to imagine that in out-of-the-way places like Wenzhou's villages there can exist nationwide specialized markets (e.g., the button wholesale market and the clock spare part market in Yongjia *xian*'s Qiaotou *zhen*, the low-voltage electrical appliance market in Leqing *xian*'s Linshi *zhen*, or the badge and label market in Yishan *xian*'s Jinxiang *zhen*, etc.). These specialized markets result from the backwardness of the commodity economy in China on the one hand, and its relatively developed state in Wenzhou on the other. The unexpected formation of a nationwide button market in a small town in Wenzhou shows that economic advance objectively requires the formation and development of this market. Given that the market was undeveloped, it was extremely difficult for all the clothing industry to buy thousands and thousands of different buttons, and for the button factories to sell their products to the whole country. The appearance of the button market in Qiaotou *zhen* solved the problem for both buyers and sellers. Thus, despite the fact that Wenzhou is very out of the way and has extremely inconvenient communications, by means principally of the scurrying around from place to place of the large number of Wenzhou traders (*gouxiaoyuan*), the buttons from all over China are concentrated here, and from here are sold all over China. If the commodity economy was highly developed, if people had better access to information, and links between suppliers and consumers could be easily established, then the buttons would be sold directly, passed by their producers to the consumers (the clothing industry) without taking such an indirect route. Therefore, although the development of the commodity economy, generally speaking, will not eliminate specialized markets, it is very unlikely that they will be found in remote areas such as Wenzhou. Of course, this will be a long process because a fully developed commodity economy cannot be created overnight. In the short-term, however, more and more of this kind of specialized market may be established; in Anhui province, for example, some have been formed recently. This is a big step in the formation and development of a commodity market in China. In Wenzhou, the specialized markets based mainly on individual business and village industry based mainly on peasant household industry are mutually supportive. With the exception of the button market (locally produced buttons account for just 200 of the total of 1,300 types of buttons found in the market) a great number of the products traded in the specialized markets are produced in local household industry. Thus, the existence and expansion of these specialized markets determines whether or not these products can be sold. As the locally produced products of household industry change, other specialized markets may be formed. There are some products which have relatively stable sales (e.g., low pressure electrical equipment), and the specialized markets will also be relatively stable.

Capital markets
As the commodity economy develops, capital flow becomes increasingly important and demands for an enlarged capital market naturally emerge. In Wenzhou, in recent years the volume of business of the Agricultural Bank and rural credit co-operatives has grown quickly. In 1985, the cumulative total of loans issued by the co-operatives alone amounted to 216 million *yuan*, though this was still very far from adequate to meet demand. Consequently, non-governmental lending has developed, including both direct lending between peasants and indirect forms of credit. There are not only various 'associations' (*hui*),[8] but also a few old-style private banks (*qian zhuang*). Due to excess demand relative to supply, as well as on account of speculation and profiteering by some people, the rate of interest on loans among the people is very high. The volume of deposits taken by the Agricultural Bank and the co-operatives has been affected by the high interest rate on loans among the people. As a result of the recently passed Banking Law, it is now illegal for individuals to run a banking business and so the various 'associations' and old-style private banks are banned. Appropriate measures have not yet been found to develop capital markets and to speed up capital flows, however. The best way to wipe out usury is to develop public financial organizations, attract more savings and make more loans. The floating interest rate practised by some agricultural

credit co-operatives in Wenzhou is also worth following, for it has played a desirable role in stabilizing the interest rate on loans among the people. Moreover, we should be discriminating in dealing with different loan activities among the people, and permit legitimate loans in this sphere. The state could set an upper limit to the level for the interest rate on loans among the people; if this rate is exceeded, the loans should be banned. The Agricultural Bank and the co-operatives should actively participate in regulating the capital market. The weakness of our undeveloped banking system has been revealed during the economic development of Wenzhou. Many peasants engaged in trading carry huge amounts of money in the form of cash when they go outside the area for business, because they cannot remit money through the financial structure. This is both unsafe and obstructs monetary circulation, as well as greatly increasing the requirements for currency, all of which produce different types of costs; this is also related to the fact that the financial organizations have not so far supplied these sorts of services. Thus, reform of the financial system is extremely urgent.

Notes

1. I am extremely grateful to the government of Wenzhou *shi* for providing the materials on which this article is based.

2. In 1983, China's total cultivated area was 1,475.39 million *mu*, and the total number of rural households was 185.232 million.

3. The category *xiangzhen* enterprises includes public enterprises only; household peasant enterprises are excluded.

4. *Zhongguo tongji nianjian 1985* (*Chinese Statistical Yearbook 1985*): 297.

5. ibid, pp. 20 and 298.

6. Dong, Fureng, 1985, 'The Findings of a Survey of *Xiangzhen* Industry in Suzhou *shi*', *Henan Jingji* (*Henan Economics*), No. 1, 1985.

7. Dong, 1985.

8. *hui:* associations of people who regularly contribute to a common fund and draw from it in turn [translator's note].

5. Developing the Commodity Economy in the Rural Areas

Zhang Lin

Against the background of China's planned commodity economy based on the socialist public ownership of the means of production, the villages in the Wenzhou *diqu*'s coastal *xian* have found a new way to develop the commodity economy. This is based on household industries producing mainly small commodities, subject fully to regulation through market forces. On the one hand, these industries have created wealth for society, developed the productive forces, and met nationwide demand for certain small commodities; on the other hand, within just a few years they have transferred about 800,000 surplus rural workers from the agricultural into the local non-agricultural sector, and helped almost all the peasants to become well off. Moreover, based on the development of the commodity economy, they have helped also to speed up rural township construction, to narrow the gap between town and countryside, and to promote urbanization and modernization of the countryside. Experience shows that this is one of the options available for expanding the commodity economy and becoming well-off more quickly in poor, remote areas with too many people in relation to arable land, and where the collective economy is not well developed.

Main features of Wenzhou's open market network

The basic precondition for the successful development of Wenzhou's rural commodity economy is the establishment of an open market network. In the past few years about 415 commodity markets of different sizes have emerged in Wenzhou's villages; each day over 400,000 'person times' of transactions are made, and in 1985 their total value came to 1,850 million *yuan*. This is a very considerable figure in view of the fact that in 1985 the total output value and the total national income produced in the whole Wenzhou area were only 3,800 million and 3,700 million *yuan* respectively.

Most of Wenzhou's rural commodity markets are located on the sites of traditional country fairs. Under the policy guidelines for re-vitalizing the economy set out at the Third Plenum of the 11th Party Congress, however, these markets have changed enormously in terms of their scope, the quantity and variety of goods traded, and their functions in socio-economic life. Currently, Wenzhou's rural markets have the following outstanding characteristics:

Most of the commodities traded there are no longer the local raw and processed agricultural products, but small-scale final and intermediate industrial products made by local family industries: The rural markets in Wenzhou are no longer the traditional country fairs based on the natural, self-sufficient or semi-self-sufficient economy, in which simple commodity exchange (selling in order to buy) takes place. Instead, they are the industrial markets based on the commodity economy, in which large-scale commodity exchange (buying in order to sell) takes place. Since the introduction of the household contract responsibility system the potential of Wenzhou's family economy has been brought fully into play, because the arable land is very limited (less than 0.5 *mu* per caput). Peasant families have steadily switched to using industrial leftovers and waste materials to produce small commodities. In Wenzhou in 1985, there were more than 133,000 individually- or jointly-run family industrial enterprises, which employed more than 330,000 workers and produced an output value of 1,136 million *yuan*. The expansion of household industries was dependent on the existence of appropriate markets, so that in areas where household industry was most highly developed a succession of markets appeared trading in those areas' products, forming production and sales bases in specialized items. Today there are about ten of these relatively large rural production and sales bases in Wenzhou. The most famous are the button market in Yongjia *xian*'s Qiaotou *zhen*, the electrical appliance market in Leqing *xian*'s Liushi *qu*, the woven plastic products markets in Pingyang *xian*'s Xiaojiang *zhen*, and in Rui'an *xian*'s Tangxia and Shencheng *qu*, the reprocessed orlon and cotton cloth market in Cangnan *xian*'s Yishan *qu*, the plastic label market in Jinxiang *zhen*, and the plastic and leather shoe market in Rui'an's *xian*'s Xiaojiang *xiang*. Of course, there are, also, some general markets either dealing mainly in industrial products (e.g., Cangnan *xian*'s Qianku *zhen* market) or mainly in agricultural products (e.g., Leqing *xian*'s Hongqiao *zhen* market). In these general markets as a whole, the share taken by industrial products is rising. For example, in Hongqiao *zhen*'s agricultural market the volume of grain and animal products transactions fell, by 63.6 per cent and 31.4 per cent respectively, from the first six months of 1981 to the same period in 1985, while for means of production the value of sales rose 291.8 per cent from 1980 to 1984 and the number of transactions rose by 148.5 per cent in the same period. This reflects the changing structure of rural production in Wenzhou, with industrial output's importance rapidly on the increase, both in relation to rising output and peasants' increasing demands for industrial products.

The main products traded in Wenzhou's rural markets are produced locally, but, in addition, some come from neighbouring provinces and xian as well as from more distant parts of the country: Only a small amount of the goods traded are sold locally; most are sold to neighbouring provinces and *xian*, and some to distant parts of China. Thus, Wenzhou's rural markets have become the collection and distribution centres for certain commodities, with the markets' scope extending into every province in China, and even including international trade. The markets' main business is nation-wide wholesale, not retailing for personal consumption purposes. These markets are no longer isolated retail markets catering mainly for the consumption needs of local people, but open wholesale markets supplying commodities to the whole country.

Part of the reason that Wenzhou's rural commodity markets are able to stretch out their antennae, not just into neighbouring provinces and *xian* but over the whole country, is that they have attracted sales people, purchasing personnel and individual peddlers from elsewhere. The main reason, however, is the colossal number of over 100,000 local peasant traders in Wenzhou itself. These people have moved out of production and into trading. They travel extensively doing business, concluding contracts, buying raw materials, selling products, and communicating market information. They have become the leaders of Wenzhou's commodity economy expansion. Many of these people were previously engaged in small businesses, such as shoe repairing and cotton fluffing, which frequently involved living in other areas. By extensive travelling, they have accumulated a wealth of social experience, and respond sharply to information. They are familiar with a great many areas' local customs, consumption habits and market conditions; they are highly proficient in commodity business. Under the relaxed policies to enliven the economy that have existed since the Third Plenum of the 11th Party Congress, they are 'like fish that have been given water', able to give full play to their skills. They bring contracts, market information, technical knowledge and raw materials to household industries, enabling them to produce according to market demand and obtain better economic returns. The household industries also rely on them to market their products. The peasant traders play an extremely important role in the expansion of Wenzhou's commodity economy. The fact that there are so many peasants doing commercial business means that raw (and other) materials and all sorts of commodities flow in an unceasing stream from all over the country into these markets and then into the multitude of households. Moreover, because these peasant traders' businesses are linked directly with their income, are flexible, have few linkages, are exceptionally efficient and have a rapid rate of turnover, circulation costs are greatly reduced. This has led to Wenzhou's markets becoming famous for their wide range of commodities, for their low prices and for their courteous service, attracting customers from all over China, so that the markets have been continuously flourishing, getting stronger over time. To exist and expand, Wenzhou's rural commodity markets need these peasant traders who are the principal promoters of the markets' prosperity. The activities of the peasant traders have brought to an end the situation in rural Wenzhou of 'tens of thousands of households undertaking production but only one channel for selling produce', and they have fundamentally solved the problem of 'hard to buy and hard to sell' which perplexed the peasants for a long period of time. Thus, it can be said with certainty that without the activities of these 100,000 peasant traders, Wenzhou's rural commodity market would have been unable to expand to the point it has reached today.

A distinctive feature of development in rural Wenzhou is the formation of specialized markets with an extremely important role to play: Wenzhou's specialized rural markets have a two-tiered structure. One tier specializes in dealing in one particular commodity, which is mostly the main product of local household industry. Thus, these markets are bound up with regional specialization. Within a single market are concentrated, for a key commodity, a wide variety of types, sizes, colours, and grades of quality, from a large number of local and national producers. This means that buyers can buy goods in a short space of time which they would formerly have had to travel to many places to buy. The button market in Yongjia *xian*'s Qiaotou *zhen* is a typical example of this. Qiaotou *zhen* is a small *zhen* in a mountain valley, but it has become the largest button collection and distribution centre in the country. The buttons produced by 130 factories and 300 household workshops within the *zhen*, as well as from over 370 factories in different parts of the country, are gathered in this market and then sold to every province in China. In the market there are twelve main sorts of button and over 1,300 different types altogether, so that practically every type of popular button can be bought in this market. Of the 1,000 individual stalls, more than 800 deal in buttons and employ over 2,000 people. The extremely wide variety of goods displayed in one location, and the fact that customers can select the goods, bargain over prices, and pay when they obtain the goods, avoiding irritating and complex formalities ('checking product type', 'approving the order', 'placing the order', 'paying in advance', 'consignment for shipping', 'checking before acceptance', etc.), is immensely attractive to those using the market. Every day there are over 2,000 purchases made by people from outside Qiaotou *zhen*, and a total daily value of transactions amounting to 200,000 *yuan* (of which, buttons accounted for 160,000 *yuan*) and an annual turnover of more than 80 million *yuan*. The appearance of specialist product markets of this scale is a new phenomenon in China's commercial history, reflecting the level of development of China's rural commodity economy.

The other tier in Wenzhou's specialized product markets is related to the division of labour in the production process. Within this category are two sub-types:

1. Specialized markets related to the regional division of labour. In this case, within a given production and sales base, different areas each have their own special superiorities and produce a specialized product and, via exchange in the specialized market, form a key point product in the production base area's structure. Leqing *xian*'s Liushi *qu* specializes in

producing low-voltage electrical appliances, of which it can produce 1,200 different types. Within the *qu* there is regional division of labour, with ten relatively large-scale specialized *xiang* and *cun*. For example, Wengyang *zhen* mainly makes components for miners' lamps, Mingdong *xiang* mainly produces electrical components (especially low pressure alternating mutual inductors), Chanxi *cun* mainly produces bakelite components, Luzhuang *cun* mainly makes automatic atmospheric switches, while Donghuang *cun* mainly makes porcelain components for electrical goods. Within each *cun* or *xiang* each household also has its own specialization. For example, in Luzhuang *cun* there are 10 big households which assemble automatic atmospheric switches, while another 100 small households each produce one or more of the components. In this fashion, the whole of Liushi *qu* basically forms an integrated whole based on division of labour and co-operation, with product specialization by *xiang*, *cun* and household. This interconnected relationship is not administratively organized, but occurs through commodity exchange in specialized markets. A further example is reprocessed textiles in Cangnan *xian*'s Yishan *qu*. Here, there are four specialized *xiang*, 58 specialized *cun* and seven large-scale specialized markets. There are those which specialize in handling leftover bits and pieces of cloth, those which specialize in reprocessed synthetic yarns and those specializing in reprocessed clothing. Different parts of the production processes are unified by exchanging labour through commodity exchange in the market.

2. Specialized markets linked to the division of labour within the production process. For example, badge production in Cangnan *xian*'s Jinxiang *zhen* is divided into more than ten different procedures (including planning, design, writing the characters, engraving, pressing out the shapes, painting, plating, making the clips, assembly, and packaging) and each family enterprise is responsible for one of them. All the intermediary inputs are passed from one stage to another through market exchange; each product in the process has its own tight cost and profit accounting with price fluctuating in line with changes in demand and supply. If the profit rate in a particular part of the process is too high then, naturally, capital and labour move there, and vice-versa, until the profit rate is roughly equal in each part.

Corresponding to household industry's production specialization and division of labour in rural Wenzhou there are some relatively large specialized markets with further division of labour. For example, within Yishan *qu* Jiangshan *xiang*'s Xihe reconstituted textile market there are three specialized markets; two are final products markets and one is a raw materials (oddments of synthetic fibre cloth and synthetic fibre yarn) market. Cangnan *xian* Longgang *zhen* Huqian *xiang*'s woven basket market is also divided into two: at the *xiang*'s eastern end and in the area along the river bank is a plastic strips market, while the *xiang*'s high street is a market for woven plastic bags. In this way, household industrial producers are able, in the several markets in one location, to sell their own products as well as purchase the materials they require for production.

Another special feature of Wenzhou's rural commodity markets is the division of labour among those who are engaged in marketing: Some become full-time, specialist travelling traders doing business all over the country, while others have fixed stalls in the market. Among the travelling traders some have specialist responsibilities for purchasing (raw materials or final products) and others have specialist responsibility for promoting the scale of their own areas' goods in other areas. Among the fixed stall holders, some are specialists in wholesale trade and some in retail trade. Sometimes there is a division of labour not only between different households but also between different members of the family. The button market of Qiaotou *zhen* has over 5,000 traders; of these, about 600 are purchasing agents who sell buttons wholesale to over 800 retail stall holders, who then sell the buttons to more than 4,000 salesmen who finally sell the buttons all over the country to the various department stores, individual pedlars and clothing factories. Thus, the Qiaotou button wholesale market has three levels. The difference between this and the state's three-level wholesale organization is that the price in each level and the distribution of profits between the purchasers, stall holders and salesmen are not determined by a higher authority or an official's subjective decision, but are regulated entirely by the market's 'invisible hand', so that the distribution between different specializations is roughly appropriate.

The benefits from Wenzhou's open market network

We have seen from the above features that a new, open and nationwide commercial network has been established in Wenzhou. The network is based on the family commercial enterprises which sell mainly small industrial commodities. It includes specialist markets working in concert with general markets, and an intertwining of large, medium and small markets. This is both the precondition, and a necessary result, of the expansion of the commodity economy in Wenzhou. The formation of this commodity network has reached a relatively high level. These markets have brought about tremendous benefits:

They have stimulated further expansion of Wenzhou's commodity production and readjusted its rural production structure: Wenzhou's rural household industries are totally regulated by the markets and, thus, are extremely dependent upon it. Consequently, the rise and fall of the market, whether sales outlets are good or bad, and prices high or low, are extremely important for them; it can be said that these are the household industries' lifelines. For just this reason, however, markets have a tremendously stimulating effect on the development of household industries. Qiaotou *zhen*'s button market began to form in the second half of 1981. In the space of just four to five years from that time, in the neighbouring two *xiang* and one *zhen*, 300 household button workshops and 130 joint household button factories started up, producing over 200 different types and with an annual value of output of 17 million *yuan*. Thanks to button production, the clothing industry has prospered increasingly. Already, there are more than 50 clothing factories in Qiaotou *zhen*, with an annual output value of around 2.5 million *yuan*.

Market competition vigorously pushes family industries to update technology, advancing from handicraft to semi-merchandized operations, and then on to equipment with even higher efficiency. This enables an uninterrupted increase in labour productivity, a steady fall in production costs and prices, and an unceasing expansion of sales. For example, in Jinxiang *zhen* the price of a school badge has fallen from 30 *fen* in 1978 to 7 *fen* today, a drop of 80 per cent, while the price of identity cards fell from 27 *fen* in 1981 to just 10 *fen* today, a 63 per cent drop. The price of reconstituted synthetic fibre thread in Yishan fell from 4–5 *yuan* per *jin* in 1979 to 3 *yuan* in 1980, 2.7 *yuan* in 1981, 2 *yuan* in 1982, and since 1983 has been around 1.7 *yuan*. The price of synthetic fibre sweaters was 3.4 *yuan* each in 1981, but today it is just 1.6 *yuan*, a drop of 53 per cent. In Xianjiang *xiang*, the profits per pair of plastic and leather shoes were 50 *fen* in 1979, 30 *fen* in 1980, 20 *fen* in 1981, 15 *fen* in 1982, and today are just 4.5 *fen*, a fall of 90 per cent. The fall in price has greatly stimulated demand so that the volume of sales continues to grow, which in turn promotes the expansion of household industry.

Market competition also forces the renewal and replacement of the products of household industry, to speed up the production of those products which the market wants and the elimination of obsolete products. The principal commodities in Wenzhou's rural markets have already been renewed two or three times; at the present time, each of the major markets is preparing a new generation of products ready for launch. In order to avoid defeat in the marketplace struggle, the managers of household industries pay extremely close attention to interpreting information. Each district's specialized market in Wenzhou has become a window for communicating information. It is through the markets that the greater part of the information about supply and demand reaches the hundreds of thousands of households, guiding their production.

Not only have Wenzhou's rural commodity markets promoted the expansion of household industry, but they have led also to growth in the tertiary sector. Around the flourishing market sites has occurred an enormous expansion of catering establishments, hotels, transport and communications, post and telecommunications, information supply, banking facilities, as well as packaging, goods consignment, advertising, repair, and other such service activities.

As more and more rural surplus labour has left the limited amount of arable land and entered the secondary and tertiary sectors, the structure of rural production and employment has become steadily more rational. In Wenzhou, from 1978 to 1985, the proportion of rural industrial and sideline output value in the total value of industrial and agricultural output increased from 17.5 per cent to 65.3 per cent, while the proportion of crop output value in the total fell from 64.4 per cent to 25.3 per cent. Over the same period the proportion of the total rural labour force engaged in industry and sidelines increased from 11 per cent to 63 per cent and the proportion engaged in crop production dropped from 89 per cent to 28.5 per cent. In the ten large production and sales base areas with especially advanced household industry, more than 80 per cent of the rural workforce is engaged in industry and sidelines, which has overturned thoroughly the old backward situation of 80 per cent of the rural population growing food.

They have enlivened the channels of circulation in the villages, and fundamentally solved the peasants' difficulties in buying and selling: The formation and development of Wenzhou's rural commodity markets have smashed the former situation of rural supply and marketing co-operatives running things in a unified fashion, with the whole country run like a single household. The single channel system of circulation has been changed into one with multiple channels. For example, in Rui'an *xian*'s Xianjiang *xiang* there already are six different channels through which to promote the sale of locally produced plastic and leather shoes, i.e., self-marketing, selling through stallholders in the local market, through local traders who sell in other areas, through the *xiang* supply and marketing co-operative, through specialized companies which set up agencies to promote the sale of goods in other areas, as well as through individuals and collectives from other areas who come to place orders in Xianjiang. Thus, as long as peasants' products meet the requirements of the market, they have no problem in selling them.

Wenzhou's rural markets also help some state wholesale units to sell goods which are over-stocked. For example, a Guangzhou department store's wholesale section had accumulated about 24 tons of buttons – equivalent to several years' sales – but after being put on the Qiaotou button market, they were sold out within some 40 days. Liaoning province's Fuxin department store had a stock of five million tons of organic black goldfish buttons sufficient to last for ten years, but when they were put on sale in the Qiaotou button market, they were all sold within ten days. Other types of goldfish buttons were sold nationally in the same way.

Moreover, the emergence of the Wenzhou rural commodity market and increasingly intense competition have, in addition, forced state and co-operative commercial enterprises to accelerate their pace of reform, to adapt to the development of a rural commodity economy, to revise old rules and regulations, old methods and the old state commerce work style. They have been forced to establish new types of organization, new rules, regulations and methods, to improve their service, to analyse their own market position and to work more professionally, thus improving their competitiveness and enabling them to play an increasingly effective role in the market.

The revenues of the state and the incomes of the peasants have both increased: In 1985, Wenzhou's ten specialized markets were the municipal government's primary source of income, handing over 74.56 million *yuan* in tax revenue. Seventy-one per cent of Cangnan *xian*'s government revenue came from the three markets of Jinxiang, Yishan and Qianku, and the market in Leqing *xian*'s Liushi *qu* supplied 60.8 per cent of that *xian*'s revenue. The revenue gathered from the market in Pingyang *xian*'s Xiaojiang *zhen* in 1984 alone exceeded that collected in the *zhen* over the entire post-Liberation period of more than 30 years. The emergence of commodity markets has also enabled the peasants to become prosperous very quickly. For example, Pingyang *xian*'s Shantou *qu* has throughout history been a poor mountainous area. In 1984, however, a rabbit fur market was established and within barely a year, the peasants had become prosperous. Peasant per capita income in Shenguanxia *cun* in 1983 averaged 105 *yuan* and the problem of ensuring adequate supplies of clothing and food was still unresolved. However, following the stimulus given to rabbit breeding by the establishment of the rabbit fur market, average per capita incomes increased to 784 *yuan* in 1984. The total income of the *cun*'s 161 households from the sale of rabbit fur was 284,000 *yuan* in 1984. Of these 161 households, two earned 30,000 *yuan*, six earned 20,000 *yuan*, forty earned 10,000 *yuan* and the remainder 3–5,000 *yuan*. 'As markets emerge, mountainous areas become prosperous' is the way the peasant masses see the impact of markets. Average per capita peasant income in Wenzhou was 417 *yuan* in 1985, an increase of more than six-fold on the 1978 level of 56 *yuan* and 1.5-fold higher than the 1980 figure of 165.2 *yuan*. Average per capita income in the ten areas where specialized markets have become established exceeds 2,000 *yuan* and, of the 6,459 households of Leqing *xian*'s Liushi *zhen*, 1,216 households had an annual income of more than 10,000 *yuan*, 296 had incomes exceeding 30,000 *yuan* and 87 households had incomes in excess of 50,000 *yuan*.

Small towns have appeared and developed: The emergence of a commodity market in rural Wenzhou has rendered obsolete the old pattern of towns suited to the natural economy. The development of the commodity economy has forced these old towns to be re-built and new towns to be established, and this process of reconstruction has been made possible by the rapid increase in the prosperity of Wenzhou's peasant households. In every place where commodity markets have been established, new towns have sprung up. At present, the number of *zhen* in the entire Wenzhou municipality is already 87 compared to its original 24. Old towns have been altered, extended and had their appearance transformed; new towns are continuously springing up, being developed and brought into action. Small towns are scattered throughout rural Wenzhou, serving as bridges between city and countryside, industry and agriculture, production and consumption, and representing the beginning of urbanization in rural areas.

The development of commodity markets in rural Wenzhou has led to the creation and growth of information, technology, labour and capital markets: These new markets, together with the commodity markets, now constitute a complete market system in rural Wenzhou. The key factors of production, without exception, are able to move around freely and are optimally combined by market forces thereby vigorously promoting the development of the commodity economy. The market is becoming an increasingly important force in rural Wenzhou's commodity economy and the centre of economic life.

Wenzhou's rural commodity markets have provided a great school for peasant education: Commodity markets have taught the peasantry the necessary skills for commodity production and management and to become strongly commodity economy orientated. The market has taught them to be courageous and to take risks in order to forge ahead and has undoubtedly given them the professional skill and management ability to run enterprises and businesses.

The emergence and blossoming of a network of commodity markets in rural Wenzhou suggests a number of important theoretical and practical conclusions for us. First, the emergence of Wenzhou's network of rural commodity markets shows us that, if we intend to realize rural socialist modernization, we must first commercialize rural production and develop and invigorate the rural commodity economy. Moreover, in invigorating and developing the rural commodity economy, it is crucial to invigorate commodity circulation. When markets are alive, the whole rural economy is alive; when markets are dead, the whole rural economy is dead. Without a flexible and sensitive system of commodity circulation, rural commodity production will remain under-developed, the phase of a self-sufficient or semi-self-sufficient natural economy will persist and rural modernization will be impossible.

Second, the emergence of a rural network of commodity markets in Wenzhou shows us that in circumstances where household management is the basic form of production, the invigoration of rural commodity circulation requires the elimination of the situation of 'Production run by thousands of households combined with commodity circulation run as a state monopoly'. We must reform our state-monopolized system of rural commerce and establish a system which is both open and has many channels. By means of multiple channels of circulation, and especially by promoting specialized markets and a comprehensive market adjustment mechanism, thousands of small household producers and consumers can be brought together, and the various kinds of household production processes fully integrated, creating a complete system of production.

Third, the establishment of a rural network of commodity markets in Wenzhou shows that if we want a multiple-channel system of commerce and a minimum of bureaucracy, we must involve each of the state, collective and individual sectors in commerce. In particular, we must shift peasants out of production and into the field of commerce where they may specialize in anything from trading, wholesale activity, retailing, shop-keeping and setting up stalls, to short or long distance transport haulage, and we must create the necessary conditions for their legitimate business activities. The transfer of peasants from production to commerce is both a necessary condition for the development of rural commodity production and historically inevitable; it will invigorate the rural economy and accelerate the process of rural transformation.

Finally, the emergence and development of a network of rural commodity markets in Wenzhou has provided us with a good illustration of a unified rural market under socialism. In it, many different economic components participate and its foundation is the establishment of both specialized and multi-purpose markets in every locality; it includes a complete set of small, medium and large markets as well as both shopkeepers and merchants, all brought together by the market. This market system has forged many links with the urban market network and together the two constitute a unified national market. The market will also provide the main channel through which the government can regulate rural production. It will control and regulate the market by the use of a variety of economic levers, such as credit, taxes and prices, as well as legal and administrative instruments, such as regulations, audits, contracts and arbitration, and hence the commodity production of more than 100 million peasant households throughout rural China.

6. The Growth of Household Industry in Rural Wenzhou

Li Shi

The model of rural economic modernization that has been adopted in rural Wenzhou differs from that of other parts of China. Its main characteristics are: making full use of the mechanisms of the market economy, bringing into play every type of resource, forming a structure of multi-level ownership and a development pattern in which rural household industry is taken as the leading sector, and which is suitable for the level of productive forces in Wenzhou.[1] As for China, which is a developing country with the typical feature of a 'dual economy', the experience of the development of Wenzhou has provided us with theoretical enlightenment and a realistic alternative in realizing economic modernization in backward rural areas.

Our investigation group toured the eastern part of Wenzhou (including Cangnan, Leqing and Yongjia) where there is a flourishing commodity economy. In particular, we made an on-the-spot investigation in some bases for commodity production and marketing, such as Liushi, Gangqiao-qiaotou, Yishan, Qianku and Longgang. On the basis of this investigation, we can analyse and summarize the general and specific theoretical features of the growth of rural household industry in Wenzhou.

The emergence of a new economic landscape

Rural Wenzhou has an historical tradition of household handicraft production. The rapid rise of household industry, however, took place after about 1980. Within five or six years, rural household industry had grown astonishingly, forming a virtuous circle of reproduction in which it played the main role; production and circulation developed concomitantly. The growth of household industry has brought profound changes to rural economy and society in Wenzhou. These changes may be summarized as follows:

Household industry holds an important economic position: According to statistics for 1984, 133,000 households and 330,000 labourers were engaged in household industry in the rural area of Wenzhou, accounting for one sixth of her total rural labour force. The gross industrial and agricultural output value of rural Wenzhou was 1,383 million *yuan*, of which the share of household industry amounted to about 60 per cent, or 800 million *yuan*. The importance of household industry was more remarkable in those areas where the commodity economy was particularly flourishing. For instance, there were more than 2,800 household factories in Cangnan *xian*'s Jinxian *zhen*. About 6,300 labourers worked there, accounting for 90 per cent of the total labour force in that town. There were also 12,822 household factories in Leqing *xian*'s Liushi *qu*, accounting for 15 per cent of the total households in the whole *qu*. The workers engaged in these factories numbered more than 60,000, accounting for 56 per cent of the total labour force in Liushi. In Yishan *qu*, 80 per cent of households were involved in the production and marketing of regenerated textiles and plastic weaving.

There has been a universal increase in personal incomes: The growth of household industry has produced a dramatic rise in the standard of living of peasants in Wenzhou. The average income of the rural population rose from 165 *yuan* in 1980 to 417 *yuan* in 1985 (higher than the average income level of 335 *yuan* for China as a whole). Since household industries were set up in Jinxiang *zhen*, incomes per capita have risen every year (70 *yuan* in 1978, 262 *yuan* in 1982, 477 *yuan* in 1983, and 574 *yuan* in 1984), increasing eightfold within six years. In the past few years, every household in Rui'an *xian*'s Xianjiang *xiang* has been producing shoes made of plastics or artificial leather. Thus, the average per capita income of the whole *xiang* rose to 434 *yuan* in 1984, four times higher than the 108 *yuan* of 1979. Within this *xiang*, the average per capita income of both Xianjiang and Hengjie *cun* reached 760 *yuan* in 1984. The rise of peasant income has changed their previous pattern of consumption. As the peasants in Yishan said, their consumption pattern can be described as 'giving first priority to nutrition in eating, to variety in dressing, to space in housing, and to high quality in articles for use'.

Employment has increased by a large margin and the structure of the labour force has changed: Wenzhou has a very large population relative to her area; therefore, before the rise of household industry, a large number of her labour force had been unable to find work, and a part of her labour resources remained unused. Household industry has more advantages than any other mode of production or management in making full use of labour resources. There were about 880,000 surplus labourers in Wenzhou before 1979, but by 1985 household industries had absorbed 330,000 of them and the tertiary sector serving household industry had absorbed another 220,000 labourers, totalling 550,000 labourers. In some *xiangzhen*, thriving household industry has not only fully utilized the local labour force, but also has absorbed many labourers from other parts of the country. For instance, the share of surplus labour was 50 per cent in Xianjiang *xiang* before 1980.[2] With the growth of the production of shoes made of plastics and artificial leather, however, employment increased every year, by 3,030 in 1980, 6,080 in 1981, 7,100 in 1982–83, and more than 8,000 in 1984. This not only absorbed the local surplus labour force, but led to more than 3,000 labourers being hired outside the *xiang* during the peak period of production. Similarly, since the setting up of household industry in Yishan *qu*, not only has it employed the whole surplus labour force of 36,000 of its own local area, but it also has employed 2,000 helpers from outside. And although the share of surplus labour in Jinxiang *zhen* was 50 per cent in 1978, all have now found a place of work, and an additional 2,000 surplus labourers have been employed due to the recent growth of household industry.

State taxes and bank deposits have increased rapidly: Statistics for the last few years show that the growth of state tax revenue is positively related to the growth rate of household industry. For instance, the total value of household industrial output (mainly from the weaving of plastic bags) has increased sixteenfold in Pingyang *xian*'s Xiaojiang *zhen* within four years, rising from 2.7 million *yuan* in 1980 to 48.73 million *yuan* in 1984. Over the same period, state tax revenue collected in this *zhen* has also increased sixteenfold, from 77,000 *yuan* to 1.69 million *yuan*. In Leqing *xian*'s Liushi *qu*, tax revenue was 12.77 million *yuan* in 1984, accounting for 60.8 per cent of the *xian*'s total revenue. Furthermore, the growth of household industry has promoted a big increase in deposits in banks and credit co-operatives, and imposed the guidance of the banking system on commodity production. Personal savings in the credit co-operative in Jinxiang *zhen*, for instance, rose from 80,000 *yuan* in 1978 to 4.27 million *yuan* in 1984. The peasants' deposits in the credit co-operative in Xianjiang *xiang* in 1984 also increased more than 20,000 *yuan* in comparison to 1983.

The development of public institutions and town construction has been rapid: Town construction and public institutions have developed rapidly in areas where household industries are flourishing. The great majority of construction projects have been completed by raising funds from the ordinary people. It is estimated that expenditure on town construction financed by collecting money directly from the population has been about 500 million *yuan* in Wenzhou in the past few years. Cangnan *xian*'s Longgang *zhen*, a new town with a population of 5,000 and comprising 15 streets, has been built by raising 120 million *yuan*. Similarly, more than 1.3 million *yuan* has been collected in Yishan recently. By means of these funds, 58 bridges, an 80-kilometre road, 5 cinemas, a park, and a waterworks have been built.

Qualitative improvement and technological transformation

Household industry, whose level of productive capacity has gone beyond the stage of traditional household handicrafts, is being transformed into a modern industry characterized by decentralized management. Compared with traditional household handicrafts, household industry in Wenzhou has been breaking away from its original structure in terms of product character, means of production, and quality of labour force; however, its unique feature, a mode of management in which each household is taken as a productive unit, has not changed dramatically. The distinctive features of this transformation may be summarized as follows:

The production of small commodities for daily use has been gradually replaced by the production of general consumer goods and means of production: Almost all low voltage electrical appliances produced in Liushi *qu* have been sold to productive enterprises as finished or semi-finished means of production. Yishan *qu* has also been expanding its scale of production of higher grade consumer goods such as carpets made from regenerated acrylic fibres, woollen blankets, lace and patterned shirts. Rui'an *xian*'s Tangxia *qu* initially produced woven plastics and elastic cords but, since 1984, automobile fittings have become one of the principal products of its household industry, and will soon be the most important product there.

Productive capacity operated mainly by manual labour has been displaced by mainly mechanized equipment: As far as each household factory is concerned, the use of machinery is both a cause and a consequence of competition as internal demand and external pressures have forced household factories to use advanced technology suitable for small-scale production. In Xianjiang *xiang*, for instance, shoes made of plastics and leather were produced by hand in the past. Since machines for pressing moulds were introduced in 1984, however, shoes have been manufactured by mechanical compression moulding and productivity has been raised; some household factories increased further their degree of mechanization in 1985 as they began to manufacture shoes by means of injection moulding. Tangxia and Shencheng *qu* now possess nearly 20,000 machines for plastic weaving, and Yishan has 37,000 textile machines. A few households have even bought imported textile machines.

The industry has changed from depending on craftsmanship to relying on technology and knowledge: In the past, some small goods made by traditional household handicraft techniques attracted consumers mainly due to their exquisite craftsmanship, but now the large majority of producers in household industry have adopted machinery and modern industrial methods. For example, there are more than 20,000 technicians in ten main bases engaged in commodity production and marketing, while amongst the 60,000 persons involved in household industrial production, or employed in *xiangzhen* enterprises in Liushi *qu*, grade-2 and grade-3 personnel account for 50 per cent of the total. There are also many skilled workers in areas which have flourishing household industries, who are continuously inventing and disseminating new technology.

Independent production and management has been replaced by specialized production: The development of specialization amongst household factories encourages horizontal links and leads to increases in labour productivity. All the household factories that have implemented a division of labour and co-operation form a 'large invisible factory' which is scattered across Wenzhou but closely connected in terms of technology and production processes. In this way, the capability of a single household factory is extended by horizontal links. For example, the production of regenerated acrylic fibre fabrics comprises six processes in Yishan *qu*, from sorting raw materials to knitting clothes, but each household factory is engaged in one process only. The manufacture of electrical appliances in Liushi *qu* is like an assembly line which involves the household factories in the surrounding *xiangzhen* supplying the parts and fittings they have produced to a central *zhen* where other household factories are responsible for combining these parts and fittings into a final product.

The product market has been extended from the local area to the entire country: There are now hundreds of thousands of buyers and sellers in Wenzhou, who have direct responsibility for the sale of the products of household industry throughout China. The buttons made in Qiaotou town of Yongjia *xian*, for instance, are sold to shops and clothing factories in other parts of China via the specialized button market, and the regenerated acrylic fibre textiles of Yishan *qu* are sold to 28 provinces, municipalities and autonomous regions by buyers and sellers. Some small items such as plastic labels and badges made in Jinxiang *zhen* are also sold throughout China by mail order.

An analysis of causal factors and key elements in the growth process

Household industry is not the outcome of factors unique to Wenzhou since it also has appeared on a different scale elsewhere, but the growth rate achieved by household industry in the *shi* is unparalleled. Here we try to explain this miracle by analysing several main elements in the growth process.

Able people with an innovative spirit have been the catalyst for the boom of household industry in Wenzhou: Economic development needs not only natural endowments and financial resources, but also many able persons who show strategic foresight and a bold, pioneering, innovative outlook, who come to prominence in a commodity economy based upon the market. J. A. Schumpeter regarded innovative entrepreneurs as the dynamic for economic development[3] and when we analyse the emergence and growth of household industry in rural Wenzhou, we can see their critical role. This type of person can be classified into two categories:
1. Buyers and salesmen who have pioneered new markets constantly. External market demand guides the emergence and growth of household industry. As far as household industry is concerned, it is impossible to

change productive techniques and to improve the quality of goods in the short term. Consequently, it was crucial for the growth of household industry that markets were explored and developed in advance. Wenzhou possesses hundreds of thousands of buyers and salesmen who buy raw materials, market products, introduce technology, and disseminate information to the household industry so as to link up local household industry with the external market, and to extend the scope of production and markets. It is estimated that the business activities of a single buyer or salesman can maintain 100 labourers in employment. Some large households engaged in buying and selling have particularly important effects in this respect. For instance, Pan Zhichao, a buyer and salesman from Yishan *xian*'s Fengjiang *xiang*, travelled around half of China to sell 100,000 products of regenerated acrylic fibres.

2. Able people who have invented new products, and introduced new technology. As learned, skilled, able and daring people, they can stimulate a rapid increase in the number of household factories through their innovative activities. For example, Chen Anjing, a peasant from Rui'an *xian*'s Hantian *cun*, set up an automobile fittings factory despite many difficulties and setbacks. Following him, many households in that village established factories to produce automobile fittings. In Yishan *qu*, Chen Guangyou and Chen Guangxi, two brothers, overcame the technical difficulty in patterning leftover bits and pieces of acrylic fibres and old Sun Acha spun the regenerated acrylic fibre yarn by modifying a spinning machine. As a result of these two technological innovations, the production of regenerated acrylic fibre fabrics by household industry has increased throughout the entire *qu*.

The process of the growth of household industry in Wenzhou has shown that innovative activity is a critical element in disturbing the equilibrium of the old system and fashioning the equilibrium of the new. The production and management activities of these innovators have determined the direction of development of the commodity economy, and of household industry throughout the *diqu*.

The multi-functioning mechanism of specialized markets has promoted and co-ordinated effectively the growth of household industry: In a closed economic system, production determines circulation and circulation reacts upon, or serves, production. This fundamental principle, however, must be modified when it is used in an open economic system in which production determines circulation and circulation and production are mutually self-determining. Their relationship can be described in the following way: production outside the system determines the circulation inside the system, and this (circulation) in turn determines production inside the system. This has been demonstrated by the interaction between household industry in Wenzhou and the specialized market. In some areas, the growth of household industry has led to the establishment of specialized markets, such as the production and marketing bases for the regenerated acrylic fibre fabrics in Yishan or for low-voltage electrical appliances in Liushi. On the other hand, the specialized market was set up before the corresponding household industry in other areas, such as the productive and marketing bases for buttons in Qiaotou *zhen* and for small articles for daily use in Qianku.

The development of a specialized division of labour, and co-operation amongst household factories promoted by the specialized market, have both changed the original pattern of production and management in household industry, and stimulated the productive forces of the whole area.[4] The specialized market is linked closely with scattered household factories engaged in different processes of production for certain products; thus, the demands of household industry for raw materials can be met, and the sale of their products can be realized. The production of regenerated acrylic fibre fabrics consists of six processes and, correspondingly, there are seven specialized markets, which form a productive system with a very specialized division of labour. The Law of Value, which functions in the specialized market, co-ordinates the quantity of products in the different household factories and their scale of production; it also guides their choice of new products and investment. Entering the market, every producer must both realize the results of the previous production process and, in deciding on the next production process, must collect the necessary information on the price fluctuations of raw materials and products, the emergence of new means of production, new technology and new products. For example, as the sales of regenerated acrylic fibre clothing in Yishan *qu* declined and regenerated acrylic blankets and carpets became bestsellers, some household factories shifted into producing these blankets and carpets. In addition, there are few fixed assets owned by household industry and so its ability to react to changing markets is high.

While it co-ordinates the production of household industry, the specialized market also co-ordinates the distribution of profits amongst the operators of household industry. In that specialized markets approximate to a state of perfect competition, changes in product demand and productivity in the productive process will affect relative product prices and so generate changes in relative incomes and output; thus, new patterns of production and of products will be introduced. If risk is ignored, the value of skilled labour can be measured in terms of unskilled labour on the basis of market signals; differences in earnings will reflect the differences in labour quality associated with the division of labour, and also differences

Table 6.1
Average income earned in each process of plastic bag production (*yuan*)

Type of process:	Cutting up	Weaving	Sewing	Cutting out	Printing
Income per day per capita	3	4–5	7–8	12	20

in labour intensity. Table 6.1 shows the average per capita income per day in different processes involved in the weaving of plastic bags in Xiaojiang *zhen*, from which we can see the relationship between the division of labour and earned income. Since the distribution of income among producers is closely related to their labour quality, their labour intensity, and their technical competence, it is beneficial in arousing the productive enthusiasm of the producing households.

Cheap product prices offer the most effective means of penetrating external markets: Compared with the products made in urban industry, the quality of the products produced by Wenzhou's household industries are at a disadvantage, but its goods have been sold in increasing quantity and variety over the past few years. One of the main reasons lies in their very low price. These low prices result from the following:

1. Low raw material prices. The raw materials for many goods came from the leftover bits and pieces produced by urban industry or other industrial sectors. Yishan *qu* has bought 34 million *jin* of leftover bits and pieces of textiles from outside each year, and a large proportion of the raw materials for weaving plastic bags has come from waste plastics in the cases of both Tangxia and Shencheng *qu*.

2. Cheap labour. Before the rise of household industry, a large proportion of Wenzhou's labour force was idle and therefore the wages needed to attract this labour into household industry were small, thus ensuring low product prices. Furthermore, the cost of labour to household industry was lower again because many household factories hired even cheaper surplus labourers from remote areas in the wake of the boom of the industry. Further, labour costs were reduced even more by extending working hours and utilizing previously unemployed labour within the family.

3. Labour productivity is increasing rapidly. Generally speaking, the productivity of household industry has increased rapidly because its productive techniques are simple, and both easy to learn and to spread. Moreover, this increase has been further accelerated by continual updating of the industry's capital stock. Thus in 1985 in Xianjiang *xiang* each worker on average produced 100-150 pairs of shoes made of plastic and artificial leather per day compared to only 10 pairs of shoes in 1979.

4. The tax burden is light. This is mainly because the small, scattered, and independent nature of household industry makes it difficult for tax collection agencies to devise suitable methods of taxation. The majority of families engaged in household industry have not registered for tax purposes while, of those that have registered, many do not keep accounts, and even those that do, fail to keep them accurately. Thus, without any accurate way of assessing tax liability, the tax bureau has had to levy a lump sum tax at regular intervals and introduce an incomes tax. According to statistics collected by the Departments concerned, tax revenue of 1.26 million *yuan* should have been levied on household industry weaving plastics located in Rui'an *xian*'s Shencheng *qu* on the basis of the value of production and

marketing in 1984, but, in fact, the value of taxation was only 0.6 million *yuan*. In Xianjiang *xiang*, household industry producing shoes made of plastics and artificial leather should have paid taxes of 3.5 million *yuan* over a period of six years according to the value of its production, but only 0.26 million *yuan* was received.

The fact that the products of household industry can sell on the market, even though their quality is not high, is closely related to the extent of product market segmentation in China. Given a set of products which have different prices and quality but the same use, consumers with different incomes will have different preferences and trade off price and quality in a different way. The bulk of the goods produced by household industry in Wenzhou is sold to remote and backward regions, where local people prefer cheap products. The regenerated acrylic fibre fabrics of Yishan *qu*, for instance, have been sold at a price equal to one fifth or one sixth of the price of the original textiles which compensates for their lower quality compared with the latter. Similarly, the percentage of electrical appliances in Liushi *qu* which reached the standard of quality set by the state was very low, but these products were still sold to small enterprises because their prices on average were 25 per cent lower than the standard prices set by the state; it is estimated that about four fifths of these goods were marketed to enterprises run by *xian* and sub-*xian* levels of government. The shoes made of plastics and artificial leathers in Xianjiang *xiang* were sold very cheaply (2 *yuan* for a pair of gentleman's shoes and 0.9 *yuan* for a pair of lady's shoes), which suited the consumption level of peasants in remote parts of the *diqu*.

Even though the bulk of goods produced by Wenzhou's household industry is characterized by low quality and low prices at present, it is not inevitable that this should be so for the products of household industry; it is possible to transform them into low price but higher quality products. Theoretically, new product price and quality changes go through three stages under the direction of the market: from goods of both low price and quality, to goods of low price but higher quality, and finally to goods of both high price and high quality. At present, some of the products of Wenzhou's household industry are making the transition to the second stage; these include, for example, badges, plastic sheets and labels produced in Jinxiang *zhen*, while in Liushi *qu* nearly 40 completed sets of goods had come up to the standard prescribed by the testing units of the province or higher administrative levels by 1985. This shows the trend towards the qualitative improvement of electrical appliances produced in this *qu*.

The wider impact of household industry

The growth of household industry must have effects on other sectors, and even on the macro-economy. Thus, the issue of external benefits or costs arising from household industry should not be neglected.

The effect of household industry on agriculture

The effects of household industry on agriculture are both positive and negative. Its positive effects on agriculture are mainly twofold. First, household industry has contributed to increasing labour productivity in agriculture since it has absorbed part of the surplus labour existing in rural areas, and thus has alleviated the contradiction between low arable area and large population. Second, local governments at all levels have transferred a small part of the income produced by household industry into agriculture as subsidies for agricultural production. This has contributed to the stability of agricultural production to some extent. In some rural areas of Wenzhou, where household industry is flourishing, however, the negative effects of household industry on agriculture have been much more obvious because the production of grain has tended to decrease there.[5] Land has even been left idle in isolated areas due to loose management. The immediate cause of this problem lies in the wide gap in income to be earned from household industry compared to agriculture. As a result, sections of the labour force, especially those who are young and mobile, have shifted into household industry. Moreover, investment in household industry has increased enormously while investment in agriculture, particularly in grain production, has declined steadily.

One important reason for relatively low incomes in agriculture lies in the very small size of family farms. According to the calculation of local farmers, optimal holding size is about 30 *mu* of land to till. Each household on average has contracted to farm only 2–3 *mu* of land to till and many able peasants want to contract more land.[6] Obviously, it is an objective necessity to concentrate land in the hands of these farmers. But the instability of production in household industry, and doubts as to the effectiveness of state policy in the long run have led to peasant unwillingness to abandon their land. Having freed themselves partly from the land, the peasants engaged in household industry regard land as their 'route of retreat'. Short-term subcontracting of land has appeared in some areas where household industry is stable, but it does not seem a good way to solve this problem because it will cause subcontractors to cultivate land inefficiently, which is not beneficial in the long run. To solve this problem, local government has already taken measures to subsidize households producing grain. For example, a peasant could get a subsidy of 30 *yuan* for cultivating one *mu* of land in Liushi *qu*. Nevertheless, because of the excessive differential in labour income between agriculture and household industry, these measures are inadequate to give peasants sufficient incentive to produce grain and, what is worse, may increase their unwillingness to abandon land. Therefore, the solution to this problem lies in a reconsideration of China's land laws. It is absolutely essential to design a set of policies which will accelerate the concentration of land in such places as Wenzhou, where household industry is flourishing.

The effect of household industry on the tertiary sector

It is obvious that the rise of household industry has brought about the growth of the tertiary sector. Many articles have considered this subject. Thus, what we want to consider here are the principal means through which household industry has affected the tertiary sector: one is the promotion of production, and the other is consumption inducement.

Production promotion refers mainly to that growth of production in household industry which has brought about the development of industries which serve it. The increasing demands of household industry for information have resulted in the establishment of a number of specialized households providing information, and consequently in the gradual formation of an information market. For instance, in 1984, Xu Fangshu, a peasant in Jinxiang *qu*, subscribed to 97 newspapers and hired five labourers to acquire and study information, by which he provided the household industry with necessary marketing information. The increase in external business undertaken by household industry has also led to a sharp rise in postal and telecommunications business in local areas. For example, the post and telecommunications office in Jinxiang delivered about 300 letters per day in 1979, but it delivered 300,000 letters in 1985, a 1,000-fold increase. In some areas where household industries are concentrated, various supply and marketing corporations have been set up, helping household industry to buy raw materials and promote the sale of its products. Furthermore, increasing trade between Wenzhou and other parts of China has promoted the development of the transport industry. For example, various parcel consignment stations have been set up. The statistics show that about 90 goods consignment stations with various forms of management had been established in Liushi, Beibaixiang, and Xiangqiang by June 1985, in which about 400 labourers worked, delivering 2,500 tons of goods per month on average. Meanwhile, there has been a large increase in the number of transportation vehicles in use. About 200 motor-powered ships and one hundred walking tractors have been used to purchase and supply means of production for household industry in Jinxiang *zhen*, for example.

Consumption inducement refers to expenditure on the products of the service sector out of the incomes earned by workers in household industry. For example, a great upsurge in new house building has resulted in the boom in the market in building materials and an increase in building workers. This kind of market has also emerged in both Qianku and Beibaixiang. The increase in consumer demand has also promoted the development of shops, eating houses, repair shops, barber shops and markets for farm products. For instance, there were 53 eating houses in Qiaotou *zhen* in 1985 compared with only one eating house in 1977.

According to the multiplier principle, the effects of household industry on other industries will form a virtuous circle and a market system which promotes and co-ordinates development.

Macro-benefits of household industry

It is comparatively difficult to analyse the macro-benefits of household industry. Here we focus on the sources of raw materials, and the use of products in household industry, trying to assess whether the latter competes for raw materials and markets with urban industry.

Table 6.2 shows the composition of raw materials, regions of marketing, and the uses of main products in seven bases of commodity production in Wenzhou. From this table, it is obvious that six products do not compete for raw materials directly with urban industry; the exception is low-voltage electrical appliance production in Liushi *qu*. Some of these products use

Table 6.2
Character of main goods in seven larger bases of commodity production in Wenzhou

Base of commodity production	Principal products	Composition of raw materials	Use of products	Main markets
Qiaotou *zhen*	Buttons	Glass, plastics	Necessary accessories for clothing	Clothing units and shops all over the country
Liushi *qu*	Low-tension electrical appliances	Metal, cooking wood	Necessary accessories for enterprise equipment	Small enterprises run by *xiangs* or lower levels
Yishan *qu*	Regenerated acrylic fibre clothing	Leftover bits and pieces from cloth-ing factory	General consumption	Rural and mountain areas
Jinxiang *zhen*	Badges, labels	Plastics, aluminium	Things for office use in enterprises and insti-tutions	Enterprises and institutions all over the country
Xiaojiang	Regenerated plastic-woven bags	Waste plastics	Product packing	Chemical fertilizer factories and cement plants
Xianjiang *xiang*	Shoes made of plastics and leather-ette	Plastics	General consumption	Rural and mountain areas
Shencheng Tangxia	Elastic cords	Cotton yarn, rubber bands	Clothing accessories	Clothing units and shops

leftover bits and pieces as their raw materials, and other inputs are not important for the state sector so the problem of them competing for raw materials does not exist. As far as their products are concerned, they are consumer goods of low quality or are necessary accessories for products manufactured by urban industry, or small articles which it does not plan to produce because only meagre gains can be earned from them. Therefore, there exists no problem of household industry competing directly for markets with urban industry. Even though some products of household industry may substitute for those of urban industry, this is beneficial in that it relaxes pressures caused by insufficient supply and sets up a buyer's market. In this sense, the macro-benefits from the production of these products correlates positively with their micro-benefits.

The low voltage electrical appliances produced in Liushi *qu* need to be analysed separately. On the one hand, they have caused external costs in the sense that consumers have suffered from their low quality and from irrational resource allocation because appliance production competes for raw materials with urban industry. On the other hand, the products are sold mainly to remote areas and grassroots units which state-operated commerce dislikes serving and thus it has been beneficial to the growth of production in these areas. This can be considered as an external benefit given the present system of commercial circulation. It is not easy to determine whether external costs or benefits are greater, however. This is the main reason for many people's doubts about this issue.

In view of the discussion above, it can be concluded that the external benefits of household industry are greater than its external costs in Wenzhou at present.

Evaluation of the growth of household industry

An evaluation of the growth of household industry can be divided into overall and individual aspects respectively.

In overall terms, there are many objective factors tending to support the existence of household industry for a long period of time. Especially in a developing country like China, with a great deal of surplus labour, the growth of household industry is an effective way to absorb this surplus and to initiate economic 'take-off' in backward areas during the long transition period from a dual economy to a unitary economy. In modern society, household industry can perform a number of roles: it can serve consumers as a complement to modern forms of social production, and can also serve urban industry. It will also develop in line with the growth of urban industry. Although the individual household factory may change its form of management during the process of development, new household factories will come into being when the necessary conditions are ripe. Thus, household industry as a whole will maintain its rightful place within the process of social production. In international terms, we can also see that, even in some developed capitalist countries, small-scale industry in which household industry predominates still exists and grows indomitably in the

Table 6.3
Enterprises by scale in Japan, 1972–1979

Number of workers	1972	1973	1974	1975	1976	1977	1978	1979
1–9	522,864	527,470	523,028	560,688	552,476	543,397	569,866	563,828
10–19	92,717	93,461	88,763	90,764	83,917	81,223	83,689	83,769
20–29	71,313	71,441	69,738	70,142	76,639	75,595	77,058	77,920
100–299	11,508	11,755	11,159	10,528	10,608	10,310	10,231	10,295
300–999	3,366	3,476	3,302	3,076	3,052	2,946	2,820	2,850
1,000 or above	819	844	805	772	735	706	673	639
Total	702,586	708,447	696,795	735,970	727,427	714,177	744,337	739,301

Source: *Small Business in Japan 1981*, edited by Small and Medium Enterprise Agency, MITI, p. 104.

face of severe competition from urban industry. Table 6.3 shows the distribution of enterprises of different scale in Japan in the 1970s, from which we can see the continued importance of small enterprises.

The recent growth of household industry in Wenzhou has highlighted the state of flux of the household sector with some factories changing into different types of organizations, others going bankrupt and new factories continually appearing.

In individual terms, each household factory faces three destinies: growth, maintaining the status quo, or bankruptcy. As far as growth is concerned, three choices are available. First, by increasing investment and the scale of production, the household factory may employ more workers and thus become a large individual household. Second, the form of joint stock management of various types may be adopted, of which the most common is for several households to join together to set up factories, hiring some labourers in addition to their own members. This form is called a joint household enterprise. Third, household management is retained, and labour productivity and profit margins per unit of output are increased by improving technical equipment, raising wages and maintaining the existing workforce. The first two approaches mean an essential change not only in the level of technology and the scale of production, but also in the mode of production and management. Representing a higher form of production and management, their emergence implies a ruthless abandonment of the limitations of the managing form of the household. Because these two forms of management have appeared in some areas of Wenzhou where household industry is flourishing, and some enterprises are of considerable scale, it is necessary to make a proper comparison of their management methods and profit allocation.

In the past two years, household industry in Wenzhou has mainly developed in the direction of joint household enterprises, that is joint-stock enterprises of several households. The members of these enterprises are both the owners of the enterprise property, and managers of its production and operations, and such enterprises are of considerable importance in some areas. For example, there were 28 joint enterprises in Jinxiang *zhen* in 1984, and 79 joint enterprises were set up in 1985, accounting for 60 per cent of the number of newly established enterprises. In Liushi *qu* there were 478 joint household enterprises at the end of 1984, but this figure had risen to 1,022 by September 1985, amounting to 6.4 per cent of all household enterprises. There were 1,017 joint enterprises of various forms in Rui'an *xian*'s Tangxia *qu* in 1985, an increase of 41 per cent in comparison with 1984 and accounting for 10 per cent of the total number of household enterprises in this area. There were 1,069 joint enterprises in Shencheng *qu* in 1985, an increase of 13 per cent compared with 1984, and accounting for 15 per cent of all enterprises there.

The reasons why joint enterprises have emerged are twofold. One is internal pressure for the merging of household enterprises. When market demand increases rapidly, and the introduction of new products needs more investment and a greater scale of production, the inadequacy of individual household enterprises in terms of labourers, funds and materials forces them to join together. The second comes from policies designed to encourage merger, which have increased the social status of joint household enterprises to some extent. Some individual enterprises have been forced to adopt the status of joint household enterprises because this sometimes is more attractive to consumers than individual enterprise status. Moreover, the joint household enterprise is more convenient in handling external business.

Compared with individual enterprises, it is easier for joint household enterprises to concentrate funds rapidly, and to control the large quantity of funds and personnel needed for production and management on a large scale. Each member in joint household enterprises, however, is both the owner of the enterprise property, and the manager of its operations. As owners, they must participate in decisions on important issues of enterprise management. Given market uncertainty, they will inevitably hold different views because of their different expectations, different desired investment and consumption decisions, and different preferences for risks. As enterprise managers, there may be conflicts of interest because of their different jobs and the inter-dependence of their decisions. In these circumstances, mutual distrust is almost unavoidable unless there is full understanding between them. In addition, objective differences in personal ability and personnel management make it difficult to compare personal performances. Thus, it is easy for different individual evaluations of profit distribution to occur and for conflicts to arise. Consequently, joint household enterprises are internally unstable. It is noticeable that these enterprises have mostly been set up by relatives or friends in Wenzhou. This helps to reduce their instability to some extent, but it also limits their further growth. Thus, it can be seen that in present circumstances joint household enterprises are an inevitable response to market pressures which make merger necessary, even though their organizational form is imperfect.

As for individual enterprise or large individual households, there is no instability of decision-making or profit allocation. Because individual enterprises have relatively stable management, and a unified decision-making structure which can take risks and earn profits, they are a form of management more adapted to the workings of a market economy. Nevertheless, individual enterprises find it impossible to grow rapidly in a short space of time due to limitations on their ability to finance expansion internally. Particularly before large individual households received approval by the state, their investment and scale of production was limited. Furthermore, the supply of bank credit cannot meet the demand for funds from individual enterprises and additionally, there has not been a fully functioning money market which also leads to difficulties for the growth of individual enterprises.

The most realistic way out of the dilemma lies in devising a better way to fund mergers, and in adopting a policy of advising and guiding individual enterprise. The issue of shares can avoid the limitation of individual enterprise or joint household enterprises to some extent because it can both raise funds quickly and ensure a stable internal structure; it is thus a preferable and better form of management. A stock market taking various forms has emerged in some areas of Wenzhou. For example, a peasant service agency has been set up for selling shares in Yishan *qu*'s Tielong *xiang*, where peasants joined the agency by purchasing shares and then electing a board of directors which takes care of routine matters. In the Pingyang woollen mill, workers join the mill by purchasing shares, with each worker investing 500 *yuan* as a share when employed to work in the mill. The mill has issued 300 shares altogether and 70 per cent of factory profits are shared out. The emergence of a general share market is inevitable, and is wholly necessary to allow the growth of individual enterprises or large labour-hiring households, at least in the short term. These enterprises will play positive roles in the formation of a comparatively stable industrial structure in the promotion of the growth of local household industry, and in the absorption of surplus labour from the surrounding backward areas. Therefore, it is an urgent matter to solve the problem of fund shortage for these enterprises. Until significant reforms to the state banking system are carried out, it is an objective demand of the development of the commodity economy to establish a managed and controlled financial market which will provide readily available funds for the continued expansion of individual enterprises.

Conclusions

On the basis of the above analysis, we can conclude the following:
1. The growth of household industry has broken away from the traditional rural economic structure of Wenzhou in which agriculture dominated, and has achieved a great economic breakthrough. This way of accelerating rural modernization is not only feasible in rural Wenzhou but also in rural

areas throughout China, especially in comparatively backward areas.

2. The economic modernization of rural China is a long-term goal. The complete transition from a dual economy to a unitary economy requires going through many stages of development, of which household industry is only the first. The evolution of household industry will itself guide the whole rural economy towards a higher stage, and the initial transition from agriculture to household industry is a great step forward in this process.

3. The main elements in the rapid growth of household industry in Wenzhou have been able people, specialized markets and low prices. Able persons are the catalysts for economic development in all forms of society. The specialized market constitutes an indispensable part of the commodity economy. Low prices are an effective strategic measure for economic take-off in developing areas. The combination of these three elements will not only have a decisive significance for the growth of household industry in Wenzhou but also a general significance for economic development in developing countries and backward areas. Low prices have also shown that it is important to make full use of advantageous conditions in an area and to choose appropriate 'intermediate techniques' of production.

4. Generally, productive forces in household industry still remain at low level in Wenzhou, but an efficient market system based on the present productive forces has great significance because it is of value to us as a reference point when we transform China's old system into a new one, and establish a flexible, effective system of macro-management.

5. The analysis of the external effects of an expanding household industry has shown that it has resulted not only in external benefits but also in external costs. Some of these reflect China's current system of management and economic policies, so their elimination will depend upon further nationwide economic reforms. As for other external costs which result from the specific nature of household industry, appropriate measures should be taken to control them.

6. Household industry as a whole will exist for a long time even in a modern industrial society, illustrating its indomitable capacity for survival and regeneration. As for individual household factories, internal demand and the pressure of external competition force them to extend constantly their scale of production. Joint household enterprises are, however, currently experiencing difficulties in dealing with the uncertainty of their external environment due to the instability of their own internal structures, and are thus not a very good form of management. By contrast, the form of share management has many advantages. The existence and development of large households using hired labourers will also play a positive role in promoting the development of the commodity economy, at least in the short run; their development should thus be permitted, though it is necessary to adopt appropriate policies to guide them.

Notes

1. Household industry here refers to form of management in which each household is a unit of production and whose members are principally engaged in industrial production.

2. The proportion of surplus labour = Surplus labour force/Total labour force.

3. Schumpeter suggested that innovations could be classified into five categories: (1) the introduction of a new good, or a new quality of good; (2) the introduction of a new method of production; (3) the opening of a new market; (4) the conquest of a new source of supply of raw materials or semi-finished goods; (5) the introduction of a new form of industrial organization.

4. 'What is operative here is not merely an increase in individual productive power by cooperation, but also the creation of a new productive power, the productive power of the masses.' Quoted from *The Collected Works of Marx*, Volume 23, p. 362.

5. A decrease in grain production is a universal phenomenon in areas where household industry is flourishing. For instance, the value of grain production decreased 11.75 per cent in 1985 compared with that in 1984 in Yiwu *xian*. Besides natural disasters and the structure of industry etc., this resulted to some extent from relatively low profit from the production of grain. Investigation revealed that earnings were 45.46 *yuan* for early rice per *mu*, and 85.03 *yuan* for late rice per *mu* in Yiwu *xian*, which were so low as to discourage grain production.

6. In Jiangshan *xiang* of Yishan *diqu* many peasant households would like to subcontract land to till themselves, or to let others till. The subcontractors of land must hand over 350–400 *jin* of grain each year to those who rent out the land.

7. Income Differentials in the Development of Wenzhou's Rural Commodity Economy

Zhao Renwei

The rapid expansion of Wenzhou's village commodity economy led to a marked change in income distribution. The widening of individual income differentials has led to widespread interest. This survey was limited in respect to time and depth of coverage and there were difficulties in collecting materials and obtaining reliable data. Consequently, it was not possible to construct a complete statistical basis for our analysis. The main source of data was sample surveys and individual visits.

Based on increased output, income has risen and differentials have widened

Following the Third Plenum of the Party's Eleventh Central Committee, the peasants of Wenzhou municipality adapted their experience in agricultural production contracting to the sphere of rural industry. This led to the expansion of household industry as well as to the opening up of specialized markets in the sphere of circulation, and took the rural commodity economy down a new path. The gross value of village agricultural output in 1980 was 1,135 million *yuan*. By 1985 it had risen to 2,531 million *yuan* – 123 per cent above the 1980 level, or more than doubling in the previous five years. In 1985, in the ten large commodity production and sales bases and specialized markets of the several coastal *xian* the volume of transactions attained 1,150 million *yuan*, occupying 62 per cent of the total value of transactions of all the commodity markets in the municipality.

On the basis of a rapid expansion of output, there occurred a high-speed increase in the state's budgetary revenue, in collectives' common accumulation and in individual income. For example, in 1985, the ten large specialized markets and production and sales bases handed over 74.56 million *yuan* to the state in tax revenue, forming an important source of budgetary income for the whole municipality. The tax revenue from the three markets of Jinxiang, Yishan and Qianku in Cangnan *xian* amounted to 71 per cent of that *xian*'s budgetary income, while in Leqing *xian* the tax revenue from Linshi *qu* amounted to 61 per cent of the *xian*'s budgetary income. In 1985, over the whole municipality, the ten large specialized markets and the production and sales bases also provided 20 million *yuan* for collective accumulation, thereby providing a substantial amount of funds for supporting agriculture and social welfare.

At the same time, the broad mass of peasants, principally those in the six coastal *xian*s where the commodity economy expanded rapidly, experienced a widespread improvement in living standards. In 1985, for the five million-odd village population in the whole municipality's nine *xian* and two *qu* the average per capita net income was 417 *yuan*, equivalent to 2.52 times the 1980 level of 165.2 *yuan*, and much above the national average per capita income in 1985 of 355 *yuan*. Prior to 1979 the masses' living standard in Yishan, Qianku and Jinxiang *qu* was extremely poor, but by 1985/6 they had almost all become well off. In Yishan *qu* in 1985, there were over 2,000 '10,000 *yuan* households', amounting to 10 per cent of total peasant households, and there were five *cun* with an average per capita income of more than 1,000 *yuan*. In this district there was formerly a village – Xinhe *cun* in Jiangshan *xiang* – which was called 'three too manys' (too many thatched houses, too many sons and daughters sold, and too many people leaving the village to beg). By 1985, it had become a new village with a good level of income and savings, and plenty of new houses. In Yongia *xian*'s Qiaotou *zhen* '10,000 *yuan* households' had reached 80 per cent of the total number of households, and 78 per cent of peasant households had built new houses, with an average of 101 square metres per house built. In Leqing *xian*'s Liushi *zhen* which is noted for its production and sale of electrical appliances, average per capita income had reached 1,000 *yuan* and '10,000 *yuan* households' were legion.

Simultaneous with the rapid rise in the rural population's average per capita incomes, however, went an expansion of the disparities in individual incomes. This was manifested principally in the following respects:

The differentials in individuals' incomes between different districts: There are differentials in individual income associated with inherited imbalances in economic development between the coastal *xian* in the east of Wenzhou municipality, and those inland in the west of the area administered by the municipality, as well as between counties and villages in plains and mountainous areas. In the past few years it is principally the coastal districts that have experienced relatively rapid growth of the rural commodity economy. Thus, it is mainly the 400,000 peasant households (amounting to almost one third of the total in the whole municipality) in the six coastal counties who have relatively quickly become prosperous. In 1985 in Cangnan *xian*'s Yishan *qu* average per capita income reached 552 *yuan* and in Leqing *xian*'s Liushi *qu* it reached 500 *yuan*, while in a small number of *cun* and *zhen* it had already reached as high as 1,000 *yuan*. But, at the present time, Wenzhou still has three *xian* and thirty-odd *xiang* which are impoverished, where average per capita income is normally about 200 *yuan*, and average per capita personal grain consumption is below 225 kilogrammes. The poorest *xian* are Wencheng and Taishun in the western mountainous district. Even in Pingyang *xian*, in which the commodity economy has achieved considerable progress, in which there are plenty of areas where there are specialized *cun* and specialized households, and where there are a few '10,000 *yuan* households', there are still some mountainous districts, old base area districts and minority peoples' districts in which the people are still poverty-stricken. For example, in Pingyang *xian*'s Mocheng *xiang* in 1984 average per capita income was 137 *yuan*, and within this *xiang*, average per capita income in Wuyi *cun* was only 105 *yuan*, and in Chaoyang *xiang* the figure was just 127 *yuan*. In an area as poor as this, some peasant households have difficulties in keeping warm and getting adequate food, and in some cases peasants even sell their sons and daughters in order to survive.

Individual income differentials between different forms of ownership system: In state-run enterprises in Wenzhou municipality in 1985 the average monthly wage (including bonuses) for staff and workers was 105 *yuan*. Wages in 'second line' collective enterprises are higher than in state enterprises; in those collective enterprises which are run relatively well, average per capita monthly wages of staff and workers can reach 200 *yuan*. As for wages in the individual ownership economy, it is necessary to analyse not only the income of individual households who established themselves in independent businesses or who hire others' labour, but also the incomes of technically skilled people who agree to work for private people. The latter's incomes are much higher than those of technically skilled workers in state-run or collective enterprises, with the incomes of some of these technically skilled workers reaching 500–600 *yuan* per month. Thus, from this examination of different kinds of workers' incomes, it can be seen that there exist different 'prices of labour'. Moreover, they form a hierarchy: state-run enterprises are lower than collective enterprises; collective enterprises are lower than privately run enterprises and, especially in regard to the 'price of labour' for technically skilled workers, the state and collectively run enterprises are both much below the privately-run enterprises.

Differentials in individual incomes between different trades and occupations: The most striking such differential is the large gap between the incomes of those engaged in agriculture and those engaged in industry and commerce. In Chooyang mentioned above, the principal cause of the low incomes is that people are engaged only in agriculture; only a tiny part of income comes from industry and commerce. In areas with advanced industry and commerce, peasants engaged in agriculture (especially those who grow crops) are in a disadvantageous economic position. For example, in Cangnan *xian*, Yishan *qu*, the average per capita annual income of workers engaged in agriculture is around 600 *yuan*, compared to around 3,000 *yuan* for those in industry, and around 7,000 *yuan* for those in commerce, i.e., the ratio of the income of those engaged in agriculture, industry and commerce

Table 7.1
Distribution of the incomes of trading (*gou xiao*) households

Average per capita household income (yuan)	Proportion of trading households (%)
< 5,000	8–9
5,000–10,000	40
10,000–15,000	30
> 15,000	'a few individuals'
'just cover costs or make a loss'	20

Among industrial or processing work households, the distribution of incomes is as seen in Table 7.2.

Table 7.2
Distribution of incomes (industrial or processing work households)

Average per capita household income (yuan)	Proportion of households (%)
< 2,000	5
2,000–5,000	65
5,000–7,000	15
7,000–8,000	13
> 8,000	'a few individuals'

is 1:5:11. Naturally, there are also income differentials among peasant households engaged in industry and commerce. It is estimated that in the above *qu* the distribution of the incomes of trading (*gou xiao*) households was as seen in Table 7.1

Differentials between hired labourers and employers of hired labour: At the present time there are some 13,000 households who hire labour, hiring a total of over 40,000 labourers, among which there are over 120 'big hiring households' hiring more than 30 workers each. According to a survey of 31 'big hiring households' carried out by the Wenzhou Municipality Policy Office, these big households hired a total of 1,500 labourers with an average of 50 per enterprise. The average annual wage of the hired workers was around 800 *yuan*, the highest being 5,400 *yuan* (processing melon), and the lowest being 540 *yuan* (making 'plastic grass'). The average income of the employers was 3,500 *yuan*, the highest reaching 150,000 *yuan*. That is to say, within these 31 'big hiring households', the differential in average income between hired workers and employers was as high as 40-fold or more.[1]

The positive aspect of widening income differentials

People have differing opinions about the increase in income differentials. China's development path and the nature of its economic system are undergoing enormous change, and Wenzhou's economic development has its own special features. Under these circumstances it is inevitable that there should be friction in the process of the new system replacing the old (especially the friction produced by having two types of prices), that there should be problems relating to unequal competition and non-labour incomes. These all complicate the issue. No matter how complex things are, however, we must still make a concrete analysis of the positive and negative features. This section examines the positive features.

They are advantageous in smashing the stagnant natural economy: Widening income differentials reflect the arousal of the economy from slumber, and are a positive force in promoting this arousal and in raising efficiency. Many development economists both inside and outside China consider that, in the early stages of development, income distribution is relatively good but, as development proceeds, it is necessary for income differentials to widen in order to raise efficiency; only when there has been a definite development of output and society's prosperity can income differentials once again become more equal. This is the so-called 'U-shaped curve hypothesis'. Wenzhou is at present basically in the early stages, with the economy rising from slumber and the former egalitarian situation being smashed. Examined from the pure 'distribution according to labour' viewpoint, expansion of income differentials attributable to development of the division of labour is both inevitable and rational. When the productive forces are undeveloped, the social division of labour and commodity relationships are not advanced, and different workers are almost all engaged in the same kind of work. Workers' abilities cannot then be brought into full play, and differences in labour contributions cannot manifest themselves; this naturally prevents the unfolding of differentials in labour remuneration. Following the expansion of commodity production and the division of labour, peoples' latent talents have the opportunity to come into full play. There is a progressive increase in different trades for them to engage in, and within each trade the division of labour becomes more and more finely differentiated. Through a massive system of division of labour connected up via commodity relationships, all individuals can reveal their different skill levels and production management abilities, and the differences in people's labour contributions are made manifest. Widening individual income differentials reflect this expansion of differentials in labour contributions, and undoubtedly play a positive role in social development. To a considerable degree, the above-mentioned expansion of differentials in individual income, both between different regions and between different trades and types of work within a region, reflects this sort of process. This expansion has a positive function in respect of those areas which are still poverty-stricken. It becomes a pressure mechanism, causing these areas to be discontented with their condition, to strive to develop their abilities and find a way out of their difficulties, struggling to become well off in the future.

They are advantageous for smashing the traditional egalitarian situation of 'eating out of the big pot' which existed under the former economic system: The expansion of individual income differentials between different ownership systems (discussed above) from one perspective is an unfair product of unequal competition. From another perspective, however, it reflects the different drawbacks of the traditional common ownership economy such as bureaucratism, low efficiency, and the 'three the sames' ('working well and badly – the same; working more or less – the same; working or not working – the same'). There are advantages to making use of the principle adopted in people's-run enterprises of 'never hesitating to reward or punish' to undermine the rigid situation of 'three the sames' in state-run enterprises operating under traditional methods. Such pressure prevents state-run enterprises from 'lying on the state's back' or relying on the soft budget to get by. It means that they can preserve their leading position only by taking up the challenge and competing. This must have a positive effect on reform of the all-people-owned economy.

They are advantageous for creating a material base for common prosperity: As I have already mentioned, allowing some areas and some people to take the lead in getting rich is a necessary path for casting off widespread poverty and ensuring common prosperity. Only in this way is it possible to raise efficiency and create still more material wealth. Although Wenzhou's economic development is still in its infancy, the rapid growth of production and the increase in society's material prosperity already has provided the means for setting up various public enterprises; quite a few areas in Wenzhou have already done this. Through macro-economic adjustment and guidance measures, Wenzhou has begun to convert still more wealth into the beginnings of public enterprises, while taking care not to affect adversely people's production enthusiasm. I will discuss this further below.

In analysing the positive aspect of widening income differentials in Wenzhou we need also to resolve the following issues:

How should one treat traders' risk income? Traders (*gou xiao yuan*) have played an especially important role in the expansion of Wenzhou's rural commodity economy. Their incomes are also especially high, which has led to intense debate. Part of the traders' income is derived from extravagant profits from taking advantage of loopholes arising from reform of the economic system (especially from loopholes in the dual price system). I shall not discuss this here but, rather, will enquire into whether or not we should affirm that traders should, indeed, obtain relatively high remuneration for risk. Wenzhou municipality supports around 10,000 traders. They are the salesmen for 'thousands of families and tens of thousands of households', as well as producers of raw materials for the 'thousands of trades and hundreds of professions'; they are the organizers of, and communicators between, specialized markets, as well as providing knowledge of and feedback to, the whole country's commodity information system. There is a direct relationship between the quantity and quality of traders, and the value of, and profits from, commodity production. In a sense, the traders play a decisive role in the development of the villages' household industries. Indeed, a principal reason for the flourishing prosperity of the whole city's ten large rural commodity markets is the 10,000 traders. The reason for the slow expansion of Taishun *xian*'s commodity economy is the weakness of its traders – there are not even 200 in the whole *xian*. According to a survey of 147 traders in different trades and professions, carried out by Wenzhou municipality's policy research office in nine *xian*, the distribution of people at different income levels is shown in Table 7.3.

Table 7.3
Distribution of people at different income levels

Annual net income (yuan)	Number of people	% of people surveyed
1,000–2,000	32	21.92
2,100–5,000	31	21.13
11,000–20,000	18	12.33
21,000–50,000	25	17.12
51,000–100,000	2	1.57
'just cover costs or else make losses'	39	'approximately 30'

Among the traders, 48 per cent basically observe the laws and have a decent, upright style of running their business; 50 per cent of them have a good style of running their business, but they 'give dinners and presents to curry favour'; approximately 6 per cent give and accept bribes, and break the law. Thus, the traditional viewpoint that 'whoever is engaged in commerce is civil, whoever wishes to become well off cannot be benevolent' needs changing. Generally speaking, traders are astute, work hard, and are mentally flexible. We should affirm their right to be rewarded for risk. That portion of their relatively high income which is legal should be guaranteed.

How should one treat the remuneration for talented producers who bring forward new ideas? During the expansion of the Wenzhou village commodity economy, a group of talented producers who possess 'the spirit of bringing forward new ideas' have assumed an extremely important role. Today in Wenzhou's villages, apart from the 100,000 traders, there are also 20,000 technically skilled personnel and 20,000 talented managerial personnel. This is a group of people with culture, ability, courage and insight, who can open up opportunities. In principle, the question of the relatively high incomes obtained by these talented people is not one about which one can have a big debate. The complexity of the question resides in the fact that among these people there are some whose business activities involve hiring labour. Apart from the exploitational aspect of employers' high incomes, there is the issue of whether or not we should affirm the relatively high income which they obtain from their activities in bringing forth new ideas. Wenzhou municipality's policy office carried out a survey of 31 'big hiring households'. It showed that the employers are not parasites who sit idle and enjoy the fruit of other people's labour. Rather, they are production managers with high ability in organization and direction; many of them study technology intensively, read avidly, and even assiduously follow specialist courses. As for the hired labourers, a fair proportion became hired labourers in order to study production technique and management methods so as to be able themselves to set up an independent business in the future. Quite a few hired labourers and employers have a master–apprentice relationship of passing on knowledge; many are relatives, friends or neighbours. Hired labour enterprises such as this are basically extensions of the household economy, and have nothing in common with the archetypical capitalist hired labour system. The relatively high income obtained by employers is rational, since it stimulates people to do those things which are useful to the economy.

The negative aspect of widening income differentials

Naturally, widening income differentials has certain negative consequences, of which the following are the main ones:

The fact that staff and workers' incomes in state-run enterprises are below those in collective enterprises, has placed the publicly owned economy, especially the all-people-owned economy, in a disadvantageous position: This has led to dissatisfaction and dissention among the staff and workers in state-run enterprises. Many people have asked to retain their posts but have their salaries stopped and look for alternative employment; quite a number of staff members and workers rely on a second occupation to supplement their incomes. According to a survey of spinning and weaving industry companies, in the knitting industry's socks and stockings factory, 79 per cent of the staff and workers in the No. 1 and No. 2 knitting plant had a second occupation; the figure of the cotton spinning and weaving trade is 37 per cent, for the silk trade the figure is 61.5 per cent, and for wool spinning the figure is 43 per cent. Because of the large number of people who have a second job, the factories' labour productivity is low and they are uncompetitive. In 1985, in the whole of Wenzhou municipality, the gross value of industrial output rose by 36.25 per cent, within which collective industrial output rose by 51.87 per cent, the villages' *xiangzhen* industry rose by 57.5 per cent, urban roadside industry rose by 130 per cent, and state-run industry rose by only 11.03 per cent. In an analogous fashion to state-run enterprises, cadres in administrative units, medical and educational personnel have also taken second jobs in order to increase their income, with some relying on household and commercial activities to supplement their incomes.

A still more important reason for this situation, apart from the problems with state-run enterprises' management systems, is the state-run enterprises' unequal position *vis-à-vis* taxation. State-run enterprises' accounts are well kept, with income tax calculated according to actual profits, but the bulk of individual enterprises simply have no accounts so that some business households have inadequate tax levels, and some basically have no taxes levied at all. Tax evasion is most glaring in the following two sorts of circumstances: the first type is that in which tax is assessed according to the individual household's stallspace. In both Yongjia (*xian*), Qiaotou button market and Rui'an's (*xian*) Chengguan industrial commodity market, taxes are levied in accordance with daily stallspace. This method cannot identify the real scope of business or the actual profit level. Under it, business households with a large wholesale trade, a large scale of management and high profit levels simply hand over a token amount of income tax. The second type is the assessment of tax according to the 'registered household' (*gua hu*) method. The so-called 'registered household' system arises because when household industrial producers and individual traders do business and wish to promote the sale of goods in other areas, they are required to have a collective enterprise which gives them a letter of introduction, which provides receipts on their behalf and is entrusted to receive funds. The 'registered household' enterprise then gives an annual 'registered household fee' (generally 10–15 per cent of the total volume of business) to the registering enterprise, and the registering enterprise then includes the 'registered household' business with its own for the purpose of paying business tax. Thus, some tax-exempt enterprises register households for other enterprises and some enterprises go to other *xian* to get 'registered household' fees. For example, the municipal district's Kaiguan factory in Donghai (a newly set up, roadside, tax-exempt enterprise) took 'registered household' fees on behalf of people from Leqing *xian*; in the first half of 1985 alone they issued receipts to the value of 790,000 *yuan*, defrauding the state of over 60,000 *yuan* in tax revenue. At the present, newly established household industries are uniformly exempt from tax for a year, leading some industrial and commercial households to study carefully the loopholes in the tax policies, transforming themselves into 'switchgear factories': that is to say, after a year of tax exemption, they change their appearance and apply for fresh registration, using this pretext to avoid paying state taxes.

Low incomes for agricultural production lead to the contraction of farm output: As was noted above, according to calculations for the Yishan *diqu*, the ratio of income for workers doing agricultural, industrial and commercial work is 1:5:11. Even when taking into account the element of reward for risk and 'blazing new trails' in carrying out commerce and industry, the income from agriculture is still too low. Naturally, such income differentials are harmful to rationalizing the structure of production and deployment of the workforce. At the present time, in the *qu* and *xian* with advanced commodity production, grain output in particular has already tended to contract. In some areas, extensive cultivation is followed, output has fallen, and land has even been allowed to revert to wilderness. The reason that some peasant households still continue with agriculture is not that they hope to sustain a high income from it, but simply because they are afraid of the instability of industrial and commercial business, and of fluctuations in policy; they wish to retain a reliable route of retreat in the agricultural sector. Thus, their philosophy of cultivating the land is, 'Don't *not* cultivate the land: don't cultivate the land *more*: don't cultivate the land *well*'. Guided by this attitude, the investment of manpower, materials and money have all declined; the quality of agricultural labour input has also fallen everywhere. The people actually working in the fields are for the most part old women and children, whom the masses call the '3861' brigade. Some people, still more fancifully, say the traders are 'heavenly generals of heavenly soldiers', those engaged in industry are 'the Yang family's female commanders', while those who work in agriculture are 'crab commanders of shrimp soldiers'.

A high level of non-labour income leads to dissatisfaction among the masses: Despite the fact that, as noted above, the relatively high income of 'big trader households' and of the 'big labour hiring households' has its positive and rational aspect, nevertheless, too high an income, especially a high level of non-labour income, causes people concern. 'Non-labour income' is of two types: 1. ill-gotten gains from exploiting loopholes in the present management system, especially those relating to price and taxation; 2. exploitative income from hiring many workers. If a way is not devised to control the large non-labour income of the 'big trader households' and the 'big construction contract households', social instability will result.

Certain measures which have already been taken and others which could be taken

Expansion of income differentials in the course of development of the commodity economy accords with the objective laws of economic development. It also accords with the party's policy of allowing some people and some areas to 'take the lead in getting rich'. A suitable expansion of income differentials helps to promote expansion of production. Affirmation of this point enables us to abolish mass poverty, avoiding the egalitarian path, and take the real path to common prosperity. We should, however, adopt appropriate effective measures to regulate excessively high incomes, especially those from non-labour sources. It is absolutely indispensable to do this, regardless of whether we are looking at things from the point of view of efficiency or equality.

Certain measures which have already been put into effect and others which could be put into effect can be outlined roughly as follows:

Promoting the commodity economy in poor areas: The poverty of Wenzhou's Wencheng, Taishun and Pingyang *xian* is not attributable to their exploitation by areas with advanced commodity economies. The reason that income differentials between these and other areas have expanded is the sluggish development of their commodity economy, i.e., it is due to unbalanced regional economic development. Thus, if we wish to reduce income differentials it is inappropriate to pull down the income of areas which have 'taken the lead in getting rich'. Rather, we must enable these areas themselves to become rich, i.e., overcome their poverty and become well off through great efforts on their own part to develop the commodity economy. According to surveys in the coastal *xian* of Leqing, Duanan, Cangnan, and Ouhai, *xiangzhen* enterprises' gross value of output in each case is over 200–300 million *yuan*, whereas in Wensheng and Taishun *xian* it is less than 20 million *yuan*. In the Pingyang mountainous district the commodity economy has developed particularly slowly; in many parts of it the self-sufficient natural economy is still dominant, while in six *xian* (including Xintian and Weixin) *xiangzhen* enterprises simply do not exist. Only by changing this situation can we enable these areas to become well off.

Rationally balancing the shift from 'using industry to support agriculture' to 'proportionate benefits': For a certain period of time and to a certain extent, 'using industry to support agriculture' is an effective way to solve the problem of low agricultural incomes and contracting agricultural production. For example, the Wenzhou people's government has already passed a regulation levying a fixed amount of 'funds to support agriculture' from rural industry and commerce. These funds are used principally to subsidize grain production, provide loans to meet agricultural production costs, and undertake farm land capital construction. Some areas also take a fixed sum from the collective accumulation fund, using it for farmland capital construction and for subsidizing agriculturalists' incomes, reducing the gap in income between those who undertake agriculture and those who undertake industry. But, we must recognize the limitation of 'using industry to support agriculture'. It is, after all, a measure in which the relative benefits from industry and agriculture are adjusted locally, while at a broader level there is imbalance between the benefits from industrial and agricultural production. Moreover, we are not even discussing here those backward areas in which *xiangzhen* enterprises lack the capacity to 'use industry to support agriculture'. In some areas in which *xiangzhen* enterprises are relatively advanced, adjustment of the industrial and agricultural advantages is achieved through the method of recruiting one industrial worker from each peasant household. This enables every agricultural household directly to benefit from industrial expansion. It ultimately restricts the rational movement, and improvement in quality, of industrial workers, however. Moreover, it constrains the growth of industrial workers' productivity and the further development of commodity relationships. 'Using industry to support agriculture' at the local level is a product of the development of commodity relationships and the division of labour between industry and agriculture. Therefore, from another point of view, it reflects the inadequate development of the division of labour and commodity relationships. In the long term, we must ensure that there is a rational balance between the benefits obtainable from industry and agriculture;[2] only then will it be possible fundamentally to prevent the contraction of agricultural production. In order to do this, we need to rationalize the relative prices of industrial and agricultural products, and take advantage of economies of scale in agriculture (especially in grain production). The latter objective requires a transformation of the situation of each household looking after small dispersed plots of land (e.g., each household has just two or three *mu* split into six or seven pieces, combining good and bad, near and far). By concentrating farmland in the hands of a few specialized households by means of 'transferred contracts', agricultural workers' labour productivity and incomes will be able to rise rapidly.

Some areas already have some useful experience in this respect. For example, a peasant called Huang Suncheng in the Yishan *qu*'s Tielong *xiang* is a past master at agricultural production, but he basically cannot do industrial work; consequently, he sank into poverty. Over the past few years, with the leadership and assistance of Tielong *xiang*'s peasant service co-operative, he has become rich through the transfer of the contract on 15 *mu* of land to be run as a family farm. The most rational size of peasant farm or specialized household depends on the local conditions. Some peasants consider that in the Wenzhou plain area a size of 30 *mu* is suitable. With farms of this scale the internal structure of agricultural production can be rationally adjusted, producing co-ordination of grain crops, economic crops and animal husbandry; it also facilitates agricultural mechanization. On the other hand, according to the relevant departments of Jinhua *diqu*, which investigated their region's natural conditions (it is a hilly area) and level of production conditions (it still operates with hand technology), about 10 *mu* is the most suitable scale of operation in this area.

Achieving macro-economic adjustment through taxation: The first task in this area is to resolve the irrational tax burden between different economic ownership systems, altering the disadvantageous position of state-run enterprises. This does not just require improvement in the tax system and in tax rates. It involves also strengthening tax management, steadily improving accounting practices and tax collection. Only when this has been done will the real level of business activity be known and profits calculated correctly, enabling taxation to take place on a reliable foundation and preventing industrial tax evasion. The tax mechanism can have two functions in regulating income distribution. First, it can restrict excessively high incomes in particular, and compulsorily depress high non-labour incomes. For example, in respect of individual employers' excessively high income, apart from progressive taxation levies, an 'adjustment tax' can also be levied, depending on the concrete circumstances. Second, it can have a guidance function. For example, a given amount of income can be used to a greater or lesser extent for consumption or accumulation. If the propensity to consume is too high, tax measures can be used to encourage a reduction in consumption and an increase in accumulation. Again, for example, certain people-run enterprises with relatively high incomes (especially 'big labour-hiring households') should be encouraged and guided towards becoming jointly-run businesses, combining the superiority of jointly-run businesses with the flexibility of household business. The present 10-step progressive income tax for the individual economy, however, inhibits the expansion of individual enterprises in the direction of jointly-run and co-operative business. Under the present tax system, if a household-run individual enterprise has an annual net income of 500 *yuan*, it should pay at a tax rate of 7 per cent, i.e., 37 *yuan*; a co-operative or jointly-run business, composed of 10 people, but with the same *per caput* net income, would have to pay 30 per cent, or 102 *yuan per caput* (i.e., 1.9 times that of the individual household); a co-operatively run business with 20 people, also with the same average *per caput* net income, should pay at 40 per cent tax rate, or an average of 141 *yuan per caput* (i.e., 3.01 times that of the individual household business's tax burden). This method fails to guide things in the desired direction and we need to make further investigations to change it.

Encouraging the setting up of public welfare undertakings and publicly constructed projects: A thoroughly feasible method of adjusting income distribution is to encourage people who have 'taken the lead in becoming rich' voluntarily to pool their funds to set up local public welfare undertakings, and to construct public projects. Some people are extremely keen to set up cultural and educational undertakings such as public parks, schools, hospitals and theatres. They are also keen to invest in building roads and bridges, and in the construction of small towns. For example, Cangnan *xian*'s Longgang *zhen* was completely newly built and Leqing *xian*'s Baixiang *zhen* was reconstructed completely on the basis of the old *zhen*, both relying on funds pooled by the masses, without a *fen* being spent by the state. As we understand it, in Wenzhou municipality there are ten relatively large small-town construction projects of the size of Longgang and Baixiang, in which the masses have pooled a total of 400–500 million *yuan*. Wenzhou's experience in small-town construction proves not only that income differentials can be narrowed progressively on the basis of some people 'taking the lead in getting rich', but, also that on this foundation it is possible to reduce progressively the differences between town and country.

Notes

1. The differential between hired workers and employers is clearly related to the number of workers hired. According to sample surveys of hired labour enterprises in Tianjin municipality, in enterprises with less than seven hired workers, the income of employers is 5.5 times that of their hired workers; in enterprises with 8–20 workers, their income is 9.8 times that of the hired workers; in enterprises with 21–40 workers, the income of employers is 27.3 times that of their workers; while in enterprises with 41–60 workers the income of employers is 57.7 times that of the workers.

2. 'Rational balance' does not mean completely eliminating the differences in individual incomes between different trades. Even though at present there is a gap in the income of those who carry out industry and agriculture, we have already produced some overall balance through the market mechanism; however, this obviously is different from the balance mechanism of 'using industry to support agriculture', or 'using the wife to support the husband'.

8. A Preliminary Analysis of the 'Big Labour-hiring Households' in Rural Wenzhou

Chen Ruiming

Labour-hiring is quite common in Wenzhou's rural areas (excluding the city proper). Hired labourers work in the following activities: temporary ploughing or harvesting in busy seasons; housework; collective fish ponds or mountain farms contracted by individuals or by partnerships; contracted building projects; individual household or joint household enterprises. Although popularly termed 'hired labourers' the first two kinds of hired labourers mentioned above (i.e., casual labourers and labourers for housework) can in fact be characterized as labour exchange among workers engaged in different branches of the division of labour. The third and fourth types (i.e., labourers working on the contracted mountain farms or in the contracted building projects) contain elements of exploitation, but they form only a small proportion of the total number of hired labourers in the municipality. Moreover, the character of the employers' business is limited, so that it is difficult for the surplus value extracted to provide the basis for further hiring of labour and uninterrupted accumulation of capital in the business. On the contrary, the surplus value is often consumed directly by the employers or diverted to other uses. Thus, this chapter does not analyse in detail these four kinds of hired labourer. Attention is focused on the fifth type of hired labourer (i.e., hired labourers in individual household or joint household enterprises): their nature, proportion, function, significance and social influence are such that they cannot be ignored.

The basic circumstances

At present there are 13,121 household and joint household enterprises running businesses with hired labour. They hire a total of 42,163 workers. They cover a wide range but the average number of hired labourers per household is very small (less than four). Some of the 'big labour-hiring households' have emerged from the ranks of the small labour-hiring households. According to Wenzhou's relevant department of economic management, a 'big labour-hiring household' refers to a large-scale household enterprise with either pooled or independent capital, owning a relatively large amount of means of production, and hiring over 30 workers. So far there are about 120 such households, with more than 5,000 hired workers in total, accounting for 2.3 per cent of the city's rural labour force and 11.9 per cent of the total number of rural hired labourers. In 1985 a survey was made in Wenzhou of 31 typical 'big labour-hiring households'. It revealed that they hired a total of 1,560 workers in 1984, the maximum number of workers in any enterprise being 110, and the minimum 30; the average was 50 hired workers per enterprise. The average annual worker's wage was about 800 *yuan*, with the maximum being 5,400 *yuan* (the technicians who processed melon seeds) and the minimum being 540 *yuan*. The total value of output of these households was 9.39 million *yuan* (the maximum being 1.18 million *yuan* and the minimum 35,000 *yuan*); the average value of output per enterprise was 300,000 *yuan*. Their total profits were 1.12 million *yuan*, and the post-tax ratio of output value to profits was 12 per cent, the maximum being 40 per cent (electrical appliances) and the minimum 2 per cent (alum). These households handed over 0.54 million *yuan* in tax. The value of their fixed assets totalled 2.23 million *yuan* (the maximum being 0.48 million *yuan* and the minimum being only 10,000 *yuan*) with an average value per enterprise of 74,000 *yuan*. The total circulating capital in these households was 3.72 million *yuan* (the maximum being 0.50 million *yuan* and the minimum 20,000 *yuan*); the average per household was 120,000 *yuan*. They obtained loans totalling 1.37 million *yuan* from banks and credit co-operatives, the maximum loan in one enterprise being 0.446 million *yuan*. Many enterprises were unable to obtain credit from banks, so the capital needed for production was obtained from credit among the people.

The income situation of the enterprises was as follows: two lost money; in seven, the annual income was below 10,000 *yuan*; five had an annual income of 10–20,000 *yuan*; ten had 30–50,000 *yuan*; four had 60–100,000 *yuan*; and three had 110–150,000 *yuan*. To sum up, most of Wenzhou's 'big labour-hiring households' hired about 50 workers, their annual value of output was around 0.50 million *yuan*, and each employer's annual income was around 50,000 *yuan*. Wenzhou has also witnessed the phenomenon of party members becoming employers, the total number being 330. Of these, 187 party members hired less than five workers each; 83 party members hired five–eight workers each; and 60 party members hired more than eleven workers each. Child labourers accounted for 20 per cent of the total number of hired workers in Wenzhou's rural areas in 1984 (though the proportion has already begun to fall). The fact that 'big labour-hiring households' in just a few years have appeared in such numbers and on such a scale, in a district with a population of around 6 million, cannot but give rise to careful scrutiny and deep reflection over the whole of China.

The characteristics

The 'big labour-hiring households' are economically and socially complex, displaying great variety; most of them have mixed and indeterminate characteristics. A small number are 'deformed', typical capitalist labour-hiring enterprises. Of the 31 'big labour-hiring households' surveyed, there were ten with self-raised capital, 20 with pooled capital, and one joint state–private enterprise. The great majority of households with pooled capital, or operated in joint state–private hands, are enterprises with mixed characteristics. Some 'big labour-hiring households' combine co-operative operation with labour-hiring by a small business. For example, the Yangdanshan gas equipment factory was established by capital pooled by five people; 80 workers were hired to work there and allocated to work under individual employers, who had an average of 16 hired workers each. These employers' income from exploitation is negligible. They themselves carry out several tasks, engaged both in manual labour and management, and their income is little different from that of highly qualified technical workers. At most they should be regarded as petty producers, and not as capitalists. Some 'big labour-hiring households' have a mixture of economic forms. Take, for example, the case of the hardware and plastics factory run by Shangtao *cun* in Leqing *xian*. The factory is under the unified leadership and management of the *cun* committee. It is divided into ten workshops, each of which is contracted to an individual. Each workshop allocates shares, assumes sole responsibility for profits and losses, and must hand over 3 per cent of its total sales value to the *cun* committee as an administrative fee. The shares derive from the capital pooled by the employers and some of the workers in the contracted workshops, and those who have contributed capital share the profits in fixed proportions. These ten workshops are, in fact, ten factories operated with funds pooled both by labour and capital, under the jurisdiction of a single village enterprise. This type of business may be regarded as a multi-form mixed economy combining *zhen* and *cun* collective enterprise, private co-operative enterprise and partially capitalist exploitative elements.

Apart from these two types of enterprise, there are a variety of other forms of labour-hiring enterprise. These include those which raise capital from mass organizations, collective enterprises, labour-hiring enterprises begun with funds pooled from peasants' own businesses, and businesses with capital derived jointly from big urban industries, scientific research institutes and universities.

None of these labour-hiring enterprises discussed above is a pure capitalist enterprise. Some of them are of a petty commodity producer nature; some are of a state capitalist nature; and quite a few are of an intermediary, mixed nature in between petty commodity production and the capitalist economy, and between the capitalist and socialist economy. The variety of forms is mainly due to 1. the fact that the collective economy is an already accomplished phenomenon; 2. the objective requirements of economic development and productive operation under the new circumstances; 3. the fact that 'capitalist hired labour business' is not a phrase that is pleasant to hear and its future is uncertain, so that it is safer to change into the mixed form of enterprise. Among the 120 'big labour-hiring households' surveyed only a small proportion have typical capitalist characteristics. Even those more typical 'labour-hiring large households' cannot be equated with capitalist enterprises under capitalism; they have many different characteristics. They have been established and evolved under the special condition that public ownership is dominant, and this has affected both their internal conditions and their external environment. Externally, they have been supervised and restricted by the socialist finance, banking and tax systems. As for supply and marketing, they must observe the relevant state policies, and accept the administration and supervision of socialist government departments. Internally, they are different from capitalists in the past.

In Wenzhou, they are composed of four types of people: skilled craftsmen; former cadres from production teams and enterprises run by communes and teams, and supply and marketing personnel; educated youth sent down to the countryside and into the mountainous areas; and, finally, ex-servicemen who have returned to the villages. Most of these people are around the age of 30. They have been living in a socialist society for a long time; they have been brought up and educated by the party and government. The majority of them are enterprising people who are literate, skilled, able, bold, adventurous, and have rich experience in running things. Quite a few young entrepreneurs have run enterprises with a view not only to making profits, but also to becoming new people in the socialist society; many have done so in order to put their talents to good use so as to realize the aspiration of enlivening their home town's economy. For instance, Ye Wengui, a 37-year-old entrepreneur, was an educated urban youth sent down to work in the countryside of Heilongjiang province. Now he runs a plastic pressing factory employing over 150 people, and helps solve the urgent problems of the raw material supply to the multitude of local household enterprises. He has personally invested over 140,000 *yuan* in the factory, and a further 12 people have contributed share capital totalling around 80–90,000 *yuan*. Now he plans to establish a non-toxic packaging materials factory with an investment of 4 million *yuan*, of which he has already raised 900,000 *yuan*. The state will not loan him money, so he plans to obtain the funds through issuing shares. He sleeps just five hours each night, and has read over 20 specialized books on plastics. He leads a simple, frugal life, and his house is furnished sparsely, except for the telephone which attracts one's attention at once. He is very strict with his children, not allowing them to spend money recklessly. He has devoted all his money and energies to the enterprise. He said:

> I can now see clearly that state enterprises are bound tightly. The only way out for them is an acceleration of reform. I intend my enterprise to compete with them and spur them forward. In the future I shall turn my enterprise over to the state; I may become a manager, or a regular state worker.

One household in Pingyang *xian* ran a crane factory hiring 106 workers. The household invested all its funds in the factory; at home they didn't even have a television set. The entrepreneur took just 5,000 *yuan* out of the business in annual wages, and even borrowed money for the business from his relatives. He still has two risks: to be called a capitalist or to become bankrupt.

Some employers use most of their profits to subsidize poor families, to nurture local factories, and to assist local cultural and educational undertakings. For example, Zheng Hanmeng, the former secretary of the party branch of Shangyan *cun* in Huanghua *xiang*, in 1980 contracted from the production brigade an almost bankrupt instrument and meter plant, and hired 60 labourers. At the end of every year, he discusses with the hired workers their intentions for the following year. For those who want to leave, he provides a copy of the product catalogue and a 500 *yuan* allowance for a business trip. If things don't go well for those who have left, he welcomes them back to work for him. Liu Youzhe, an employer who runs the Hongqiao television components factory in Hongqiao in 1984 provided 2–3,000 *yuan* in subsidies to families in difficulties. He handed over part of his business to some people who had attempted to earn a living outside but had made losses, and he arranged for children of poor families to work in his factory. Liu also admitted to work in the factory two people who were reckless gamblers with evil habits; in one year they earned 10,000 *yuan*, and they were transformed into workers earning their own livings. As a result of these things both the government and the people had a good opinion of Liu Youzhe. Many employers have set up systems of labour insurance and welfare for staff and workers, arranged for their hired workers to study culture and technology, and initiated pension funds.

The employees are not the proletarians of a capitalist society. Around 30 per cent of hired workers are the children, apprentices, and neighbours of employers' close friends. If the friends of employers' friends and the relatives of employers' relatives are included, the proportion, perhaps, could be as high as 90 per cent. Seventy per cent of the girls work to earn money for dowries. Many employees work in order to learn productive skills and obtain experience in order to run their own businesses afterwards. The relationship between the employers and the hired workers for the most part is one of imparting knowledge, assistance and guidance; the employment process is one of study and nurturing talents. Employers and employees have an equal political status. Even the workers in Liushiqiaotou waiting to be hired have cheerful expressions, are well dressed, healthy and strong, and continually laughing and joking. Surely they cannot be mentioned in the same breath as the terrified proletarians described by Marx in *Kapital*, who followed despairingly as the capitalists strode forward with their heads held high. They are not proletarians with invisible chains around their necks; they are extremely independent. If they consider that the income they obtain as hired workers is less than they could get at home, then they don't have to hire themselves out. Some hired workers said, 'We are transferring happily from agricultural to industrial work.'

Now let us look at the means of production controlled by the employers.

If the employer is just a contractor, then he has power only over the use of means of production. If the employer's investment is financed by state bank loans, then he must accept the bank's supervision and run his business in accordance with socialist policies. Even if the investment is all self-financed, it has nothing in common with 'primitive capitalist accumulation', since most of it comes from legitimate labour. Thus, the 'big labour-hiring households' under socialism have a different nature from the capitalist enterprise. To some extent, the former can be characterized as labour and capital mutually benefiting and working together to develop the local economy in backward areas. Because of many subjective and objective conditions in socialist society, expansion of this kind of enterprise will not result in polarization. Rather, able and more hard-working people get rich first. Then they lead along the people behind them to become rich afterwards, and finally, the whole village becomes rich. Take the case of Ye Changqing, a young entrepreneur in Liushi *zhen*'s Liuzhuang *cun*. He introduced a new product to his village, hired 80 workers, taught local people the skills, lent them money to set up family factories, and helped them to sell the products. He helped the whole village to become rich; 80 per cent of the formerly poverty-stricken households have built beautiful, multi-storey houses. When this 'young capitalist' died in an accident, the whole village – young and old, men and women – attended his funeral in tears.

The degree of exploitation of hired workers, and the amount of surplus value gained by the 'big labour-hiring households' is very complex and extremely difficult to measure. For example, in Wenzhou, only a few 'big labour-hiring households' obtain annual profits of 50,000 *yuan*. Now let us do some calculations. Generally, it needs at least 300,000 *yuan* of capital to make 50,000 *yuan* of profit. If the employer puts the same amount of money (300,000 *yuan*) into a bank he can earn about 20,000 *yuan* of interest in a year. The interest cannot be considered as an exploitation, so we must deduct 20,000 from 50,000, leaving 30,000 *yuan*, from which a further deduction (rent) is needed as the employer runs the factory in his own house. Three or four members of the employer's family work together in the factory, each earning 4,000–5,000 *yuan* a year. The employer himself works as a manager but holds many other posts at the same time, such as purchasing agent, accountant, storeman, and skilled worker. His annual income is over 10,000 *yuan*, or just twice that of a highly skilled worker (over 5,000 *yuan* a year) who has been invited to come from outside to work in Wenzhou. The employer's income is seven to eight times – and his family members' four to five times – higher than an average worker's income (about 1,200 *yuan* a year). As we have seen from the calculation, the so-called 'capitalists' in the 'big labour-hiring households' in Wenzhou are pitifully small and are in an entirely different league from the big capitalists in the old China, in the United States and Hong Kong. In fact, the reason they earn more than ordinary working people is mainly that they work much harder, both physically and mentally. To sum up, we should analyse objectively the capitalist nature of the 'big labour-hiring households'; we should not make dogmatic judgements and jump to conclusions without proof. We should not exaggerate things nor feel unduly anxious about these things.

The trend of development

The 120 'big labour-hiring households' have a total of about 5,000 workers, which accounts for only 2.3 per cent of Wenzhou's total rural labour force. The total output value of those households is only about 40 million *yuan*, or 7 per cent of the gross value of output produced in Wenzhou's rural areas. Therefore, their proportion and economic strength in the local economy are very small. Moreover, labour hiring occurs only in some parts of the area. State and collective enterprises are still in a dominant position in Wenzhou in terms of both the number of workers and their economic strength. According to the 1985 statistics, of the total industrial product value produced in both urban and rural areas of Wenzhou, the state enterprises produced 18.43 per cent; the collective enterprises 70.17 per cent, and the private economy only 14 per cent. Labour hiring in Wenzhou is strikingly developed compared to other parts of the country due to a series of special historical and objective factors. Within the national economy as a whole, labour-hiring enterprises are just a drop in the ocean. Even if in the future the role of Wenzhou's relatively large-scale labour-hiring enterprises becomes much bigger, it still will be unable to change the whole structure of the national economy, with public ownership in the dominant position. Although the 'big labour-hiring households' will be allowed to exist and grow for quite a long time, looked at from the point of view of objective necessity and their trend of development, it is absolutely impossible that they will be able to play a pivotal role, controlling either the economic base or the superstructure. First of all, they will be obstructed by the socialist economic base in which public ownership is dominant; China's land, mines, sea, ports, and large and medium-sized enterprises are all in the state's hands and cannot freely be bought and sold. Their growth will not be as unimpeded as at present. As the reform of large and medium-sized state enterprises deepens, and the collective economy steadily improves, they will be challenged by vigorous competition from enterprises which have much greater economic strength and possess much more advanced equipment than they do. Second, we know clearly from our socialist superstructure guided by Marxism and Leninism and based on public ownership, that labour hiring is just a factor that is used temporarily under specific circumstances to stimulate the development of the productive forces. If we allow labour-hiring enterprises to develop without check to the point where they form a class force, then China will once again sink into a society with class antagonism and the productive forces will be destroyed. Thus, both the socialist state authorities and the economic management organizations should keep a close watch on the trends in labour hiring, and try to adopt well thought out measures to restrain and guide enterprises with hired workers, so as to ensure that they take the socialist path.

The advantages and disadvantages

Naturally the socio-economic nature of the 'big labour-hiring households' is an important aspect of this question. Another important aspect is their micro- and macro-economic results, i.e., the issue of whether or not they make a positive contribution to the current socio-economic expansion. If the present labour hiring only benefited the employers and was of benefit to the local Wenzhou area, but had a negative effect on national economy's growth and upon macro-economic results, then we could not permit its existence and expansion. There are big disputes about this question. My personal view is that Wenzhou's 'big labour-hiring households' are not only relatively highly efficient from a micro-economic point of view, but also that, at the national level, the economic benefits exceed the costs.

The micro-economic efficiency of the 'big labour-hiring households' themselves is clear at a glance and doesn't need much analysis. The following sequence of events occurs frequently. As soon as a nearly bankrupt collective enterprise is contracted to a private employer, it immediately becomes invigorated and within a year earns a profit of over 100,000 *yuan*. State-run enterprises producing the same product as hired labour enterprises, and having much better equipment and access to credit, often have considerably lower economic efficiency than the local hired labour enterprise. In Cangnan *xian*'s Yishan *qu* there is a private enterprise recycling spun and woven textile products, which has a ratio of investment to output of 1:10, and a ratio of fixed capital to profits of 1:8.5; a state-run enterprise producing the same products has a ratio of investment to output of 1:2, and of fixed capital to profits of 1:2.9. When we visited private employer Wen Guishi, he said:

> Yesterday I went to look at a state-run factory and a collective factory both producing the same products as my factory. They receive electricity at parity price. Their equipment is better than mine, and the rate of interest they pay on loans is lower than mine, but they are in a muddle. From above there are lots of regulations and checks. Internally, costs are high, with many disputes over trifles. They 'eat from the big pot' and there is no way to galvanize their enthusiasm. The factory managers continuously complain of being hard done by. My own factory makes high profits. A lot of people vie with each other to enter it, but it's very difficult since I require my workers to have a high cultural level and a good bearing. The kind of enterprise I want to run has not yet come into being.

It is much more complex to analyse the 'big labour-hiring households' from the perspective of the whole economy and their macro-economic efficiency. Some people maintain that 'big labour-hiring households' have the following deficiencies:

1. Their profits are too big and are made too easily. They have relied principally upon exploiting the loopholes which have appeared in the course of the economic reform. They evade taxes, passing off fake goods as genuine, buy and sell illegally, and possess much greater autonomy than state and collective enterprises. Consequently, each brick with which they build their high buildings is extracted from the foot of the socialist wall.

2. They simply seek profit, so that their production is anarchic, and damaging to the state plan. This not only results in much wasteful duplication in construction and production, but also exacerbates the already extremely tense situation in transport, power and raw material supply.

3. Unless we pay serious attention to the cruel exploitation of hired workers, antagonistic social contradictions will result.

4. On account of the limitations of private individuals' capital, a big expansion of private enterprises will lead to an undesirable reduction in the size structure of China's enterprises.

These shortcomings do, in fact, all exist to some degree. We should, however, distinguish between minor shortcomings which certainly can result in the midst of something that is of big overall benefit, isolated deficiencies which can be controlled and overcome, as well as problems which exist across the whole country and are not just associated with 'big labour-hiring households'. In respect to the first of the alleged short-comings mentioned above, the 'big labour-hiring households' do have large tax and marketing advantages compared to the average state-run or collective enterprise. They can invest their capital as they choose in products for which the price is worthwhile. There are, however, many respects in which they are in a worse position than state and collective enterprises. Their electricity costs 50–60 *fen* per kilowatt-hour; their raw materials are bought at market-determined high prices, and they have to borrow from non-institutional sources at high rates of interest. Compared to scattered individual households, 'big labour-hiring households' are rather more regularized and less often sell fake goods as genuine. Their profits reflect the valuable functions they perform in running their businesses well, providing information, working hard, taking risks, daring to start up new undertakings, and in myriad different ways satisfying multiple social needs. As for problems of 'blindness' and waste through duplication, in the future as the autonomy of state enterprises increases and directive planning is replaced by guidance planning, these problems also will come to affect state enterprises. The crux of the matter is that we must improve and strengthen indirect macro-economic regulation and the regulatory functions of key cities' economic management departments. The products of Wenzhou's 'big labour-hiring households' mainly make use of left-over bits and pieces, and fill in deficiencies and gaps. It is not at all clear that they compete fiercely with state enterprises for energy and by producing the same type of products, and thereby undermine the state plan. If, in the future, they do compete with state enterprises in the same product markets, then this in fact is beneficial since the superior product will defeat the inferior in a competitive struggle. If the commodity economy did not have duplication of products, then it would be difficult to launch competition.

As for the third alleged problem, namely cruel exploitation, this can be solved in the future through legislation. In fact, exploitation in Wenzhou today is not widespread, and up to the present there have been no disputes between employers and hired workers. In respect to the question of abnormally small scale, I consider that, in general, the best role for private labour-hiring enterprises is 'filling in the gaps'. In our system, very large-scale, private, modern, hired labour enterprises cannot grow; nor is it appropriate to encourage them. The appropriate role for private labour-hiring enterprises is in the relatively small-scale sector. One can anticipate that in future 'big labour-hiring households' will not account for a large proportion of hired labour nationally, so they certainly will not be responsible for any abnormalities in the size structure of industrial enterprises across the country as a whole. The 'abnormalities' associated with 'big labour-hiring households' relate to the origins, level and manner of use of their profits. Not only may a portion of their excessively high incomes be irrational, but these incomes can, moreover, given the present level of popular consciousness, easily cause resentment and damage the production enthusiasm of a very large portion of the population. Thus, we must adopt measures to regulate and restrict these incomes (the issue will be discussed in detail later).

From the point of view of national economic development, the 'big labour-hiring households' have the following positive roles:

1. They help to promote the integration of the huge surplus labour force with dispersed, idle capital. Not only do they increase society's wealth, but they also contribute to social stability. The expansion of household enterprises has absorbed about 800,000 surplus workers over the whole area and takes in 100,000 new workers each year.

2. They fill the gaps in the output structure which the large or medium-sized state enterprises cannot, or do not, wish to meet. In this way they satisfy multiple social needs.

3. They provide the multitude of local individual household businesses with raw materials, simple equipment and components for them to assemble. They have led the process of local industrial development, and to a considerable degree have transformed the structure of production in a backward area.

4. Through market competition they exert external pressure on state and collective enterprises, contributing to the sense of urgency about their reforms. The experiences of 'big labour-hiring households' in production, management and marketing can be used as examples for state and collective enterprises to learn from.

They discover and nurture a large number of daring entrepreneurs who understand technology and are good at management. This enables the numerous talented people who were suppressed and stifled under the old system to have ample scope to bring their abilities into play in the great cause of China's Four Modernizations. When people in the different trades and occupations bring all their physical energies and talents into play according to their specializations, and the people have ease of mind, then there can be a stable national unity of the component parts.

Overall, the advantages of 'big labour-hiring households' in Wenzhou outweigh the disadvantages. We should, however, reflect soberly that they are able to expand smoothly and play a positive role in China's economic development on account of the present special circumstances under which they run their businesses. They can raise their own capital, run their businesses independently, decide how they distribute their income, and are solely responsible for their profits and losses. The 'superiority' of private enterprises with hired labour is conditional; it should not be made a fetish of. Nor should we draw the erroneous conclusion that 'public' is not as good as 'private'. From an overall point of view, at the present stage of social development, a society with public ownership and without antagonistic class struggle is greatly superior to a society with private ownership. This is an objective truth which has been proved by Marxist theory, and the practice of thousands of millions of people across the world. Moreover, we should note that the macro-economic integration of state and collective enterprises can generate a series of superiorities peculiar to public ownership, which a private ownership society does not possess. The individual public enterprises, however, possess less independence, autonomy and vitality than private labour-hiring enterprises. Consequently, if suitable measures are not taken to restrict and guide the 'big labour-hiring households' with 'differential advantages', then even if there was basic equality in respect to markets and equipment, it would be very hard for the former to compete with the latter. Over time, this could lead to private economy eating away at the public economy, corroding both the base and superstructure of the socialist economy. Moreover, if objective factors lead to higher incomes in labour-hiring enterprises than in state and collective enterprises, then the morale of staff and workers in the latter will be affected. Thus, the correct policy is both to make use of the positive role played by labour-hiring enterprises at present, and appropriately to restrict and guide them; that is to say, we cannot *not* restrict them, but nor can we restrict them completely.

The following are the measures that we should adopt towards the labour-hiring enterprises:

1. The transition from the old economic system to the new one should be accelerated, and the independence of large and medium-sized state and collective enterprises increased further, so that the market system can be perfected, and indirect macro-adjustment can be carried out well. During the current economic transition, however, when various regulatory mechanisms are incomplete and far from perfect, and legislation regarding

labour-hiring enterprises has not yet been enacted, the development of labour-hiring enterprises should be suitably restricted. Certain enterprises should be denied access to credit. Taxation should be tightened up rapidly. Administrative measures must be strengthened, preventing swindling and other illegal activities. These measures will prevent the enterprises from utilizing loopholes appearing while the system changes track to obtain excessive illegitimate profits and thereby produce imbalance in socio-economic life. We cannot proceed from traditional ownership theories (collective enterprises have greater autonomy than state enterprises, and private enterprises have more autonomy than collective enterprises) under which artificial superiority is created for private enterprises. If, however, labour-hiring enterprises are superior to state enterprises, even after these restrictive measures are adopted, then this will act as a considerable spur to state enterprises.

2. The economic management departments in cities of all sizes must put into effect measures to supervise and regulate labour-hiring enterprises. A set of regulations about the responsibilities, rights and benefits of these departments should be enacted in order that they handle these matters in accordance with the spirit of central policies, and control flexibly the labour-hiring enterprises on the basis of concrete conditions.

3. The enactment of laws about labour-hiring enterprises must be speeded up in order to avoid the detrimental effects on economic development arising from their short-term behaviour.

4. After the economic system has basically completed its change of track from the old to the new system, and competition between state, collective and private labour-hiring enterprises has been put on an equal footing, it will still be necessary to adopt measures to restrict labour-hiring enterprises, though, naturally, these will be very different from those at present.

There are several different viewpoints worth considering in respect of restrictive measures. Some comrades propose restricting the number of hired workers in labour-hiring enterprises. Document 1 of 1984, issued by the Central Committee of the Chinese Communist Party, placed a limit of seven on the number of hired labourers in one enterprise. Perhaps this is based on Marx's observations in *Kapital*, in which he considered that a small owner became a capitalist if he hired more than eight workers. This was purely hypothetical, however, and had great qualifications. It cannot be copied mechanically. The key questions concern the nature of the industry, the rate of exploitation, the level of exploitation and whether or not employers participate in labour, rather than the number of hired workers. Ota Sik, who advocates allowing the expansion of small, private, labour-hiring enterprises in a socialist society, believes that it is unscientific to regulate the number of hired labourers, since a given number of hired labourers is of different significance in different trades. For example, an employer hiring two or three workers in commerce might make a lot more money than someone hiring the same number of workers in industry, and within industry the conditions vary from branch to branch. Moreover, we should recognize that restricting the number of hired workers affects economies of scale for labour-hiring enterprises.

Some people advocate a policy of 'withholding' from labourer-hiring enterprises on all occasions. For example, they should be restricted through the credit mechanism. Supply and marketing facilities should be 'withheld', and they should be restricted through administrative measures. This is inappropriate. When the objective conditions have become equal for the various components of the economic system, adopting such policies towards the labour-hiring enterprises is equivalent to providing biased advantages to the state and collective enterprises. Such enterprises cannot then become competitive and energetic, and, consequently, this is harmful to increased efficiency.

Some people consider that restriction should be achieved mainly by controls on profits. I think this is a very worthwhile suggestion. Ota Sik advocates that a limit should be set to labour-hiring enterprises' profits (e.g., the employer's income out of profits cannot be more than twice that of a skilled labourer). Any profits beyond this amount cannot be retained by the employer, and the major part (80 per cent, for instance) should be handed over to society. This 'handing over' should not be through taxation, but should be through transfer into enterprise investment. Since the capital formed by this investment is under the control of the workers collectively, rather than the employers, and since a new enterprise may be formed in the process, in which there is both individual and collective capital, Sik calls this a 'compound company'. Since the collective capital therein is not based on contradictory relationships between capitalists and proletarians but belongs to labourers themselves, Sik calls this 'neutral capital'. Sik's tentative ideas are very worthy of study, but in certain respects are insufficiently integrated. For example, his proposition that an employer's income should be not more than twice that of a skilled worker will not work. He has not considered the interest which the employer ought to receive on his initial capital, or the question of risk income. If the employers' incomes are as low as in Sik's scheme, then employers would prefer to invest their capital in a bank and obtain interest rather than to invest in setting up a private enterprise.

Lin Qingsong and others have considered this question more thoroughly. They propose that employers must participate in work, and receive wages according to the complexity of their work. On that part of their dividend income which exceeds the interest from depositing the funds in the bank and is in excess of three times the average worker's wage, the state should levy a progressive dividend income tax. I would like to add that the employers' dividend income not only includes appropriate interest on capital, but also includes risk income and reward for setting up the enterprise. Looked at in this light, employers' incomes should be allowed to exceed the average worker's by rather more, perhaps fivefold. Only by so doing can the employers' pioneering enthusiasm be preserved. The suggestion of Lin Qingsong *et al.* that employers ought to participate in labour should be altered to a requirement to participate in either labour or management. Sik's suggestion of the 'mixed company' and 'neutral capital' may create a theoretical problem, whether or not there is a flavour of 'distributive determinism'. In my view, we shouldn't worry any further about this. In a socialist society where the public economy is in the dominant position, and in a society where the broad mass of workers are the masters in their own house, private employers are highly controllable and malleable. The socialist superstructure has the power, whenever needed, to change the nature of the feeble private enterprises by altering the method of profit distribution (or even confiscating the profits) according to the objective necessity of national economic development. In the final analysis, this type of change is determined by the economic base of public ownership, and not purely by distribution. This is because only if the superstructure is based on public ownership will it be able to change the nature of private enterprise, according to the whole society's developmental needs. Of course, it is utopian to apply mechanically to capitalist society the theory and practice of changing the nature of private enterprise through the method of profit distribution, since capitalism's economic base and superstructure are different from those of socialist society. Under capitalism, any encroachment upon the economic interests of capitalist enterprises will lead to forceful opposition; profit distribution is acceptable only if it is to their benefit. According to Engels, capitalist society is one in which 'people plan their affairs but the realization of their plans depends on God' (meaning that it is impossible for capitalists self-consciously to utilize economic laws), whereas socialist society is one in which 'people plan their affairs and the realization of their plans is in their own hands'. Certainly, there is no way in which socialist society is able completely to achieve 'realization of human plans in people's own hands', but people's subjective initiative is much greater than in capitalist society. One reason is that, armed with Marxist scientific theory, people have a better understanding of objective economic laws. Another is that socialist society does not have two classes with sharply conflicting interests.

5. This concerns guidance. Many comrades have discussed methods of promoting the conglomeration of different types of funds and state share-holding in private enterprises. In my opinion, if basically we can adopt Sik's methods of guiding the development of private labour-hiring enterprises towards 'mixed companies', then there is no immediate urgency to conglomerate funds, or for the state to hold shares. Conglomeration of funds will cause many conflicts of interest. Especially difficult to resolve is the issue of 'the one who speaks is the one who is taken seriously'; this will impede greatly the pioneering spirit of capable people. Therefore, in Wenzhou, as long as individuals are able to run their own enterprises, they are absolutely unwilling to form joint companies with conglomerated funds. Many conglomerates exist in name only; some conglomerates disintegrate very quickly. As for share-holding by the state, if the state

intervenes in employers' decision-making and affairs of management, then the competitive superiority of private enterprises will be reduced substantially. But if the state pays no attention to the private employers' management and only supplies funds and collects dividends, will this not foster artificially the strength of private economy?

Frankly speaking, there are three aspects to the superiority of the private employers: first, there is an extremely direct relation between the enterprise's production results and the employer's income; second, the employer is a managerially and administratively talented person rich in innovative, risk-taking and pioneering spirit, developed in the course of fierce competitive struggle; third, unlike state and collective enterprises' plant managers, employers' managerial activities are not constrained in every respect. These issues provide theoreticians with an extremely important theoretical problem: how can state and collective enterprises' plant managers achieve what the private employers have achieved regarding the development of production and management, without changing the nature of public ownership (while, naturally, breaking away from a great many traditional, erroneous concepts)?

There are, perhaps, people who say that this will result in macro-economic chaos. I do not think this is so. The crux of the matter is whether it is true that the more developed the commodity economy, the higher the degree of economic anarchy. The system of macro-economic guidance should be altered in step with the development of the commodity economy, with indirect regulation greatly enhanced, and the role of core cities in enterprise regulation considerably strengthened. The core cities should become the intermediaries between the centre and the myriad enterprises. Following the expansion of the commodity economy, people's consciousness and concepts of value should change. We must not only break away from the system of workers eating from the enterprise's 'big rice bowl' and enterprises eating from the nation's 'big rice bowl' but also break away from the situation of the state eating from the enterprises' and the workers' 'big rice bowls'. To achieve this it is necessary to specify the responsibilities, rights, and benefits of all personnel in the superstructure; decision-making departments must be made legally and economically responsible for their decisions. Only then can cadres in economic management concentrate their energies on economic construction, rather than on trifling matters unrelated to either material or spiritual construction. This is another way of saying that reform of the economic system is a grand project embracing the whole society. Unless the economic base and the superstructure are reformed as an integrated system, the benefits from different aspects of the reform may cancel each other out; tensions and conflicts will appear ceaselessly, creating enormous ideological confusion, and people will find it increasingly difficult to understand the situation. Only if we advance resolutely towards the goal of developing the socialist commodity economy, can we maintain the socialist path with public ownership in the dominant position. Only by taking this path can people's intelligence and wisdom be brought into play as never before, the productive forces advance at a high speed, both micro- and macro-economic efficiency rapidly increase, the non-antagonistic classes give full play to private incentives as well as realize the public sector's superiority. Only by taking this path will the socialist system, which is the one best suited to combining organically concentration and dispersion, reveal its radiant glory.

9. Small Town Construction: an Alternative Path

Pei Xiaoge

Small town construction in China is the only way to make the transition to a unified economy from a dual economy with an advanced industrial, and a backward agricultural, sector. Exploring the patterns of small town construction and development is an important task in carrying out socialist modernization.

The past development of the Cangnan area is a typical example of China's method of small town construction. It has relied upon small town collective enterprises to provide accumulation funds to supplement state investment, and upon using both in combination with rural labour power and publicly owned industrial means of production for small town construction. This is one path to small town construction in China, but this chapter examines the possibilities for following a different path in the light of an analysis of the experience in Longgang *zhen*.

Longgang's economic and geographical situation

Longgang *zhen* is located in Wenzhou municipality's Cangnan *xian*. Its construction only began at the end of 1983 but already it covers an area of three square kilometres and has a population of 30,000. Before Longgang's construction began, the site consisted of five villages from Longjiang and Yanjiang *xiang* with a total population of a little over 6,000; their backward and impoverished conditions were typical of rural areas throughout Wenzhou municipality.

Longgang's construction was the result of important economic and geographical factors. The central role played by individual household industry in the all-round development of the rural commodity economy helped to initiate Longgang's construction. After 1979 and the implementation of a combination of production responsibility systems and other appropriate policies, many of Wenzhou's peasants discovered that the path to the elimination of poverty and the creation of wealth lay in the promotion of individual household industry by relying on supply and marketing teams and specialized commodity markets. Individual household industry and specialized markets developed particularly quickly in Cangnan *xian*. For example, the *xian* saw the successive emergence of a spinning and weaving industry in Yishan, aluminium and plastic product processing in Jinxiang and firework production in Qianku; in all, some 18 specialist *xiang* (*zhen*) appeared, comprising more than 44,000 specialist households and more than 54,000 joint economic undertakings. By 1984, the value of individual household industry accounted for 50 per cent of the gross value of industrial and agricultural output and links had been achieved with twelve specialist markets at a national level. In Yishan, Qianku, Jinxiang and other such areas, more than 80 per cent of the total rural labour force was employed in individual household industry and trading; living standards of the masses were high, and more than 80 per cent of households had built multi-storeyed houses.

The emergence of individual and joint household industry throughout Wenzhou municipality has meant that the former dominance of the natural economy has gradually been replaced by that of the commodity economy. The desire of Cangnan's peasants to 'take the lead in getting rich' by engaging in industry and commerce has led to a demand for more convenient means of transportation and the more extensive infrastructure offered by towns and cities so they can set up more factories, establish shops and expand their scale of operation. From this point of view, the construction of Longgang *zhen* was begun at the right time.

The Longgang area is located in the lower reaches of the Ao river, one of Zhejiang province's eight large river systems, and has a hinterland of around 4,000 square kilometres. Its port facilities on the southern bank of the Ao river's lower reaches are good, and there is an extensive network of rivers and waterways extending in all directions. The main Zhejiang–Fujian road crosses Cangnan *xian* and road travel is generally easy. Longgang is only 50 nautical miles from the mouth of the Ou river in Wenzhou municipality and from the port of Shacheng in Fujian province; it has longer-distance links with Shanghai, Lianyungang (Jiangsu province), Dalian, Fuzhou, etc., whilst close by along the coast are the ports of Bajin, Yanting, Shiping, Chixi and Xiaguan. By means of inland waterways, it is linked to Mabu, Shuitou and other ports in Pingyang county, as well as to Lingxi, Qianku, Jinxiang and Yishan; roads link the town with Wenzhou and with Fujian province. Because of these transport advantages, Longgang is the economic centre of both Cangnan and Pingyang *xian* and is also a centre for the distribution and collection of goods and materials to and from Taishun and Wencheng *xian*, as well as for several ports in northern Fujian province. It annually handles more than 400,000 tons of goods and over two million passengers. In addition, Longgang is the main fishing centre for Wenzhou municipality with fishing grounds abounding in prawns, groupers, herring etc.; aquatic product output totals more than 35,000 tons per annum, of which much is exported.

The central role played by individual household industry in the rural commodity economy has necessitated an expansion of small town construction in Cangnan *xian*. Moreover, Longgang possesses many locational advantages for commercial expansion. Therefore, it was a wise decision for Cangnan *xian* to choose Longgang for the construction of a new town.

Financing small town construction in Longgang

Longgang *zhen* is similar to other towns and cities in that it is the economic centre of a region, a focus for commodity circulation, and has followed a similar pattern of development. But it is also unique because its construction has taken place in Wenzhou against a background in which individual household industry has played the key role in the development of the commodity economy. Its construction has relied neither upon state investment (whether by national, *xian* or *zhen* government) nor upon funds from collective industry; instead, it has relied upon the strength of the industrial and commercial enterprises of the individual peasant sector.

The construction of Longgang *zhen* on a piece of sandy ground needed a large number of enterprises to initiate it, and therefore the question of its funding needed to be solved urgently. Cangnan *xian* had been newly created in only 1984 from part of Pingyang *xian* and therefore its basic construction needs were many. Its state budget for basic construction investment was, however, limited to 10 million *yuan* per annum. According to an estimate produced by the Longgang *zhen* committee, the town's construction would involve a long gestation period (eight or nine years) even if this entire county budget was allocated to it. The construction of basic roads, water supply and sewerage alone would require some 6 million *yuan*. Given this lengthy time horizon and other demands upon the county budget, it was decided that local conditions meant that there was no choice but to rely upon direct funding and investment by the individual household sector.

Longgang's construction has relied upon all kinds of investors for the bulk of its investment funds. Over a period of more than two years, the number of people investing in Longgang grew progressively greater whilst the scope of investment broadened from an initial emphasis on housing towards shops, industry, transport, etc. The investors themselves initially came mainly from four areas of Cangnan *xian* located on the southern bank of the Ao river, but again, this gradually widened to include investors from other counties and even from outside the province. So far, Longgang has attracted more than 5,000 households drawn from three provinces and from eight *xian*. Total investment has amounted to 133 million *yuan*, of which 12.16 million have been provided by the state, 6.865 million by pooled capital, and 114 million by individual households. The combined share of individual households and pooled capital has thus amounted to more than 90 per cent of the investment total, and specialized households with assets of more than 30,000 *yuan* have featured prominently amongst the investors. Large numbers of entrepreneurs and skilled traders from Cangnan *xian*'s Yishan, Qianku and Jinxiang *xiang* (*zhen*) have moved to Longgang, whilst most of those that did not move established branches in the town. These specialized households are the leaders in commodity production and have particularly strong management skills, and have provided the main impetus during the brief two-year period of Longgang's construction. Many types of specialist areas of production from neighbouring *xian* are now concentrated in Longgang; these include shipbuilding, machinery, clothing, arts and crafts, glass fibre, light spinning, printing, coloured plastic prints, fine synthetic fibres and other industries. There has also been strong expansion of transport companies and tertiary industry. The gross value of industrial production totalled 15.5 million *yuan* in 1985, compared to just 1.48 million in 1984. Another source of finance has been funds provided by the masses. According to the cadre in charge of the project, Longgang has used funds from a variety of sources including grants, loans and pooled investment.

Grants have come mainly from Wenzhou municipality itself, raised by business taxes, public utility charges and land taxation. The town government offered a settlement allowance of 5,000 *yuan* for every *mu* of land taken over from the peasants for development. The taking over of development land has been conducted in a co-ordinated manner by the *zhen* government, which has divided up the town into industrial, commercial and recreational zones to produce a rational layout. The government stipulated that, in order to rationalize land use and ensure a well laid-out street plan, every building was to be of three storeys in height and was to occupy 42 square metres. Following construction, a municipality service fee of 1,900–5,600 *yuan* per building was levied, the amount depending on the zone; in addition, a fixed public utility charge per building and a one-off real estate tax of 4,000 *yuan* per building were also levied. Individually constructed and used buildings, as well as jointly constructed and used buildings, could be used to set up factories or shops, rented out, or used for dwellings. Many of those constructed have combined dwellings in their top half, with shops in the bottom part. Construction costs were to be met entirely by the investors. The municipal government's income from service fees, etc., is used for public welfare: road construction, water supply, waste disposal, schools and public toilets, etc. Revenue from this source has amounted to 7.6 million *yuan*.

Funds raised by borrowing have been of many types. For example, in order to fund the construction of a food market, the town government drew up a regulation stipulating that anyone wanting to set up a stall for trading must first obtain a commercial enterprise licence from the town committee and, when setting up the stall, had to place a deposit of 300–500 *yuan* which was to be repaid monthly, free of any interest payment. Using this method, 76,400 *yuan* was raised in only three days from 220 persons and, after 28 days, a concrete site and a roof structure of steel and glass fibre with an area of 1,638 square metres for the food market had been constructed.

The investment funds for Longgang's construction have come from many different types of business enterprises including large ones, such as the Chuanlong limited company, the Jilin electrical wire company

(Longgang branch), the Longhua woollen sweater company, the Hubei province Shiyan city daily necessities company (Longgang branch), the aquatic products' market, the building materials' market, the cinemas, etc. Some of the funds pooled by enterprises have been loans and some have been grants.

Longgang's construction has been a splendid achievement. Up to the end of August 1985, 75 million *yuan* had been invested and 750,000 square metres of buildings had been started, of which 300,000 square metres had already been finished. In one year, investment totalled 92.03 million *yuan* and completed buildings covered 433,600 square metres, 27 roads were finished, of which five ran north–south, and 22 east–west; the longest of these was the Longgang circular road of 3.5 kilometres and the shortest was People's Road at 30 metres. Eleven road bridges have already been completed as have 1,000 multi-storeyed dwellings, totalling more than 300,000 square metres. Fifteen sets of public toilets have also been built, as well as a middle school covering 3,000 square metres, two primary schools of more than 2,000 square metres and a kindergarten covering over 600 square metres. In the first half of 1985 alone, the middle school enrolled 200 pupils whilst the primary schools and kindergarten enrolled 1,800 and 300 respectively. The pumping station is already capable of producing 2,000 tons of water daily and, beginning from New Year's Day 1985, a 35,000 volt electricity substation has been in operation. The whole town has now been provided with a basic road, water, electricity and sewerage network. At the moment, there are 37 engineering teams in the town working on the construction of new items such as three cinemas, a concert hall and several hotels. Longgang's achievements are remarkable; no wonder some say that in the future it will be a city comparable to Wenzhou and that some people have even given it the new name of 'Sanjiang' (Three River) city because it is close to the town of Aojiang (Ao river) and the *xiang* of Longjiang (Long river) and Yanjiang (Yan river). The experience gained in the construction of Longgang has provided valuable material for our exploration of which route to follow in constructing small towns in China.

The lessons from town construction in Longgang for other parts of China

In a short two-year period, and without relying on either foreign capital or state investment funds, Longgang has been transformed from a poor village into a forest of tall, regular and beautiful buildings with the appearance of an elegant and modern town; it is a masterpiece of small town construction. This process suggests the following lessons in analysing the path that China should take in small town construction:

Developing the rural commodity economy is a powerful force for promoting small town construction

Even in the early years of China's feudal society, the buds of the commodity economy existed in the countryside but, for several thousand years, these buds were held in check by the self-sufficient and semi-sufficient nature of the rural economy. Things changed somewhat after Liberation but, because of continuous restriction on the growth of the commodity economy, self-sufficient and semi-sufficient production continued to predominate. No fundamental change occurred in the backward rural economy in which 800 million peasants were involved in grain production and consumption, and thus there was no stimulus to small town construction, which remained stagnant. The experience of Longgang shows that, from the time of the smashing of the self- and semi-sufficient economy by the commodity economy, peasant commodity producers needed small towns to provide a location for market exchange and in which to set up businesses. This provided a powerful force for small town development. The pushing forward of small town construction by the growth of the commodity economy is shown very clearly by the way Longgang's buildings combine dwellings at the top and shops at the bottom. The town's construction on such a large scale could not have been possible without the growth of the rural commodity economy and the demand for small town construction that it led to. Therefore, in practice, we must promote simultaneously the development of the rural commodity economy and the construction of small towns. The commodity economy must be used to promote small town construction and, simultaneously, small town construction must be adapted to the requirements of the commodity economy. In this way, expansion of the commodity economy will complement the construction of small towns. Together they will provide a powerful catalyst in transforming China's rural backwardness and her rural industrial structure.

The individual economy must be fully brought into play in the process of small town construction
Wenzhou's economic boom and Longgang's construction have both relied upon the strength of individual and joint household industry. The mechanization of Wenzhou's individual and joint household handicraft industry shows not only that individual and joint ownership is suitable for the handicraft industry in backward areas, but also that it can make use of advanced machinery and be innovative in its use of such machinery. The traditional view, that the individual economy could only serve as a complementary sector in China's economy because it was unable to exploit the benefits from division of labour – in contrast to big and powerful collective enterprises – and so would gradually wither away, is not correct. By means of expansion and the fact that producers are responsible directly for profits or losses, their enthusiasm has been stimulated. Consequently, Wenzhou's economy has boomed and Longgang's construction has been rapid. It has, however, also been partly attributable to the fact that the expansion of medium-sized markets caused by the reform of China's economic system has been exploited by individual sector enterprises, but not by state enterprises in which reform is incomplete, and because

loopholes in macro-economic indirect enterprise control have not yet been eliminated. Nevertheless, their rapid development is certainly also because the individual economy has played a big and important role in bringing into play production enthusiasm. The implementation of the rural production responsibility system has led to a large increase in the share of the individual, relative to the collective, sector and also to the possibility for peasants in the individual economy to switch to industry and commerce. It has destroyed the old system of most peasants tied to the land in self-sufficient production working from sunrise to sunset, and allowed peasants to manage production themselves and use their labour time flexibly. These trends are all advantageous for the promotion of rural commodity development, the expansion of small town construction and for establishing a unified rather than a dual economy in China. Also, because state and collectively run enterprises can only absorb a limited amount of labour, the share of the individual sector in the Chinese economy is likely to grow quickly for some time to come.

Undoubtedly, the growth of the individual economy in Wenzhou has posed some problems. Personal income differentials have grown, the state economy has taken a pounding, standards of living are unstable and product quality is not easy to control. This shows that the requirements of the individual economy must be adapted to the needs of the state sector and that we must press ahead with the transformation and development of the banking and public finance systems. Longgang's experience shows that if we blindly restrict or abolish entirely the individual economy because it is a form of private ownership, then we will lose a force of the utmost importance for the development of the rural commodity economy and the construction of small towns.

We must pay attention to science, and co-ordinating the leadership of *xian* and *zhen* in small town construction

In making a good job of small town construction, it is particularly important to bring into play all types of enthusiasm and to strengthen leadership co-ordination. On the question of small town construction, the approach of the leaders of Cangnan *xian* and Longgang *zhen* has been completely different from that usually adopted; they have paid a good deal of attention to, and worked very hard at, the balanced development of small town construction and the commodity economy in order to make the transformation from a backward to a modern countryside. In collaboration with other relevant departments, they selected a suitable location for the town's construction and drew up a co-ordinated plan. A set of eight standard regulations suitable for the real situation in Longgang were drawn up with regard to site, housing and energy, and the procedures for peasants wishing to move to the town were simplified. A propaganda team of more than 30 people was sent four times in succession to every district to publicize Longgang's favourable geography and general development prospects; the question of the demolition of old housing in Longgang was also appropriately solved. Moreover, the county's relevant departments, to cut down on time wasted on red tape and trifling disagreements, settled many issues on the spot. The choice of an appropriate location, fitting in with the general provincial situation and the town's rapid construction, avoided the usual 'too much land so water must be increased, too much water so land must be increased; demolish then build, build then demolish' problems encountered in small town construction, which cause an unfavourable cycle and lead to an unsystematic layout. Problems were avoided thanks to the active role played by the leaders of Cangnan *xian* and Longgnan *zhen*.

Small rural towns can serve as local centres of government, economy and culture, promote the development of rural commercial and industrial enterprises, satisfy peasant cultural, scientific, health, educational and sporting requirements, absorb surplus rural labour and make agricultural production more scientific and specialized. Unfortunately, in many places at present, there is little popular or leadership awareness of the role to be played by small town construction. This is perhaps an important reason why the development of small town construction has been sluggish and their layout badly planned in many places. If the leaders of every county and township were able to observe the approach of the leaders of Cangnan *xian* and of Longgang *zhen*, the transition from a traditional to a modern economy would quickly give rise to small town construction and also increase the pace of China's agricultural modernization.

Summarizing the above, we can see that the traditional strategy of small town construction has been to rely on the capacity of collective township enterprises and the state. But there is also the alternative strategy in which, under the unified leadership of *xian* and *zhen*, an expanding individual and joint household economy promotes the development of small town construction by fully bringing into play the individual economy and by using every economic sector to provide direct investment and to raise money. The former strategy is appropriate where the state and collective sectors are strong (for instance, Sunan). Its advantages are that it involves few risks, allows income differentials and product quality to be easily controlled, and enables the proportions between agriculture and other economic sectors to be easily adjusted. Its disadvantages are that state and collective funds are limited, as is the ability of these sectors to absorb surplus labour and stimulate productive enthusiasm. Moreover, the speed of construction is slow. This strategy would also require hard work to mobilize the enthusiasm of individuals and the individual economy.

The alternative strategy is suitable in areas where the state and collective economy is weak, but where the individual economy is strong (like Wenzhou). This strategy avoids the problems of the former strategy, but private ownership also gives rise to a number of difficulties, such as income distribution, the problem of taxation and controlling product quality. Popularizing this strategy at a national level also requires a comprehensive reform of the economic system, especially the banking and public finance sectors, while the question of how to combine the individual economy with state and collective economies is a complicated one. But, regardless of this, the experience of constructing Longgang *zhen* shows that this latter strategy is feasible.

China is a vast country with highly diverse economic conditions. Therefore, making the transition from a dual to a unified economic structure will require more than a single, unique approach; similarly, small town construction should not be limited to a single approach. Each area must select the small town development strategy which is best suited to its own particular conditions. This is important not just for small town construction, but also for the immense task of developing the entire Chinese economy.

10. Privatization, Marketization and Polarization

Lin Zili

Wenzhou's household industry accounts for 60 per cent of the total gross value of industrial output in the city. The great majority of household businesses are of the expanded form, that is to say, they employ workers or apprentices. Wenzhou *diqu* at present has over 400 people's (*minjian*) markets of different sizes, including ten famous large commodity production and sales bases; these have begun to form a system of people's markets within the area, including markets both for means of production and for capital. The market mechanism is beginning really to make itself felt. The all-round expansion of household enterprises and the beginnings of the formation of a market system, albeit one that is far from mature, have enabled Wenzhou's commodity economy to advance dramatically. In eight years, the whole city's gross value of industrial and agricultural output has doubled twice over. In 1977, the average per caput income of Wenzhou's peasants was just 55 *yuan*; by 1985 it had risen to 480 *yuan*, with one third of the peasants having an income of over 1,000 *yuan*. Simultaneously, income differentials among the people obviously increased.

The special characteristics of the 'Wenzhou model' – household industry and people's markets – have led to widespread interest and intense debate. Is Wenzhou a 'privatized' economy? Is it 'marketized'? Are Wenzhou's villages 'polarizing'? This is what I mean by the so-called 'components' issue in Wenzhou's commodity economy. The problems that Wenzhou faces exist in China's villages wherever the commodity economy has advanced rapidly and has spread its influence widely. Over the past few years, comrades involved in practical village work, as well as some theoreticians, have thought deeply about these issues. The facts make it clear, however, that these questions cannot be answered by using traditional socialist doctrines as the theoretical base. Whenever these questions are debated right through to their logical conclusion, people cannot avoid taking these issues to a higher plane of discussion: what is socialism? In the final analysis, what does one understand by the 'socialist commodity economy'? If the discussion does not progress to this higher plane, then the so-called 'privatization' question cannot be comprehended.

Concerning socialist scientific knowledge

In Marx's conception, socialism is unity among the workers, and exchange of equal amounts of labour. In Lenin's view, socialism meant equal pay for equal work, which is also the meaning of exchange of equal amounts of labour. Marx's exchange of equal amounts of labour is, however, the direct exchange of labour using natural time as the criterion. Moreover, different qualities of labour cannot be measured by the criterion of natural labour time; society's requirements for different types of labour cannot be grasped directly and fully understood. The exchange of labour among producers and the distribution of social labour between different spheres both need the assistance of the market, via value's tortuous channels. Thus, the exchange of equal amounts of labour must be characterized by the exchange of commodities of equal value, becoming a new form of equal exchange of value relationship: this is the socialist commodity economy.

This unifying of the exchange of equal amounts of labour with the exchange of commodities of equal value, the theory of unifying socialist production relationships with the commodity production form (i.e., the theory of the socialist commodity economy) has broken through the traditional doctrine of only being able to have exchange of equal amounts of labour via the direct exchange of labour. It has enabled the abstract principle of exchange of equal amounts of labour to become united with reality.

The 'exchange of equal amounts of labour' includes only labour (i.e., the exchange of different types and different qualities of labour) eliminating the influence of differences in material conditions of production upon the exchange of labour, i.e., it eliminates the fact that some producers have superior material production conditions to rely on so that they can 'possess' (*zhanqu*) other people's labour. This is the basic difference between it and ordinary exchange of equal values. In Marx's view, the exchange of equal amounts of labour is the essence of socialist economic relationships. This is precisely because he, in principle, eliminated the 'possession' of other people's labour, getting rid of class exploitation.

Where there is exchange of equal amounts of labour through the market (i.e., normal exchange of equal value) the market cannot spontaneously eliminate the influence of differences in material production conditions upon exchange relationships. This can occur only through the state's macro-economic adjustment mechanisms, such as regulating the income from natural resources and capital.

Since the exchange of equal amounts of labour must be mediated by the market, and possess the characteristics of ordinary exchange of equal values, then the 'equal amount' 'can only exist in the sense of an average amount within the total, and does not exist in each and every instance'. The state's regulation of different levels of income also cannot be absolutely precise but must be in terms of 'the average amount'. Moreover, in order to encourage the adoption of advanced production methods, income differentials cannot be removed completely by society. At the same time, expansion of the commodity economy requires the concentration of funds, so we ought not to oppose the payment of interest to those who supply funds (including savings and deposits). Therefore, the exchange of equal amounts of labour is complex. It includes the exchange of unequal amounts of labour, with producers who have relatively advanced material production conditions still able to obtain a certain differential income, and the suppliers of capital able to obtain interest. These things are both unequal exchange of labour, involving the 'possession' of other people's labour, though they generally do not occupy an important position. If at a certain time their role expands, then we can regulate and control them through macro-economic measures, so that polarization and class antagonism do not result. Therefore, we consider it inappropriate to speak of unequal exchange of labour in the socialist commodity economy as 'class exploitation'. Rather, it is more appropriately termed 'non-labour income'. 'Eating out of the big pot' also is an aspect of some people 'possessing' other people's labour. If a state enterprise makes persistent losses, and the state keeps providing it with subsidies, we should reflect on where the subsidies come from. Since they also come from social labour, shouldn't this equally be termed 'exploitation'?

The above income differences, interest and other non-labour income must all be regulated through the state's macro-economic levers. This mechanism also has the crucial function of balancing social supply and demand, however. Therefore, the socialist economy is inevitably divided into two administrative layers. All producers and businesses, whether they be state enterprises, co-operative organizations, or households, individual businesses or other forms of enterprise, are micro-economic units. They must all enter the second tier of the two-level structure. Their economic income and activities must all accept the restrictions imposed by the macro-economic levers.

All relatively advanced commodity economics require macro-economic regulation so that they all possess two-tiered structures. Treating the regulation of income differentials and non-labour income as the main function of macro-economic regulation (of course, it also has other functions) is one of the special characteristics of the socialist commodity economy. Income differentiation is an extremely important question. Only if it is suitably regulated will the conditions exist for equal competition (*pingdeng jingzheng*) among micro-economic units under the principle of exchange of equal amounts of labour: this is the basic requirement of the socialist commodity economy.

Obviously, the present situation does not conform fully with the above discussion of the socialist commodity economy. Economic relationships are 'twisted' (*niu qu*); not only are there income differentials and interest, but also there is plenty of 'abnormal' non-labour income which comes from evil practices. This is because the socialist commodity economy is still lacking certain necessary characteristics. The principal of these is that socialist market relationships have still not formed, while macro-economic mechanisms and regulatory measures are still very weak. Moreover, the surges in demand and supply shortages which occurred under the old system still exist. These are temporary irregularities which will be eliminated gradually with the success of the overall reform.

What is the significance of the present widening of income differentials?

In respect of the three issues raised hereafter in this chapter (i.e., 'privatization', 'marketization', and 'widening income differentials') the one about which people are most concerned is also that which is the most concrete, namely, income differentials.

For this, we need to analyse the structure of people's income in the socialist commodity economy. Irrespective of whether we are considering household enterprise business, ordinary staff and workers, or other workers, their income first and foremost is from labour, including remuneration for skill and business labour. Some comrades do not acknowledge that business is a form of labour. In fact, not only is business a form of labour, but it is complex labour, and it is a form of labour which still is scarce in China's villages. This form of labour ability is an essential factor in production, but it is hard to come by. In China today it is obvious that there are differences in the quality of labour, between talented and ordinary labour. Thus, relatively large differentials (tenfold, or even wider) in remuneration for labour cannot be regarded as departing from the principle of exchange of equal amounts of labour in a socialist commodity economy. Naturally, these differentials must be arrived at through the market, i.e., through social evaluation an objective, realistic outcome is arrived at. With the present incomplete socialist market system and macro-economic levers, this cannot be attained fully.

In Wenzhou, on the other hand, market-determined differentials in labour income produced are fairly realistic because there the market mechanism has already begun properly to manifest itself. It is difficult for people to obtain abnormal, additional income through the market. Improving the market mechanism acts as a restraint on abnormal non-labour income and income from evil practices. Naturally, some Wenzhou businesses earn such income. Mostly, however, it is not obtained from the Wenzhou markets themselves, but from the inter-relationship with other areas, e.g., obtaining low price materials from other areas' state enterprises or other units' personnel by means of giving (or receiving) bribes, or selling inferior or even fake goods. Until the whole macro-economic reform has advanced considerably, it will be hard to eliminate these activities. Wenzhou cannot solve this problem on its own.

As well as remuneration for labour, income includes also interest on capital. As the commodity economy expands, all micro-economic units, whether state or co-operative, household or individual, accumulate capital. In addition, there is some saving from labour income. All these funds, whether deposited in banks or entering financial circulation through other means, obtain some interest. Indeed, even using one's own capital to avoid paying interest is equivalent to obtaining interest. Excluding that portion necessary to account for increases in the price level, interest is simply a form of non-labour income from capital.

Apart from interest, obtaining income from undertaking business or risking capital is also a regular part of the commodity economy, e.g., interest on shares in share enterprises includes both interest and risk income.

Generally speaking, leaving aside not only making use of certain temporary, abnormal factors (i.e., distorted prices and imperfections in the tax and credit system) to obtain a cheap advantage but also obtaining abnormal income through evil means, in the socialist commodity economy people's income includes not only labour remuneration but also interest on capital, risk income and certain normal income differentials from non-labour income.

The market objectively appraises differentials in labour quality, leading to widening differentials in labour income. This conforms with the principle of exchange of equal amounts of labour and distribution according to labour; distribution according to labour begins with the exchange of equal amounts of labour in the production process and is continued in the sphere of distribution, i.e., it is exchange of equal amounts of labour seen from the point of view of distribution. Widening income differentials is an unavoidable phenomenon for a certain period of time in the development of the socialist commodity economy. When the socialist commodity economy is more advanced, differentials of labour quality and remuneration inevitably contract.

Part of the widening of income differentials is attributable to increased non-labour income. To a certain degree, increased non-labour income is unavoidable as the socialist commodity economy expands. Amongst household businesses (and their expanded form) there are a few big households. They are relatively efficient, have high incomes, and their accumulated funds expand continuously. Some of them have abundant funds, and obtain considerable interest income. In particular, in the Wenzhou people's (*min jian*) capital market the rate of interest is in a dominant position, with an average monthly interest rate of 3 per cent, which includes a high figure for risk income. Therefore, there is a tendency for non-labour income to swell. We should use socialist macro-economic measures to regulate non-labour income. Apart from needing to investigate a tax on income differentials, we also need to investigate the question of a tax on interest to regulate income from interest. Naturally, a tax on interest can also be encompassed by an income tax. We must investigate thoroughly the question of the points at which the tax is to be levied, the tax rate and the progressive method. We must ensure that the relatively large labour incomes accord with the legally specified differentials. The present income tax does not distinguish between labour and non-labour income. Nor does it distinguish between that part of income used for consumption and that used for investment. We should investigate these questions.

The principle of exchange of equal amounts of labour involves equality in buying and selling different amounts of labour and in exchanging different average values. This causes people's economic benefits to depend on the amount and efficiency of their labour so that this kind of equality encourages efficiency. For the reasons discussed above, however, (i.e., the requirements of the expansion of the commodity economy and the need for even greater efficiency) we must permit a certain amount of legal, regular non-labour income. The extent of such income may vary depending on society's conception of what is fair. This 'concept of fairness' must be distinguished from the equality principle discussed above. It is not an economic relationship, but is an issue of what society regards as an acceptable differential between rich and poor. The extent of the differential is elastic. There is no single differential appropriate to all economies and every level of cultural development.

The expansion of Wenzhou's commodity economy has led to a widespread, high-speed increase in people's incomes. Moreover, Wenzhou has witnessed the lively phenomenon of those going first to get rich dragging along others behind them to become rich; a great many household enterprises have been pulled along in this fashion. Widening income differentials in Wenzhou have been based on widespread progress towards prosperity, even if the degree and speed has differed. Wenzhou's increased income differentials reflect the exchange of equal amounts of labour. Provided macro-economic levers can be provided and perfected, enabling appropriate adjustment of non-labour income, then the situation will accord with the requirements of the socialist commodity economy; this is not 'polarization'!

'Privatization' or diversification of micro-economic forms?

Within Wenzhou's micro-economic structure, household enterprises (including their expanded form) are in the great majority. People regard this as a change in the 'structure of ownership', and speak critically of it as 'privatization'. Although this view is quite widespread, I consider that we need to make a breakthrough in our thinking on this issue.

Today, when people constantly discuss the ownership system, there are two meanings. The first is production relationships, that is to say, the ownership system which Marx repeatedly spoke of as the 'sum total of production relationships', or 'the totality of social relationships subsumed within the ownership system'. The second is property relationships, that is to say, the question of ownership rights or who disposes of the means of production (*shengehan ziliao gui shei*).

Both of these, whether a 'change in the structure of ownership' or 'privatization', are unscientific. I have noted already that an advanced commodity economy requires macro-economic regulation. Indeed, macro-economic regulation possesses an extremely important function in the socialist commodity economy. The socialist commodity economy has a two-tiered structure. All commodity producers, irrespective of their form, are micro-economic units in the second tier of the socialist economy. They must all accept restraints from the first tier, i.e., macro-economic levers. This restraint influences and transforms economic relationships. This is an undeniable phenomenon and is an undeniable trend of development.

To put things concretely, I shall begin by examining the first aspect of the ownership system, i.e., production relationships. It is quite inadequate to exclude the macro-economy and only discuss the ownership system from the micro-economic viewpoint. This does not enable one to appreciate the essence of the ownership relationship.

If we disregard the macro-economic levers of Wenzhou's control, then according to the traditional viewpoint Wenzhou's household enterprises are the 'individual economy' or 'petty proprietors'. After examining the restraints imposed by the macro-economic levers, however, things appear differently. This is the case even if we ignore the regulation which their economic activity (including production and exchange) is subjected to, and consider simply the allocation of their income. According to the temporary rules and regulations of the State Council concerning income tax on urban and rural individual industrial and commercial households, if household enterprises' annual income falls between 4,000 to 6,000 *yuan*, then on that portion of their income they pay tax at the rate of 30 per cent; on the portion of income which lies between 12,000 and 18,000 *yuan*, the tax rate is 45 per cent; on the portion which is above 30,000 *yuan*, the tax rate is 60 per cent; if the income surpasses 50,000 *yuan*, then on that part which surpasses this figure, there is an additional levy of between 10 per cent and 40 per cent. In other words, at the highest tax rate they are paying over to the state around 80 per cent of the top portion of their income. This is higher than the highest rate at which state enterprises hand over income to the state. Thus, state enterprises can obtain favourable treatment; also, they may obtain cheap supplies of means of production from the state, which is out of the question for household enterprises. Up to the present, if state enterprises make losses, they also get subsidies from the state, whereas if household enterprises make losses, they must bear the whole burden. So, if we examine the issues from the point of view of the two-tier structure rather than from the point of view simply of the micro-economy (i.e., production relationships) then, examining the whole set of relationships, including production, exchange and distribution, we can see clearly that household enterprises are different from the individual economy or 'petty proprietors' of the traditional viewpoint.

Moreover, even from the micro-economic point of view it can be seen that Wenzhou's household enterprises are different from the individual economy of the traditional viewpoint. Most of Wenzhou's household enterprises adopt the 'household operating under the auspices of the big enterprises' system. This method enables peasants to enter the national market (which is necessary for expanding the commodity economy) so as to become 'well off'. The enterprises under whose auspices they operate were formerly just responsible for 'renting out the official seal and account number', but today the 'households operating under the auspices of the big enterprises' system has provided a sound basis for direct or indirect macro-economic control (including tax, credit regulations and supervision of industrial, commercial and financial affairs).

Speaking further of the 'ownership system' (ownership rights) and who property is controlled by, within the socialist two-tiered economic structure, the whole of the micro-economy, irrespective of its form, must accept the unified socialist market and be regulated by macro-economic levers. Thus, property ownership rights are incomplete. The significance of property resides in obtaining economic benefits and income from it, not in whose name it goes or who it is under legally. If economic benefits and income cannot be derived from it then, as Marx said, its significance 'amounts to nothing'. According to the tax rates discussed above, after household enterprises have paid their taxes, the benefits they obtain from their property ownership rights are relatively limited, and their property ownership rights in practice are incomplete.

We must now discuss the question of accumulation by household businesses. This possesses a much broader significance which surpasses the question of the businesses' income, since accumulation promotes social advance. Household businesses include the capital accumulation of some large households, serving as the material conditions of production. As long as the savings enter the process of expanded reproduction, and continue circulating, their role is no different from that of public accumulation, and has the same characteristics as socialized property. It also has the characteristic of private property, however. Since the businesses can lend at interest and obtain share dividend income, and these activities can be fairly extensive, they also must be regulated by macro-economic levers. These are all concrete forms of incomplete ownership rights.

Generally speaking, businessmen cannot freely switch funds from production to consumption. There are pressures resulting from the law of the commodity economy and from market competition. We cannot, however, prevent such transfers taking place. In this respect, macro-economic counter-measures are of great significance. If the state taxes funds transferred from production to consumption, (i.e., a capital or funds transfer tax) and, moreover, sets up suitable levying points and progressive tax rates, then it can pressure commodity producers themselves to prefer accumulation, in addition to being greatly restricted by macro-economic levers. Consequently, the private characteristic of this form of socialized property is relatively limited.

Under the two-tiered social economy, not only household enterprises, but the property ownership rights of all economic forms are similarly incomplete. For example, in the case of state enterprises, there is not the slightest doubt that their property belongs to the state. Following the implementation of the reforms, however, the enterprises' 'free capital' has expanded steadily. This became especially marked with the change from financial allocations to bank loans to the enterprise. Thus, there are people who say: haven't state enterprises really changed into collective enterprises owned by the enterprise personnel? The enterprise personnel cannot, however, dispose of the enterprise; they cannot split it up and dissolve it. Those who consider its ownership rights are subordinate to the state should note that the state cannot, without compensation, transfer the enterprise to another unit. When the enterprise is used, that is to say, united with labour, it is continuously producing social wealth. No party has exclusive ownership rights in respect to these matters.

Ownership rights are the legal manifestation of property relationships, and property relationships are decided by production relationships, i.e., by production, exchange and distribution. Marx repeatedly explained: production relationships are the 'cause' and property relationships are the 'effect'. If we wish to explain a type of property or ownership right, then we need to 'describe the whole of production's social relationship'; it is simply 'a metaphysical, legalistic fantasy' to imagine that one can separate ownership rights from production relations.

The traditional economic philosophy of the past few decades views the question of under whose jurisdiction property lies as superseding production relationships, and, moreover, it considers that this determines the whole of production relationships. This theory cannot make sense of practical economic life; it cannot explain real production relationships, and cannot make sense of actual property relationships. For example, the system of state ownership existed in feudal society, and, moreover, the present day capitalist countries have plenty of state ownership, but that doesn't explain these countries' economic essence. If we reverse things, and proceed from production relationships to explain property relationships, then all becomes clear. The result of the exchange of equal amounts of labour is that each person can obtain only the income from their own labour; the material conditions of production (i.e., property) are irrelevant to each person's economic benefits. The fact that property loses its meaning for the individual is precisely the significance of the socialization and public ownership of property. Socialism is the unity of labour and the common ownership of property. Because the exchange of labour in the socialist commodity economy must be impure, with non-labour income still unavoidably in existence, the socialization of property and the common ownership of property cannot but be incomplete and impure.

The final completion of the socialization and common appropriation of property requires a long historical process. The current existence of a wide variety of different forms of incomplete property rights is an inevitable product of this transition. The 'socialization of property' is a transitional process in which property loses its significance for the individual; ultimately, there is no longer any meaning to property or any significance to ownership rights.

As I have explained in the foregoing analysis, I consider that the dominating position held by household industry in Wenzhou is a component part of the micro-economy and is part of the process of diversification of forms in the transition. Moreover, we cannot speak of the changes occurring during household industry's continued expansion (e.g., the vigorous advances in *xiangzhen* construction has played an important role in the advances in household industry) as a 'transformation of the ownership structure' or 'privatization'. Diversification of micro-economic forms is required by the socialist commodity economy; since certain forms possess exceptional vitality, for a while they will occupy a commanding position, and this follows a regular pattern in social development. Although this form has the characteristics of the private economy, it is different from the traditional private economy since its individualistic and private ownership characteristics are incomplete and limited. The socialist commodity economy inevitably has a diversified micro-economy and a unified macro-economy. Only if the macro-economic functions become progressively more extensive and more complete will the micro-economic forms enter the system of socialist commodity economy and follow its trajectory. Today, in terms both of theory and policy, we need to examine things more from the macro-economic point of view, and not resist certain micro-economic forms. It is incorrect to regard the components of the micro-economy as an 'ownership system', that is to say, a complete economic relationship.

The necessity of 'marketization' for the socialist commodity economy

The so-called 'marketization' in Wenzhou's economic development can be considered as authentic, since there is widespread competition between producers and sellers. This is a market beginning to form into a system; it is the market mechanism in embryo. These things are absolutely necessary for the socialist commodity economy.

At present people can regard a socialist economy as a commodity economy without attracting censure. There still are some doubts about whether or not a socialist economy is a market economy, however. What, in fact, is the ultimate difference between a commodity economy and a market economy? One cannot have a commodity economy without markets just as one cannot have a market without a commodity economy. If we wish to distinguish between the two, then we can say that the commodity economy is the market economy's essence, and the market economy is the form which the commodity economy assumes, just as value is the essence of price, while price is the form which value takes.

The essence of the capitalist market economy is the capitalist commodity economy. The form assumed by the socialist commodity economy is the socialist market economy. The socialist market is one in which there is equal competition based on the exchange of equal amounts of labour, and in which there is macro-economic regulation in accordance with this principle (i.e., the socialist economic principle).

The Wenzhou experience makes it clear that if we don't have a market system and its mechanisms, then we can raise the quality neither of our enterprises, nor of the managers and workers, and we cannot have the labour efficiency, speed of circulation and economic efficiency such as are found in Wenzhou today. The expansion of market relationships also has caused people's viewpoints to change. People in Wenzhou today are strongly independent; they don't 'lie down on the state's back', and are accustomed to market fluctuations. They dare to take risks. Where they are mutually involved in issues concerning incomes it is already very rare to see them have no regard for the results of each other's labour. These things are all appropriate to the expansion of the socialist commodity economy.

If we can say that the experience of Wenzhou's commodity economy has created 'marketization' then that is a very considerable 'good thing', since it creates the basis for the provision of the means for macro-economic regulation. Simultaneously, it provides the conditions for further progress in rationalizing micro-economic behaviour. In this way, we feel that the formation and possession of the socialist market system and its mechanisms have already become the key points in socialist economic reform.

Glossary

bao gan dao hu = contracting work to the household
cun = village
diqu = district
qu = administrative district
shedui = commune and brigade
shi = municipality
Sunan = Southern Jiangsu province
xian = county
xiang = township (formerly rural peoples' commune)
xiangzhen = township
xiangcun = commune and brigade
zhen = small town

Notes on the Contributors

Dong Fureng is former Head of the Economics Research Institute, Chinese Academy of Social Sciences, Beijing; he is currently the Honorary Head of the Economics Research Institute, and Vice-Chairman of the Financial and Economic Committee of the National People's Congress.

Zhao Renwei is Head of the Economics Research Institute, Chinese Academy of Social Sciences, Beijing.

Chen Ruiming, Li Shi, Pei Xiaoge and Zhang Lin all are Research Fellows at the Economics Research Institute, Chinese Academy of Social Sciences, Beijing.

Lin Zili has played an important role in developing the theoretical underpinnings of China's current economic reforms. His collected writings on the subject are being published in a multi-volume work under the general title of *The Socialist Economy* (*Shehuizhuyi jingji lun*).

Peter Nolan is a Lecturer in the Faculty of Economics and Politics, Cambridge University, and a Fellow of Jesus College, Cambridge.

Christopher Bramall is a Research Fellow of Sidney Sussex College, Cambridge.

Index

able people, 124, 132, 150, 154, 168
absorption of surplus labour *see* surplus labour
Afghanistan, 67
Agricultural Bank, 80, 95, 96
agricultural output, t21, 47; decline of, 91-2
agriculture: effect of household industry on, 117; institutional changes in, 3; subsidization of, 91
aluminium industry, 157
apprentices, 14, 90, 165
automobile parts, production of, 111, 113

backward ideas, elimination of, 80-1
badge market, 94
badge production, 78, 101, 116, t119
bank deposits, growth of, 110
Banking Law, 95
bankruptcy, 4
bankruptcy law, 59
banks, 103, 141, 145, 152, 168
bao chan systems, 8
birth rates, 33
black market, 2
blankets, production of, 114
bonus payments, 12
Botswana, 67
Bramall, Christopher, 6
Brazil, 62
Bretton Woods, 69
brewing, 53
bribery, 73, 88, 132
bridges, building of, 160
building workers, 118
Bukharin, Nikolai, 2, 5, 36
Bukharinism, 1, 7, 34, 37
bureaucracy, 106, 131, 163
business, as form of labour, 168
button market, 5, 38, 94, 95, 98, 100, 102, 104, 134
button production, 103, 112, 114, t119

canals, 49, 50
canned food production, 88
capital, neutral, 153
capital markets, 95-6
capitalism, 'restoration' of, 28
capitalist characteristics of labour hiring, 142
carpets, production of, 111, 114
cash, money as, 96
cassette recorders, 17
catering, 103
Central African Republic, 67
ceramics production, 53
chemicals industry, 53, 57
Chen Ruiming, 5
children, employment of, 85, 141; sale of, 128
circulation, 104
class antagonism, 91, 146, 150, 167
class relations, in villages, 30
clock spare parts market, 94
clothing industry, 88, 94, 95, t119, 103, 159
clothing, reprocessed, 101
co-operative purchasing, 36
co-operatives, 10, 13, 15, 36, 44, 84, 87, 91, 93, 104, 142
coal, 24; shortages of, 88
coal mining, 88
collective enterprises, 4, 12, 13, 14, 16, 19, 30, 55, 56, 58, 83, 128, 142, 147, 148, 151, 154, 161, 162, 163, 173
collective farms, 2, 7, 10, 28, 34, 35-6, 38
collective welfare institutions, 16, 32
collectivization, 50
combine harvesters, t23
commodity economy, 161; development of, 89, 92, 95, 97-107, 123; expansion of, 78, 79; promotion of, 136, rural, 77-96; socialist, 154, 165, 169, 171, 174
commodity exchange, 98
commodity markets, 94-5; emergence of, 105

Communist Party of China (CCP), 9, 60; intervention by, 12; limitations on, 9; role of, 9
competition, 1, 3; absence of, 2
competitiveness, 104
compulsory purchase, 18, 19
condensed milk production, 53
construction, 65, 93; of small towns, 92-3, 156-64
consumer durables, 13, 17
consumption patterns, changing, 109
contract systems, t8, 15
contracting of farmland, 3
contracting work to households, 8-9
contracts, expansion of, 9
cotton fluffing, 99
cotton: t21; purchases of, 18, 19
craftsmanship, 111
credit, 37, 123, 136, 141, 145, 151, 152, 172; expansion of, excessive, 83
credit co-operatives, 95, 96, 110
crop spraying, 37
cultural revolution, 5

de-collectivization, 8, 15, 22, 29, 32, 33
demand: elasticity of, 54; excess, 66
desert, 49
diet, transformation of, 27
differentials *see* income differentials
disparities between cadres and workers, 90
distribution, 11
diversification, industrial, 53
division of labour, 100-1, 102, 112, 114, 130, 137, 161; rural, 78-9
Dong Fureng, 4, 5
division of land, 9-10
dowry, 144
drainage, 16
dress, conformity in, 58
drought, 49
dual economy, 81, 108, 120, 124, 156, 162
dual price system, 131

economies of scale, 1, 31, 38, 58
economy, socialist, 7-37
education, 16, 32, 37, 72, 73, 89, 138, 144, 163
education facilities, 9, 27, 30, 35
egalitarianism, 5, 30, 135, 170; smashing of, 130, 131
electrical appliance market, 94, 95, 98, 127
electrical appliance production, 101, 111, 114, 116, t119, 120
electrical components, 101
electricity, costs of, 148
electronics industry, 57

employment levels, 109
employment: agricultural, 79, 81; in industry, 104, 108, 137; non-farm, 14; part-time, 90
energy efficiency, 2
energy. problem of, 87-9
Engels, Friedrich, 153
engineering industry, 53
Enterprise Bankruptcy Law (1988), 4
enterprise size, 15
entrepreneurs, innovative, 112-13
exchange of labour, 166, 170, 174
exchange rates, 69
exploitation, 14
exports, 157

factories, rural, 54
fairness, concept of, 170
fairs, country, 97, 98
family enterprises, 46, 56, 102
farm inputs, t23
farm output: contraction of, 134; growth of, 27, 28
farm sector: profitability of, 48, 52, 55; role of, 48
farmland: concentration of, 137; distribution of, 30
fashion accessories production, 66
feedstuffs, animal, 29
Fei Xiaotong, 54
fertilizer, 9, 22, t23, 30, 48, 92
firework production, 157
fishing, 157
Five Year Plan: First, 2; Fifth, 65; Sixth, 65
flexibility of production, 93
food: intakes of, t25; growing of, 104
foreign investment, 55
Four Modernizations, 150
fraud, 89
full employment, 2

Gang of Four, 3
Germany, West, 69
goldfish buttons, 104
Gorbachev, Mikhail, 2
grain coupons, 25
grain procurements, 50
grain, t21; production of, 10, 65, 117, 136; purchases of, 18, 19; regulation of, 29; supply of, 92
growing conditions, in Wenzhou, 49
growth rates, t17, 56; in China, 47, 48, 73; industrial, 2; of household industry, 112; of Japan, t69; of Wenzhou, t47, 48, 66, t74; rates of, 43, 46; unequal, 38
gufen qiye, 44

health, 16, 37, 72, 73, 163
health facilities, 9, 27, 30, 32, 35
heavy industry, growth of, 3, 17
hired labour, 14-15, 20, 80, 90, 129, 133, 140-55; exploitation of, 148, 149; treatment of, 91 *see also* labour hiring
Hong Kong, 145
hotels, 78, 103
house building, 118, 127
household contract system, 15
household enterprises, 46, 57-60, 70, 84, 85, 89, 90, 94, 95, 99, 100, 102, 103, 156, 157, 158, 161, 165, 170, 172, 174; development of, 87; effect on agriculture, 117; effect on tertiary sector, 118; growth of, 44, 78 (in Wenzhou, 108-24); productivity of, 115; prospects for, 93-4; taxation of, 70
households, specialized, 11
housing, 82, 92, 109, 159, 162
Hundred Flowers, 34
Hungary, 3

immiserization, 60-6
import tariffs, 71
incentive goods, t17, 20
income ceilings, 15; removal of, 30
income data, 43
income differentials, 15, 20, 30, 45, 46, 61, 62, 68, 70, 71, 73, 80, 84, 89-91, 117, 162, 167; in Wenzhou, 126- 38; negative aspects of, 133-5; positive aspects of, 129-33; significance of, 168-70; tax on, 169
income levels, t132
income, growth of, 4, 86, 109, 126-9; in Wenzhou, t50; national, t51; non-labour, t74, 167, 168, 169, 170
incomes, 47, 133; distribution of, t129; incomes in Wenzhou, t45; increase in, 13; rural, 60 *see also* peasant incomes
India, 71, 74, 82
industrial output, 47
industrial products: final, 98; intermediate, 98
industrialization: in China, 55; in Wenzhou, 55; rural, 58
industry: employment in, 104, 108; urban, growth of, 120
inequality, 36-8
inflation, 43, 48
information, 103, 106, 118; access to, 95
inheritance, 10
institutional change, 56-9
instrument production, 144
insurance, 37, 91
intensity of labour, 12, 60, 83; rural, 27

interest, 167, 169; rates of, 27, 80, 95, 148 (floating, 95); tax on, 169
investment, 1, 2, 16, 32, 82, 84, 92, 121, 122, 123, 138, 148, 152, 158, 160, 170; agricultural, 135; industrial, 48, 117; non-farm, 65; rural, 72
irrigation, 16, 22, t23, 30, 33, 37, 49, 72, 92

Japan, 57; growth rates in, t69; scale of enterprises in, t121; war with, 55
Japanese colonialism, 73
Japanese competition, 53, 55
jianye nonghu, 44
jiating gongchang, 44
joint enterprises, 122; household, 44
joint stock management, 121

kibbutzim, 35
kulaks, 36

label market, 94, 98
label production, 78, 116, t119
labour costs, 56, 57
labour force, structure of, 109
labour hierarchy, 128
labour hiring, 121, 135; in Wenzhou, 140-55
labour migration, 61, 62, 64, 65, 82; restrictions on, 62, 82
labour mobility, 25
labour shortages, 61
labour: cheapness of, 93; exchange of, 166, 170, 174; skilled, 55, 62, 82, 85, 99, 111, 114, 143; trained, 53; transfer of, 81-2, 84, 86, 144
labour-hiring enterprises, 44; as a class force, 146
labour-hiring households, big, 129, 140-55
labourers, rural, numbers of, 30
lace making, 53
land contract period, 10
land rent, 36
land: concentration of, 92; contracting of, 33; cultivation philosophy of, 135; division of, 9-10; left idle, 117; quality of, 49; scarcity of, 54, 80; subcontracting of, 92, 117; urban, scarcity of, 83
land-locked countries, 67
leadership co-ordination, 162
leasing, 59
left-overs, industrial, use of, 98, 115, t119, 120, 148
Lenin, Vladimir Ilyich, 30, 166
Lewis, W.A., 81
Li Shi, 5
lianhe qiye, 44

lifestyle, changes in, 79-80
Lin Qingson, 152-3
literacy, 143
living standards, 3, 21, 24-5, 61, 82, 127; of peasants, t26
Longgang, situation of, 156-64
luxury goods, 71

machinery, agricultural, 22
macro-economic policy, 46-8, 54, 154, 162, 167, 170, 172, 174; and taxation, 137
managers, position of, 12
manual labour displaced, 111
Mao Zedong, 3, 7, 14, 15, 16, 81
Maoism, 2, 7, 22, 32, 54, 58
Maoist political economy, demolition of, 7
market economy, capitalist, 174
market mechanism, 38, 168
market relations, expansion of, 175
market: black, 2; changes in, 80; unified, 107
marketing co-operatives, 44
marketing, 37; agricultural, crisis of, 18; farm, 17-18
marketization, 165-75; necessity of, 174-5
markets, people's, 165
markets: elimination of, 2; problem of, 87-9; specialized, 124 (opening of, 126; formation of, 100)
Marx, Karl, 5, 14, 30, 144, 151, 166, 170, 172, 173
Marxism, 55, 150
mat weaving, 53
material prices, 115
means of production, ownership of, 10
meat, t21; consumption of, 29; prices of, 29
mechanization, of agriculture, 33, 49, 56
mergers, funding of, 123
Mexico, 62
migration, 26, 31 *see also* labour migration
miners' lamps, production of, 101
misallocation, 88
mixed companies, 153
modernization, 87; rural, 65, 67, 68, 77-81, 80, 97, 106, 108, 123
money-making, obsession with, 33-4
monopoly, 1, 17, 66
mountain areas, 27, 31, 49, 61, 128, 136, 143

natural economy: importance of, 136; stagnation of, 130
Nepal, 67
neutral capital, 153
New Economic Policy (NEP): in China,

37; in USSR, 2, 34, 36
Nolan, Peter, 5
non-farm sector, growth of, 19, 29, 44, 48, 49
nutrition, 109

obsolete products, elimination of, 103
oil, edible, 19
One Child Family campaign, 33
open market network, of Wenzhou, 97-102
organizational forms in rural industry, 44
output, growth of, t64
over-investment, 87
overstocking, 87
ownership: rights, 173; system, 172; types of, 58

paper production, 53
Paraguay, 67
parcellization of land holdings, 10
peasant consciousness, 38
peasant households as unit of production, 77
peasant incomes, 47, t48, 51, 54, 79, 85, 88, 89, 91, 105
peasants, 10, 14, 15, 25, 32, 35, 44, 55, 80, 82, 85, 90, 97, 104, 116, 117, 123, 127, 156, 162; education of, 106-7; living standards of, t26; transfer of, 107
Pei Xiaoge, 5
pensions, 57, 59
people's communes, 7, 8, 33
petty commodity production, 7-37
piecework, 12
planning, 2, 4, 28
plastic bag production, 101, t114
plastic injection machinery, 94
plastics industry, 98, 143, 157
plastics weaving, 109, 110, 111, t119
ploughing, 92; mechanical, 22
polarization, 38, 165-75
pollution, 83
population: growth of, 33, 62, t63, (in Wenzhou, t74)
port facilities, 52, 157; in Wenzhou, 52
postal services, 118; expansion of, 78
pottery production, 53
poverty, 4, 21, 25-7, 31, 35, 37, 86, 127, 128, 131, 135, 136, 145, 156
precision instrument production, 57
price mechanism, 16
price policy, 29
prices, 60; food, 20; low, 115, 124; of farm products, 19; state-fixed, 4, 13, 18, 19, 20
primitive accumulation, 145

printing industry, 159
private economy, 174
private property, 172
privately owned enterprises, 84
privatization, 33, 165-75
production relations, socialist, 166
productivity: agricultural, 7, 22-4; labour,
    31, 59, 79, 81, 82, 93, 94, 112, 115, 117,
    121, 133 (agricultural, 137; industrial,
    136; rural, 27); of land, 35
profit allocation, 123
profit-seeking behaviour, 12
profitability, 101; of farming sector, 46,
    48, 52, 55
profiteering, 95
profits, 33, 147, 149; control of, 152;
    excessive, 151; taxation of, 68
proletarians, 144
property relationships, 173
property, common ownership of, 173
public ownership, 87
purchasing, 102

quality of product, 57, 58, 89, 110-12, 120

rabbit fur market, 105
railways, 52, 68
rainfall, 49
rationing, 19, 25
raw material problems, 87-9, 148
refrigerators, 17
remittances from migrants, 25, 31, 61
Renwei, Zhao, 5
reserve army, 61
restaurants, 78, 118
retail sales, composition of, t44
rice growing, 49
rice milling, 53
risk: income from, 169; rewards for, 132;
    daring to take, 175
river systems, 157
roads, 52, 92, 157, 158, 160; building of,
    27, 138
running water, 92
rural economy, 161; non-farm, 7, 11-14,
    t24, 70; performance of, 20-8;
    structure of, 29-33
rural income, t31
rural industry, 52; growth of, 47
rural non-farm employment, growth of, 72
rural reform, 36-8
rural technical services, 11

sales, mail order, 112
sanitation, 80
savings, 1
scale of production, 121

schools, 159, 160
science, 162
second jobs, 133
separatism, regional, 74
sewerage networks, 160
Shanghai, economic impact of, 54
share-issuing enterprises, 44
shares, 142, 169; purchasing of, 123
shedui enterprises, 54, 55, 58
shipbuilding industry, 159
shoe market, 98
shoe production, 83, 94, 103, 104, 109,
    111, 115, 116, t119
shoe repairing, 99
shortages, 87
Sik, Ota, 151, 152-3
silk industry, 55
siren gugong qiye, 44
skills *see* labour, skilled
small businesses, t57
social relations, changes in, 79-80
socialism, 4, 5, 91, 173; municipal, 5
socialist economy, 1, 7-37
Socialist Education Movement, 34
socialist modernization, 77-81, 106
socialist science, 166-8
specialized households, 11
specialized markets in Wenzhou, 94-5
spinning industry, 133, 157, 159
spraying of crops, 30
stagnation, 43; of natural economy, 130
Stalinism, 1, 3, 7, 34
stalls, market, 159; taxation of, 134
starvation, 55
state, role of, 146
state aid, 45
state enterprises, 1, 13, 54, 57, 59, 71, 83,
    84, 90, 120, 128, 131, 133, 134, 143,
    147, 148, 151, 154, 162, 173; problems
    of, 59
state sector, 44, 163; reform of, 59
stock market, 123
sub-contracting, 13, 57; of land, 92, 117
subsidization, 16, 54, 117, 136, 144; of
    agriculture, 91
sugar cane, t21
Sunan model of development, 14, 84
sunlight, 49
surplus labour, 15, 81, 82, 83, 84-6, 97,
    103, 109, 110, 120, 149
synthetic fibres production, 159

Taiwan, 71, 72, 73
talented people *see* able people
tariffs, import, 71
tax evasion, 69, 70, 71, 88, 137, 148
tax exemption, 56

tax revenue, 45, 54, 105, 126; in
    Wenzhou, t70
taxation, 5, 18-19, 30, 32, 56, 68, 86, 90,
    107, 110, 115-16, 134, 135, 137, 151,
    152, 169, 171, 172; according to
    household, 134; according to
    stallspace, 134; agricultural, 19, 25,
    92; business, 19; enterprise income,
    25; exemption from, 88; indirect, 71;
    of household enterprises, 69; on
    income, 18, 30, 115, 169, 171; on
    income differentials, 169; on interest,
    169; progressive, 19, 71, 73, 90, 138;
    property, 71; registration for, 115
tea firing, 53
technological transformation, 110-12
technology, 82, 93, 103, 106, 121, 150;
    new, 113; spread of, 91
technology transfer, 53, 54, 55
telecommunications, 103, 118; expansion
    of, 78
telegrams, 78
telephones, 78
television, 17, 32
television components production, 144
terms of trade, agricultural, 18
tertiary sector, 65, 103; effect of
    household industry on, 118
textile industry, 66, 83
textile machinery, 111
textiles, 57; reprocessed, 101, 109, 112,
    113, 114, 116, t119, 147
Tibet, 66, 68
toilets, building of, 160
town and country, differences between, 80
towns: construction of, 97, 110, 138; new,
    growth of, 105-6; small, construction
    of, 156-64
tractors, 22, t23, 36
trade unions, 12
trade, international, 99
traders, 31-2, 158; peasant, 99-100
training, 82, 85
transfer of labour, 97, 144
transport links, 55
transportation, 11, 13, 22, 37, 65, 67, 71,
    72, 84, 89, 103, 107, 118; costs of, 66
    (on water, 67); development of, 78;

rail, 67; sea, 67
trucks, t23

umbrella production, 53
unemployment, 61
Union of Soviet Socialist Republics
    (USSR), 1, 3, 7, 34, 67
United States of America (USA), 45, 145
urban centres, 50; as source of nightsoil,
    50
urbanization, 97; problems of, 84
US aid, 73
usury, 36

volunteer service brigades, 27

wage labour, 36
wages, 45, 54, 56, 60, 128; of workers, 12
waste, 3, 148
water conservation, 16
water supply, 36, 80, 158, 160
waterways, navigable, 52
weaving industry, 133, 157
welfare, 32, 91; of workers, 56
welfare undertakings, 138
Wenzhou 'miracle' assessed, 43-75
Wenzhou model, 5, 14, 32, 77-96;
    applicability of, 66-74
Wenzhou: backwardness of, 52; climate
    of, 49; growth of household industry
    in, 108-24; income differentials in,
    126-38; industrial tradition of, 53
women, employment of, 85
working conditions, 60
woven plastic products market, 98

xiangcun enterprises, 12, 13, 14
xiangzhen enterprises, 24, 46, 47, 54, 55,
    56, 57, 58, 59, 60, 83, 84, 86, 87, 89, 91,
    136

Yugoslavia, 3

Zambia, 67
Zhang Lin, 5
Zhao Ziyang, 14
Zimbabwe, 67